O E T I C

M E D I C I N E

THE SLEEPLESS ONES

What if all the people
who could not sleep
at two or three or four
in the morning
left their houses
and went to the parks
what if hundreds, thousands,
millions
went in their solitude
like a stream
and each told their story
what if there were
old women
fearful if they slept
they would die
and young women
unable to conceive
and husbands
having affairs
and children
fearful of failing
and fathers
worried about paying bills
and men
having business troubles
and women unlucky in love

and those that were in physical
pain
and those who were guilty
what if they all left their houses
like a stream
and the moon
illuminated their way and
they came, each one
to tell their stories
would these be the more troubled
of humanity
or would these be
the more passionate of this world
or those who need to create to live
or would these be
the lonely
ones
and I ask you
if they all came to the parks
at night
and told their stories
would the sun on rising
be more radiant and
again I ask you
would they embrace

—Lawrence Tirnauer

ALSO BY JOHN FOX

FINDING WHAT YOU DIDN'T LOSE: *Expressing Your Truth and Creativity Through Poem-Making*

POETIC
MEDICINE

The Healing Art of Poem-Making

JOHN FOX, CPT

Jeremy P. Tarcher / Putnam   *a member of Penguin Putnam Inc.*   *New York*

Most Tarcher/Putnam books are available at special quantity discounts for bulk purchases for sales promotions, premiums, fund-raising, and educational needs. Special books or book excerpts also can be created to fit specific needs. For details, write or telephone Putnam Special Markets, 200 Madison Avenue, New York, NY 10016; (212) 951-8891.

Jeremy P. Tarcher/Putnam
a member of
Penguin Putnam Inc.
200 Madison Avenue
New York, NY 10016

Library of Congress Cataloging-in-Publication Data

Fox, John, date.
    Poetic medicine : the healing art of poem-making / John Fox.
       p.   cm.
    Includes bibliographical references and index.
    ISBN 0-87477-882-4 (alk. paper)
    1. Poetry—Authorship. 2. Poetry—Psychological aspects.
I. Title.
PN1059.A9F686   1997   97-8832 CIP
808.1—dc21

Book design by Chris Welch
Cover design by Lee Fukui
Cover illustration © by Celia Johnson/SIS
Photograph of the author by Paula Leslie

Printed in the United States of America
10 9 8 7 6 5 4 3 2 1
This book is printed on acid-free paper. ∞

TO HOLLY

CONTENTS

Appreciations   *xi*

Preface   *xiii*

CHAPTER ONE

HEART, WHO WILL YOU CRY OUT TO?

Giving Silence Words   *1*

CHAPTER TWO

THE SAME RIVER TWICE

Merging the Healing and Creative Processes   *31*

CHAPTER THREE

POETIC TOOLS FOR YOUR HEALING JOURNEY

Creating with the Elements of Poetry   *57*

CHAPTER FOUR

THE FRAGILE BOND

Expressing Poems of Pain and Love Between Parent and Child   *93*

CHAPTER FIVE

LANDSCAPES OF RELATIONSHIP

Reflecting on Intimacy, Marriage and Longing   125

CHAPTER SIX

WHEN GOD SIGHS

Making Poems About Loss, Illness and Death   159

CHAPTER SEVEN

THE PEACE OF WILD THINGS

Embracing the Earth to Tell Your Story   191

CHAPTER EIGHT

POEMS OF WITNESS IN A CONFLICTED WORLD

Speaking the Truth, Going to the Heart   223

CHAPTER NINE

THERE IS A SECRET ONE INSIDE US

Using Your Spiritual Voice to Heal   249

Resources   279

Suggested Reading   282

Bibliography   285

Permissions   288

Index   297

APPRECIATIONS

My deep thanks to these friends and colleagues for their friendship, insight, encouragement and inspiration:

Jim Fadiman, who has a knack for seeing what wants to happen.

Beth Carmack, who expresses through her fine ear and heart the gift for noticing the essential.

Lisa Friedlander, who lives the language of healing. Her encouragement and faith helped me to go deeper and make the spirit of this book strong.

Kimberley Nelson, who dedicates herself to the poetic voice that is great within troubled children, and in serving them, inspires me.

John and Lynett Petrula, who listen carefully and offer excellent comments that give greater clarity to my text.

Jack Winkle, who calls with enthusiasm to tell me he just wrote his second poem on the train home.

Dorothy Fadiman and Susan Thompson, who love silence and voices of the soul. Meditation partners for over eleven years, these friends are fearless in their enthusiastic love for what matters.

Kay Adams, who shares her joy of creative exploration and the healing power of words.

Lois Tucker, who is prepared, looks for words, sends quotes, and knows wonders on long hikes in Marin County.

Eleanor Fox, my mother, who offers her example and support.

For the marvelous groundbreaking work they do in the healing art of poetry therapy: Joy Shieman, my mentor and a pioneer in the healing art of poetry. And with gratitude to: Jack Leedy, Arleen Hynes, Peggy Osna Heller, Sherry Reiter, Alicia Seeger, Steve Rojcewicz, Jennifer Bosveld, Alma Rolfs and Ken Gorelick.

✴

Kris Haas, Jacquelyn Cenacveira and Gail Parenteau for their help, comments, suggestions and encouragement.

I also extend my deep gratitude to the following people whose contributions are integral to the publication of this book:

Jeremy Tarcher for his faith, thoughtfulness, solutions and vision. His example inspires me in my personal and professional life.

My superb editor, Laura Golden Bellotti. Her keen insight, care, attention, love for poetry and editorial gifts draw excellence out of my writing so that it appears on the page.

Rachel Naomi Remen for her wise and lovely preface.

Joel Fotinos, Publisher at Tarcher/Putnam; Irene Prokop, Editor-in-Chief at Tarcher; and Joanna Pinsker, my fine publicist; Maria Liu, in marketing; David Groff, associate editor—all have given their friendly support and attention to this project.

Maggie Farley, my permissions-gathering angel, who dealt with many details and my innumerable requests, worries and questions with grace and calm.

And above all, I want to thank . . .

Each person who has contributed poem and personal story to this book. These include:

Students of my course *Poetry Therapy: Reclamation of Deep Language* at John F. Kennedy University. The beautiful people who attended the *Poem-Making as Healing* workshop at Omega Institute in the summer of 1996. Children and young adults who take part in classes through the California-Poets-in-the-Schools Program. Workshop students and poet-friends across the country. All poets from around the world and translators of poetry, well known or unknown, who inspire my work.

My deepest gratitude to each of these people. Whether their poems and stories appear on these pages or not, their willingness to share their lives and the healing power of poetry gives these pages Life.

PREFACE

As a girl, I hated poetry. So, much more the irony that I have spent hours, even whole days, writing and reading poetry with people with cancer, with their doctors and their nurses, and with their family members. But this poetry is different from the poetry of my youth. Much of the old poetry was pretentious and erudite, full of references to mythology or the ancient Greeks, poetry whose words I could not easily understand. The poetry of my youth made me feel diminished.

But this poetry, this poetry makes me proud to be a human being.

Poetry is simply speaking truth. Each of us has a truth as unique as our own fingerprints. Without knowing that truth, without speaking it aloud, we cannot know who we are and that we are already whole. In the most profound way, speaking our truth allows us to know that our life matters, that our viewpoint has never existed before. That our suffering, our joy, our fears and our hopes are important and meaningful. One of the best kept secrets in this technically oriented culture is that simply speaking truth heals.

Often the first poem is the hardest, the one caught by a lifetime of being smaller than you are, trapped by your ideas of what art is, what an artist is, immobilized by the judgments of teachers whose names you may never again remember. How did we come to forget that anything true is beautiful? How young were we then?

Writing poetry is contagious. Once past the first, we may discover that we have written poetry for years without knowing. Because no one was listening, not even we ourselves. Those of us on the Commonweal Cancer Help Retreat staff began by listening to the poems of people with cancer, then joining them in the writing sessions, and finally writing for ourselves just because we too are alive.

Our poetry allows us to remember that our integrity is not in our body, that despite our physical limitations, our suffering and our fears, there is something in us that is not touched, something shining. Our poetry is its voice. To hear that voice is to know the power to heal. To believe.

The first poem I ever wrote took me by surprise. Between one breath and the next, there was the truth of my own decades of chronic illness.

> *O body—*
> *for 41 years*
> *1,573 experts*
> *with 14,355*
> *combined years of training*
>
> *to*
> *cure*
> *your*
> *wounds.*
>
> *Deep inside,*
>
> *I*
> *am*
> *whole.*

A lot of healing lies in the recovery of a personal sense of meaning, that capacity which enables us to endure difficulties, to find and draw on unsuspected strength. In times of crisis, meaning *is* strength. But the deepest meaning is carried in the unconscious mind, whose language is the language of dreams, of symbols and archetypes. Poetry speaks this language, and helps us hear meaning in illness, in the events of our lives often for the first time. Finding such meaning feels like revelation. Like grace.

Writing poetry together heals loneliness. What is true for someone on the deepest level is often true for us all. Reading a poem aloud and listening to the poems of others can heal the alienation which is so much a part of our world. These days, much in life is masked. Poetry wears no mask. In taking off the

masks we have worn to be safe, to protect ourselves, to win approval, we become less vulnerable. Less alone. Our pain becomes just pain. It is no longer suffering.

We may have lost faith in our ability to write poems, just as
we have lost faith in our ability to heal. Recovering the poet
strengthens the healer and sets free the unique song that is at
the heart of every life.

—RACHEL NAOMI REMEN, M.D.

CHAPTER ONE

EART, WHO WILL YOU CRY OUT TO?

Giving Silence Words

In its origin a poem is something completely unequivocal. It is a discharge, a call, a cry, a sigh, a gesture, a reaction by which the living soul seeks to defend itself from or to become aware of an emotion, an experience. In this first spontaneous most important function no poem can be judged. It speaks first of all simply to the poet himself, it is his cry, his scream, his dream, his smile, his whirling fists.

—Hermann Hesse

SACRED PLACE, COMPANION AND NATURAL MEDICINE

> The world is poetical intrinsically and what it means is simply itself. Its significance is the enormous mystery of its existence and of our awareness of its existence.
>
> —Aldous Huxley

*P*oetry is a natural medicine; it is like a homeopathic tincture derived from the stuff of life itself—*your experience.* Poems distill experience into the essentials. Our personal experiences touch the common ground we share with others. The exciting part of this process is that poetry used in this healing way helps people integrate the disparate, even fragmented parts of their life. Poetic essences of sound, metaphor, image, feeling and rhythm act as remedies that can elegantly strengthen our whole system—physical, mental and spiritual.

Poems speak to us when nothing else will. Poetry helps us to *feel* our lives rather than be numb. The page, touched with our poem, becomes a place for painful feelings to be held, explored and transformed. Writing and reading poems is a way of seeing and naming where we have been, where we are and where we are going with our lives.

> *P*oetry gives you permission to feel.
>
> —James Autry

Poetry provides guidance, revealing what you did not know you knew before you wrote or read the poem. This moment of *surprising yourself* with your own words of wisdom or of being surprised by the poems of others is at the heart of poetry as healer.

Surprise is a kind of revelation, resurrection and rebirth—a creative, joyful, luminous, physical experience of being disinterred from limitation. Experiencing this sense of surprise rolls away the stone of the mind's harshness and self-doubt, allowing us to recognize a voice that has been discouraged, or hidden away, or perhaps is yet undiscovered.

Writing poetry is a way to bring your voice to life. Nourishing surprise deepens our contact with life, our capacity to heal ourselves and others.

The rippling chorus of "ah's" sounded out from the lips of listeners of poetry around the world signifies universal agreement: poetic language allows us to say something directly *from* experience, with words that go straight to our core. Poetry allows both writer and listener to discover new possibilities of who they are.

You make a poem with words—but you also build an *interior place* when you write, a place where your *intuitive voice* may awaken and thrive. This workshop student wrote about why poetry was important to her following the suicide of her father when she was eighteen:

> *I was living through death, moving towards wholeness, working to navigate in the darkness surrounding me. The writing gave form to formlessness, it gave validation to the view of the inner eye, helping me to navigate through darkness. Writing the poem gave the inner world where I was focused a stronger sense of reality, the way throwing dust on the Invisible Man reveals his presence. This allowed me to have greater appreciation and compassion for my experience when all I knew for certain was darkness.*
>
> —Glo Lamson

As others write, they too build their own unique, interior place. When we listen to one another, we meet not only on an outer physical level, but inside our hearts, in the place of intuitive knowing.

Expressing our experience through poetry, we connect to a widely varied community of poem-makers and kindred spirits. In this inner/outer place of relatedness and communication, it is possible to recognize profound healing and wholeness:

I think there is a great renaissance of poetry in this country, and I think that we are beginning to remember that the first poets didn't come out of the classroom.

—Lucille Clifton

By making us stop for a moment, poetry gives us an opportunity to think about ourselves as human beings on this planet and what we mean to each other.

—Rita Dove

I ask all blessings,
I ask them with reverence,
of my mother the earth,
of the sky, moon, and sun my father.
I am old age: the essence of life,
I am the source of all happiness.
All is peaceful, all in beauty,
all in harmony, all in joy.
—Anonymous Navaho
(nineteenth–twentieth centuries)

Poetry is a companion through dark times. The poem is the friend who calls you at just the right moment on a bad day when above all *you feel the need to be known.* The poem is a voice that makes it clear *you are not alone.*

Whether reading or writing poetry, applying the lines of a poem to your life experience helps uncover the meaning within your questions, problems and crises.

Sacred place, companion and *natural medicine*—poems are all of these and each will support your process of healing.

EXERCISE
Finding Your Sacred Place, Companion and Natural Medicine

* **Sacred Place.** Imagine or recall in detail the place or places you feel most able to let your writing emerge. It doesn't have to be just one place. This place could be in your present home—or a home that you design to support your creativity. It could be an interior place shaped by your imagination or a spiritual realm you visit. Nothing is too mundane or exotic to name as your sacred place. Workshop students say things like: the kitchen, a coffee house or a rookery where blue herons live and feed. What kind of objects are in your place? Things from childhood? Things from nature? What common objects are in this place? What other signs or expressions of life are there? What particular vegetation, animals or people thrive here?

I surround myself with objects that carry with them a personal history— old books, bowls and boxes, splintering chairs and benches from imperial China.

—Amy Tan

✳

What colors, smells and textures? What is the shape of your place? What feelings exist here? What is the quality of the light and dark in this place? Turn your acute observations into a poem of place, a place that invites your poems.

> *This is the field where the battle did not happen,*
> *where the unknown soldier did not die.*
> *This is the field where grass joined hands,*
> *where no monument stands,*
> *and the only heroic thing is the sky.*
>
> *Birds fly here without any sound,*
> *unfolding their wings across the open.*
> *No people killed—or were killed—on this ground*
> *hallowed by neglect and an air so tame*
> *that people celebrate it by forgetting its name.*
> —William Stafford

✳ **Companion.** Consider poetry or the poetic spirit as your companion. Imagine this poetic spirit befriending you. Listening to you. Speaking to you. How and where does this Muse appear? What does your Muse look like? If you've never thought of a "muse" before, consider someone who is important to you—perhaps a spouse, child or friend. Possibly it is an animal you take as a symbol for yourself or as your protector. It may be a helpful person you recall from an earlier, significant time in your life or someone you recall more recently who best embodies this Muse. Some figure may come to mind that has appeared spontaneously to you, in a dream or otherwise.

It could be a particularly inspiring poem that has the evocative qualities of the Muse. Read that poem now to yourself or have a friend read it to you. Listen to the sounds, images and rhythms. Reflect on your experience. Why does this poem touch you so deeply?

When did this poetic "friend" enter and touch your life? How does this friend relate to your experience now? What does this Muse know about reaching your heart? Where do you feel the

Poetry came before language, for it was the poetic spirit in man that made language.

—Hazrat Inayat Khan

Muse in your body? Does it help you in particular circumstances? What is it like to have this companion as part of your
life? What would it be like if this Muse, if the poem, if poetry
itself vanished from your life? Be specific rather than general.

MY FAMILIAR

Just off
A bustling sidewalk
Tonight in Chinatown she
Appeared again
Wearing a hooded parka
Of soft grey squirrel fur
Looking at me still and straight
Above the people passing
Then was gone

She comes every year;
Finds me. Once her
Eyes ebon-dark
in a weatherbrown face
Gave me assurance
Before I traveled alone
To a remote shadowed region.

At home, I often sense her;
Feel a flash
Of motion behind my shoulder,
See an angle of light
Where was none before.
Her husky voice speaks
In the secret bones of my skull.
I know only this: she
Was there when I was born.
I know the eyes,
The deep, the timeless,
The wild eyes.
        —Mary TallMountain

*For us, there is not just this world,
there's also a layering of others. Time
is not divided by minutes and hours,
and everything has presence and
meaning within this landscape of
timelessness.*

        —Joy Harjo

✳

✳ **Natural Medicine.** Reflect on poetry as a natural medicine. What is your medicine made of? This medicine is not like a drug, intended to suppress and cover over pain or illness. It has the quality of a naturopathic or homeopathic remedy made to permeate, support and enhance the natural healing abilities of your immune system.

> *Homeopathic medicines . . . may be able to sift through the blood-brain*
> *barrier which normally impedes large and potentially dangerous mole-*
> *cules from entering the brain; perhaps homeopathic medicines are able to*
> *affect brain chemistry and thereby disease in significant ways.*
>
> —*Dana Ullman*

What sort of physical, mental and spiritual attributes do your poetic medicines have? What kind of recipe might resilience, humor and calmness be found in? How do you make this potion? What would you like its effect on you to be? If you could make a natural, poetic medicine using anything at all—what is essential to mix together? General ingredients for an elixir of healing poetry might include: musical language, sensory awareness, feeling and concrete images. Also try ingredients that are even more concrete and personal.

For instance, what particular pieces of music, natural objects and places, flowers, animals or personal items are energizing and healing? Name them.

The great Spanish poet Federico García Lorca, known for his childlike sweetness and powerful imagery, named these poetic medicines for recovering his spirit of childhood:

> *My heart of silk*
> *is filled with lights,*
> *with lost bells,*
> *with lilies and bees.*
> *I will go very far,*
> *farther than those mountains,*
> *farther than the oceans,*
> *way up near the stars,*

*

to ask Christ the Lord
to give back to me
the soul I had as a child,
matured by fairy tales,
with its hat of feathers
and its wooden sword.

Lorca brings us his childhood through lilies and bees, stars and oceans, his hat of feathers and his wooden sword. These kinds of things can be your poetic medicines, too.

THE LANGUAGE OF RELATIONSHIPS: "ACROSS THE AIR BETWEEN US"

A workshop student wrote a poem about language as a path for deepening relationship. Her words show us why poetic language is so powerful when shared in the context of relationship:

> *. . . I ask for a human language*
> *to make its flying sound*
> *across the air between us,*
> *coming from me and then*
> *separately from you,*
> *and then to see the shape*
> *of our words forming above our heads*
> *like blessings held in their own bodies . . .*
> *—Georgia Robertson*

Poetic language expresses what plain language cannot, and thus helps us heal in a very unique way. Georgia speaks of the bridge that poetry can be—a bridge for joining and healing in relationships.

A woman who rarely wrote poetry sent a poem to a close male friend. She could have sent a letter, but the poem expressed her feelings best and she took a risk. To her surprise she

Every relationship between conscious adults is unique, needing freedom to blossom into its own individual flower. We can only attend and cherish the bud with all our care, waiting for the flower to open and declare itself.

—Irene Claremont de Castillejo

received a reply back from the man in the form of a poem. They began to correspond in poetry. It immediately deepened their friendship. Language had made its "flying sound" between them. Their poems invited a more creative kind of communication.

EXERCISE
Poetry and Relationships

Fill in the following sentence stems. You may need to ask a few questions of those close to you.

If I wrote and sent a poem to someone, that person or persons would be _____

_____ .

My favorite poem I'd give as a gift to a spouse, family member, lover or friend is_____

_____ .

The favorite poems or poets of my spouse, family members, lover or friend are_____

_____ .

If I wrote a poem to help heal a particular relationship it would be for my relationship with _____

_____ .

The issue in that relationship I would most like to write about is _____

_____ .

WHAT IS PRECIOUS IS
NEVER TO FORGET

More than "curing" or "solving" particular problems, communicating truth in the spare lines of a healing poem gives life to a healthier spirit, a whole spirit able to meet the challenges of a difficult world: a spirit rooted in integrity, simplicity and a sense of compassion.

Integrating these basic, foundational qualities will help sustain you in the midst of crises, illness, painful experiences and challenging life transitions. We strengthen the whole healing process by remembering and communicating the essential character and original nature of who we are. When nothing can be done to change the hardships of life, we are still reminded:

> *. . . What is precious, is never to forget*
> *The delight of the blood drawn from ageless springs*
> *Breaking through rocks in worlds before our earth.*
> *Never to deny its pleasure in the morning simple light*
> *Nor its grave evening demand for love;*
> *Never to allow gradually the traffic to smother*
> *With noise and fog the flowering of the Spirit.*
> *—Stephen Spender*

These "things" called poems—incandescent lamps of language come in all shapes and sizes—offer us profound encouragement. A poem or even a fragment of a poem may serve as the balancing point which your eyes focus on in order to walk over difficult terrain. Keeping your eyes on that balance point can prevent you from falling upon rocks of despair and sadness that can afflict our daily lives:

> *. . . Shake off this sadness, and recover your spirit;*
> *sluggish you will never see the wheel of fate*
> *that brushes your heel as it turns going by,*
> *the man who wants to live is the man in whom life is abundant . . .*
> *—Miguel de Unamuno*

You can call upon poetry to provide insight into your specific problems. This book will offer you poems to read—and help you write your own. Perhaps no one else will know that the lines of a poem move you with inspiration, or touch you with comfort and joy, but you will know. To the man or woman who *wants to live*, this is all that matters.

THE PRESENCE OF PARADOX

> *Joy & Woe are woven fine*
> *A Clothing for the Soul divine*
> *Under every grief and pine*
> *Runs a joy with silken twine*
> *It is right it should be so*
> *Man was made for Joy & Woe*
> *And when this we rightly know*
> *Thro the World we safely go*
> —*William Blake*

Your life is valuable whether you feel well or ill, joy or sorrow. You may experience joy and sorrow in a single day, in the space of one hour. Allowing room for this paradox is an essential part of living a whole life. It can be difficult because our culture places value on the mythological happiness of advertising: eternal youth riding high and beautiful in a brand new-Bronco.

Finding a way to "talk" in a poem about your real life experience, experience that includes paradox, is to embrace your *whole* life. In the process, you may intuit the subtle thread of joy that is within you, always.

Because the feeling-oriented, nonlinear logic of poetry allows for paradox and even celebrates it, familiarity with poetry will expand your range of possible emotional choices. Sadness *and* exaltation each help in the process of healing. Less in conflict about the presence of paradox in your life, you can experience life from a gradually calmer, intuitive center. You'll be able to develop the emotional stability and agility needed to respond to difficult experiences.

Paradox reveals our link with a *greater* reality. Your true nature and worth is more dynamic, mysterious and beautiful than "self-

Poetic language honors polarities. We use the language of poetry to provide the many levels of feeling, facets of knowing, simultaneously, so we can examine them and move forward.

—*Peggy Osna Heller*

esteem" and "positive thinking" books communicate. Joy and pain happen within the context of this much larger poetical, albeit paradoxical, reality:

> *I am the poet of the Body and I am the poet of the Soul,*
> *The pleasures of heaven are with me and the pains of hell are with me,*
> *The first I graft and increase upon myself, the latter I translate into a*
> *   new tongue.*
>
> —*Walt Whitman*

Embracing paradox is a good strategy for tapping into healing creativity. Intuition, generated by this dynamic embrace, enables us to see possibilities for growth. We sense that good comes from taking risks with expressing our creativity. The risks we need to take to grow require us to accept and live with paradox. Audre Lorde, in her book *The Cancer Journals*, writes about risking to live for the truth:

> *Maybe this is the chance to live and speak those things I really do be-*
> *lieve, that power comes from moving into whatever I fear most that can-*
> *not be avoided. But will I ever be strong enough again to open my*
> *mouth and not have a cry of raw pain leap out?*

Lorde senses that her truth-speaking will gain power as she faces her fears. She does not know what the outcome will be; nevertheless, by saying what she most longs for—the opportunity to speak truthfully about her experience—she quickly names her greatest fear: that she may *only* be able to cry out. Crying out is the act of reclamation.

CRYING OUT ON THE PAGE

> Heart, who will you cry out to? More and more alone, you
> make your way through the unknowable human beings . . .
> —Rainer Maria Rilke
> Paris, July 1914

*

And what if a cry of raw pain *does* emerge? It's okay. You can spill out that cry of pain on the page. Noel releases her cry of loneliness onto the page:

> I miss you
> in no articulate way,
> no civilized words for now.
> And though my lips
> curl around their fastidious sounds,
> my heart, through a ragged hole,
> howls Why? and
> What if? and
> I'm lonely!
> I'm lonely!
> I'm lonely!
> Now, there is nothing to do
> but put the wailing child
> to bed and wait
> either for reason or a
> numbing sleep to over take
> this grief . . .
>
> grief that is so
> unquietly working
> over all the little
> broken things.
>
> —Noel Beitler

The present findings, along with those from conceptually similar experiments, suggest that the disclosure of trauma is simultaneously associated with improvement in certain aspects of immune function and physical health.

—Dr. James Pennebaker

Give yourself permission to cry out. Avoiding what is confusing and painful may exact a far greater toll on you physically and mentally than *not* expressing what is gnawing at your soul. Attempts to explain or discuss or analyze your painful experience may not be enough to free the energy and insight you need to heal and move forward.

A more visceral, spontaneous language, originating within you, may open the gateway to greater intuition, insight and energy for dealing with your problems. This language can benefit you in a number of ways. Your poems can be brought to therapy sessions to provide material for therapeutic work; or you can reflect on them in private to mark the steps and resting places of your journey, the twists and turns of your life.

Cathy's need to "cry out" was rooted in physical pain. For several years she had suffered from severe lower back pain that persisted despite various medical treatments. She wrote the following poem during a workshop I gave many years ago. She was thirty-four and working as production director for a textbook publishing company. Cathy had not written a poem since high school:

Pain's terrorwide eye
stares at me unblinking
lidless
as summer noontime sun.

I barely dare to dream
of escape.
The eye might see my pluck
and sear its stare
into my back forever.

Twinkling love-lit star eyes,
motherlove my longing for your gaze
shapes the faceless space
I call my heart, breaks

like fever, aches
into my consciousness   mama, mama   pain
is for heroes not little girls   or grown women
to bear   nowhere

my shadeless heart to hide.
                    —*Cathy Willkie*

Cathy began to mother herself, tending to her body's needs and offering herself a greater care—a conscious care that remains with her to this day. The raw energy of her poem served as a place of emotional connection with her therapist:

Until I wrote this poem I did not know how much the constant pain had frightened me. I didn't know there could be words for the pain, because it felt like a disaster of unspeakable proportions. I remember taking the poem to a therapist whom I had sought out for help with the feelings that surrounded the knifelike pain which had persisted in my lower back.

I felt self-conscious as I read this poem out loud to her, keeping my eyes on the paper. I hardly knew this person nor she me. We had met only once or twice before. When I looked up I saw tears filling her eyes, and in an instant, I fell headlong into a world I had felt separated from by intense physical pain; the world of being known, seen, understood and cared for.

After writing this poem and reading it to this therapist, something changed. I didn't feel helplessly speechless about hurting even though I still had pain.

Sometimes today, even years later, it is hard for me to tolerate seeing the nakedness of longing for comfort that I expressed in this poem, but when I push through my embarrassment and share it anyway, people usually respond with deep understanding. So the not being alone is a world I keep getting to visit like a great gift that keeps on happening and surprising me.

Cathy and Noel do not give easy answers for their pain. Answers are not what they seek. They want to be heard! These poems are stark. They bite. As I write in *Finding What You Didn't Lose*, it is good to "leave the roots on your writing." Charles Olson puts it so well—his poem *These Days* bears repeating here:

> *whatever you have to say, leave*
> *the roots on, let them*
> *dangle*
> *And the dirt*

Just to make clear
where they come from

Words and images are strong, uncomplicated and clear in Noel and Cathy's poems. Struggle is *felt*. They leave us with no doubt that loneliness and pain demand their attention. They do not intellectualize or try to soothe us with naively hopeful words. Words jangle and burn on the page, catch our attention and draw us into the poignancy of loneliness and pain.

Line breaks and subtle word spacing in Cathy's poem are a way for her intense feelings to condense into their true shape. Her lines form a body that moves. This body of feeling reveals Cathy's life at that time of writing. Noel shouts her loneliness—unstopping the flood that spills through the "ragged hole" of her heart. Once her loneliness is sounded out on the page, Noel sees that loneliness is like a wailing child. She knows what usually happens to that child: numbness and reason quickly stand in the place of care and attention. Now that she knows these things, she can act in a way that is more healing.

For each of them the poem is a way to see the truth and in that process, healing change becomes possible. Treat your own writing with this kind of care as you shape and polish the raw material of your poem.

I have never cut feelings off. I never learned that you were supposed to contain your feelings if you were an educated person, a sophisticated person. I did learn that I had to see things wholly and I learned to feel wholly as well, especially the complexities of what it means to be human and the complexities of what it means to be me.

—Lucille Clifton

EXERCISE
Words That Cry Out

I ask workshop students to speak strong and vibrant words out loud, words that leave the roots and dirt on. As they are spoken, I write the words with colored markers on a large pad. These are not necessarily words that shock or have a coarse edge. They're magnetic words that stir attention and feeling. The potent energy contained within such words ignites the authentic development of your poem. Dive into these words.

Noel uses *lonely* and *ragged*. Cathy made a new word, *terror-wide*, and she uses *sear* in a compelling way. What words can you say and write that show "dirt" on the roots of your poem?

*

Choose words that interest you, that have impact, that reveal something about you and your state of mind, problem or hurt right now. Choose words that are related to the body, to nature and your emotions. Pay attention to how the sound of a word communicates the feeling of that word.

Here are some examples of vibrant words that resonate with me. Now come up with your own.

restless, jagged, wreckage, ruthless, abandon, frighten, turbulent, bruised, caress, fertile, pungent, empty, moist, ache, rotting, stormy, scream, rage, shatter, odor, exhausted, thorny, cavernous, molten

_____

_____

_____

WHERE ARE YOU GLUED TOGETHER? (THAT'S WHERE YOU CAN HEAR GOOD SINGING)

Rainer Maria Rilke suggested not just telling about our pain *but singing it.* Rilke invites us to a more intimate, compassionate relationship between human beings—an intimacy that renders ordinary expression inadequate. Courage to express our suffering could serve us well:

> *It's O.K. for the rich and the lucky to keep still,*
> *no one wants to know about them anyway.*
> *But those in need have to step forward,*
> *have to say: I am blind,*
> *or: I'm about to go blind,*
> *or: nothing is going well with me,*
> *or: I have a child who is sick,*
> *or: right there I am sort of glued together. . . .*
>
> *And probably that doesn't do anything either.*

They have to sing; if they didn't sing, everyone
would walk past, as if they were fences or trees.

That's where you can hear good singing.
People are really strange: they prefer
to hear castratos in boy choirs.

But God himself comes and stays a long time
when the world of half-people start to bore him.
                              —Rainer Maria Rilke

EXERCISE
Expressing Your Suffering Courageously

Be detailed and specific!

What painful things do you most want to speak out about?

_____

_____

What is it you can no longer avoid?

_____

_____

What do you want to courageously sing about?

_____

_____

Where are your places of being "glued together"?

_____

_____

What do you want to invite into your life right now?

_____

_____

Shape your responses into a poem.

★

LOSS AND METAPHORS OF LOSS: THE LEAF-SHAPE REMAINS

When I was eighteen my right leg was amputated just below the knee. It happened at the end of my freshman year in college. A poem I wrote during that period of physical pain, loss and confusion in my life made an enormous difference to me. I'd like to tell you some of my story.

Although I was walking on a prosthesis within a month after the amputation (I even played on a softball team of former high school friends that summer—a friend ran for me as I stood up to hit!), the pain remained intense even a few years after the surgery. Doctors prescribed strong pain relievers but to no avail. Nothing alleviated the pain that burned in my leg like streamers of fire. The medical phrase for this is "phantom pain."

Rationally speaking, my right ankle shouldn't have hurt since it was no longer there. But "phantom pain" is a phantom phrase. Nothing is phantom about this pain! We can talk about scar tissue irritating severed nerve endings as a reason for this pain. We might look into the holographic nature of brain circuitry. We could explain my experience by imagining Kirlian photographs that show the aura of cut leaves . . . the leaf is cut away, but an energetic light form of the leaf-shape remains.

These all offered plausible explanations for my pain from scientific and spiritual perspectives. But they did not allow me to wrestle with my experience. They didn't allow me to investigate the lesson of my pain, and they certainly didn't make the pain go away!

Pain in itself may not offer a useful message, *but* if we perceive its *purpose* in our lives, we can learn valuable lessons. We can realize our potential to heal and grow. I needed to move into this dark loss. Poetic language became my blind man's stick.

Anyone who has been through a severe loss knows how *real* the phantomlike pain of loss is. Explanations won't do. "Get over it" and "time to move on" are just irritating, exasperating, empty words.

My "empty" space of loss was filled with hurt. Chimeric out-lines and poignant hints of my leg's presence haunted me. Those hints provided a powerful contrast to the obvious ab-sence of the leg.

As bizarre as it sounds, I sometimes sense wetness on my in-step when I put my prosthetic foot in a puddle of water. It *feels* like a moment of water touching my bare foot. A strange trick of my mind? I'm not just kidding myself. It *feels* as if I am able to wiggle my big toe. The joy of that! It's just that I don't experi-ence these things, really. But that does not change my *feeling* that I experience these things as true.

With a sudden rattle of quills a flock of pigeons broke out of one of the towering peepul trees. Green-winged and coral-billed, their breasts changing color in the light like mother-of-pearl, they flew off towards the forest. How beautiful they were, how unutterably lovely! Susila was on the point of turning to catch the expression of delight on Dugald's upturned face; then, checking herself, she looked down at the ground. There was no Dugald any more; there was only the pain, like the pain of the phantom limb that goes on haunting the imagination, haunting even the perceptions of those who have undergone the amputation . . .

—Aldous Huxley, from Island

Someone who has experienced the death of or separation from a loved one might imagine that loved one smiling or walking around a corner or hear their voice say "hello" when answering the phone. What they discover is that sunlight has hit upon a stranger's face at a certain angle leaving a shadow of hope, or that it was just a misunderstood inflection of voice or a wrong number.

Amputation and phantom pain are excellent metaphors for loss. What you lose never really goes away. The leaf-shape re-mains. What does one do with that grief? Poetry enters into the severed places in life that explanations and reason cannot touch. The open nature of the blank page allows you to exper-iment with releasing that hurt. What does it feel like—when we release pain like this?

I will call the world a School—and I will call the Child able to read, the Soul made from that School—and I will call the world a school instituted for the purpose of teaching little children to read—I will call the human heart the horn Book used in that school—and I will call the Child able to read the Soul made from that School and its hornbook. Do you not see how necessary a World of Pains and troubles is to school an Intelligence and make it a soul? A Place where the heart must feel and suffer in a thousand diverse ways! Not merely is the Heart a Hornbook. It is the Mind's Bible . . .

—John Keats

✳

I write a poem and say what I need to say. That's it—it is finished. Sometimes it takes time and work getting at what I want to say in a poem. Hard won is their nature. Sometimes I come in contact with an essential joy behind the pain by writing. Writing these poems feels like receiving grace. At other times, I can only let my heart cry out because it hurts.

After I lost my leg, I wanted to take the "next step," to move through and past the pain I felt. My confusion was so deep and the pain so unrelenting that I could do nothing else but cry out.

EVEN TO THIS

> *What my thoughts have troubled about*
> *all through the night after night!*
> *It's so very scary*
> > *sometimes*
> > *I feel*
> > > *would rather*
> *what's the worst that could happen?*
> *because it just hurts too much*
>
> *or having had enough of my own hatred*
> *against myself, lonely is*
>
> *nowhere else to go—*
> *time to stop feeling sorry*
> *for myself,*
>
> *time to open my heart*
> *even to this*
> *and call to God.*

I did not know what my next step was until I wrote it. I threw fragments of my troubled thoughts down on the page. I let them *appear* fragmentary. I wrote the shape of the hurt down. I moved right into my inner struggle. I discovered my next step was not about *getting rid* of the pain.

Pain was a warning to me. I needed to put my attention and care *toward it*, not, in my case, to drug and dull the pain. My poem told me: making a place in my psyche for the loss of my leg must be a priority. If I did not make it a priority, something else less healthy would move into that space of loss and claim my life energy.

My grief about the loss, my fear of the future, the self-hatred and loneliness woven into my turbulent feelings and thoughts— all of these asked not for painkillers but for *opening*— for opening *"even to this."*

There *was* nothing else for me to do. First I had to tell myself there was "nowhere else to go." Not accepting my loss, I could fail to see the potential for something even more insidious and debilitating than physical pain: *self-pity.* Self-pity had no point, no message. The only function of self-pity was to keep my heart tightly contracted and my soul hopeless. Feeling sorry for myself allowed no room for seeing *what is*—or for letting God into my life.

The more I looked at my poem months after writing it, I re-alized what a deep relationship existed between accepting *what is* and *help from God.*

Coming to an emotional awareness of what I needed—a sense of caring acceptance for myself *and* help from God— made my last four words of the poem, "and call to God," feel true, unexpected, deeply felt, natural. I experienced a sense of breaking through—without disowning myself.

Accepting paradox made it possible to feel a relationship be-tween my life and God. After writing this poem, I tried other healing exercises in place of painkillers. I visualized rose petals falling . . . floating down over my stump. Using this vibrant im-age eased the pain considerably and helped gently open my heart to the reality of my loss. I did this with real rose petals too: to see my stump strewn not with hot embers of rejection and self-pity but the soft petals of care. In crying out to God *with all my pain and confusion* I began to make my own song.

What saves a man is to take a step. Then another step. It is always the same step, but you have to take it.

—Antoine de Saint-Exupéry

*

> *I don't have much knowledge yet in grief—*
> *so this massive darkness makes me small.*
> *You be the master: make yourself fierce, break in:*
> *then your great transforming will happen to me,*
> *and my great grief cry will happen to you.*
> *—Rainer Maria Rilke*

It's better for the heart to break than not to break.

—Mary Oliver

My "grief cry" made room for my loss—and initiated transformation. You may not want to use the word "God." That's fine. As Rumi says, "There are hundreds of ways to kneel and kiss the ground." The question still echoes for me and you: "Heart, who will you cry out to?" It's probably not a question we can answer. The questions will change. The answers will be different as we grow and move through our lives.

As Rilke said, we must "live the questions." We must make those questions personal. We must ask them again and again. Dive more deeply into the questions of your life. Writing will help you to make room for your questions, and for the unanticipated insights creativity brings.

Poetry offers a worthy container for our most profound feelings and uncertainties. Whether you've never written a line of poetry before or have won the Nobel Prize in Literature—the poem creates a place for you to *live* your questions.

FACING EXISTENTIAL CRISES: THE-RAG-AND-BONE SHOP OF THE HEART

William Butler Yeats, at seventy-two, was two years from death. He had come to a time when his enthusiasm for life, his spiritual quest, his long-held desire for a relationship with a particular woman, his political work, his imaginative and poetic inspiration, his sexual energy—all felt inadequate. His past life seemed but a fading dream to which he clung. Mortality

weighed heavily upon him. He struggled and found a new perspective through a poem.

Fragments from his poem *The Circus Animals' Desertion* reflect
the powerful experience of existential crisis:

> *. . . Maybe at last being but a broken man*
> *I must be satisfied with my heart . . .*

> *Players and painted stage took all my love,*
> *And not those things that they were emblems of . . .*

Why does this powerful realization of needing to find satisfaction with our own hearts rattle us so profoundly? The poet
Charles Olson said: "I have had to learn the simplest things last,
and this has made for difficulties." We know what he means.
Though we are able to listen for signs of life at the furthest edge
of the universe, the only thing still out of reach of our listening
may be our own hearts.

Whenever your time of struggling with existential meaning
occurs, when it does, if you are open to let that struggle work
upon you, something begins to shift from background to foreground. A shift in priorities may become intensely important.
What matters to you? Working for money without any passion
may seem of less value, while spending time with a spouse
and/or children may take on greater importance. Pursuing the
work, projects or avocation you care about becomes imperative
even if it means leaving a well-paying secure job that does not
satisfy your soul.

What happens to us when we listen to the deepest place
within us? What do we feel when we experience loss, family
problems, midlife crises, broken relationships, illness, work difficulties and the problems of the planet?

Yeats realized that coming to terms with his own heart was
important, that the deepest satisfaction is found not in richly
poetical "players and painted stage" but finally in those things
that lay in the shadows of his human experience: the alley, the
commonplace rubble, raw and useless old things:

As a tool of cognition, poetry beats any existing form of analysis (a) because it pares down our reality to its linguistic essentials, whose interplay, be it clash or fusion, yields epiphany or revelation, and (b) because it exploits the rhythmic and euphonic properties of the language that in themselves are revelatory.

—Joseph Brodsky

✳

> *A mound of refuse or the sweepings of a street,*
> *Old kettles, old bottles, and a broken can,*
> *Old iron, old bones, old rags, that raving slut*
> *Who keeps the till. Now that my ladder's gone,*
> *I must lie down where all ladders start,*
> *In the foul rag-and-bone shop of the heart*

Yeats wasn't rejoicing in these things. He was not valuing garbage. He saw that for all his exquisitely lyrical, powerful writing about life and the history of the Irish people, these "old bones" and "broken cans" and "old iron" were also part of his life. All those difficult things we try to push out of our lives.

Again, I am not talking about seeing ugliness or illness as something wonderful. Discovering what is most essential to us involves acknowledging, often embracing, the totality of our experience. Poetry enables us to tell our real-life, "rag-and-bone," paradoxical experiences without forcing us to draw conclusions or make false "painted" pronouncements. When Joe Milosch's wife became ill with breast cancer he had no choice but to face the "foul rag and bone shop" of their experience together.

TOUCHING THE EXPERIENCE OF CANCER: "I DON'T KNOW"

Before teaching writing to children through California Poets in the Schools and to adults at the San Diego Writing Center, Joe Milosch worked as a trail locator and heavy equipment foreman for the National Forest Service. He wrote the following poem about his wife's cancer exactly when he was *not* trying to write it:

> *Why is a scar on a man a mark of distinction,*
> *on a woman a mark of disfigurement?*

I don't know.

Why is it funny when a man loses his hair,
and tragic when a woman loses hers?

I don't know.

What will you tell her
when the X rays turn the scar
on her breast raw–
hamburger red?

I don't know.

When she's bald, lost the hair
from her eyebrows,
and lies with closed eyes,
with a skeletal look,
will you kiss her
and tell her
she's beautiful?

I don't know.

What do you do
in the bedroom,
when she is thinking
of death,
and she cries?

I hold her hand, and I breathe.

Joe tried to write this poem for three years. Earlier poems he had written about his wife's illness were not satisfying. Although his earlier efforts served as stepping-stones to reach the poem here, Joe felt he had not gotten to the heart of the matter. Something in the experience of *how* Joe and his wife worked

If we were to examine our diseases poetically, we might find a wealth of imagery that could speak to the way we live our lives.

—Thomas Moore

out the experience of her illness *together* remained elusive in his writing. It took time to get there. Something as devastating as the possible death of his wife required Joe to do other work before he spoke clearly. Joe says:

My first poems about Patsy's illness were not experiential—they did not communicate the feeling that someone very close to me might die. It was frustrating, I could not touch the actual experience. I started to write poems about my dad. I wanted to remember him as he was, in a sense, because I had this love for him I wanted to remember. I wanted to paint our relationship as it was rather than immortalize him as a perfect father. I had been struggling to write these poems about a sometimes brutal and at other times extremely gentle relationship. This was in the midst of my wife's illness.

My dad had died a year before the diagnosis of my wife's illness and so with all of this working around inside of myself I studied performance poetry with Juan Felipe Herrera. We were trying to put ourselves in an area of the unknown and write a poem about it. Juan had me sing and play percussion instruments which I had never done before. I wrote a poem about my father walking naked into my bedroom. As I was working on this poem, which turned out to be a love poem to my father, Juan, who is very flamboyant, came up with an idea that he would give each student a line or a phrase as a gift at the end of class and we would write this poem using that line for the next day. Juan came up to me and whispered "I don't know" into my ear.

I wandered about after class trying to think of a poem. I didn't have anything to go with his words. I was so wrapped up in my father and thought the poem would be about him. So as is my practice, I got up around 5:30 the next morning to write and came up with nothing. I decided I would go to class and do an impromptu poem based on Juan's phrase. As I was waiting outside of the class the whole poem about my wife's illness arrived in just a few minutes.

I knew there was something in this poem. I called Patsy immediately to share it. She was the first to hear it. It was so intimate that I felt I needed to have her permission to read it to the class. She was very moved. She liked my honesty and ambivalence. She felt happy and wanted me to share it with others.

I tried to read it at first like it was an angry poem. Some people in the hospital cancer group had been very confrontational and graphic in asking me questions about how I would deal with issues surrounding Patsy's cancer. These tactics had made me angry and the poem was, I first thought, my angry response to their questions. But then I realized it wasn't really an angry poem. Instead, I was telling myself that I didn't know what I was doing or would do—but I knew how I had to be open.

Writing the poem helped me drain off my rage. Once I got the rage out of me, I had a different way of looking at Patsy's illness. I see more of her beauty.

With cancer, you keep hoping for answers or someone to blame. But there are no answers or anyone to blame. "I don't know" still plays a big part in our lives. We are more tolerant of one another. There is more blurriness and less edges in our relationship. That's okay.

When I read it to Patsy, it became a love poem. That's what it is, a love poem.

POEM-MAKING AS A GUIDE IN YOUR LIFE

To Know the Dark

To go in the dark with a light is to know the light.
To know the dark, go dark. Go without sight,
and find that the dark, too, blooms and sings,
and is traveled by dark feet and dark wings.
                              —*Wendell Berry*

Poetry can be a safe guide, a wise presence, so you don't feel alone while moving through the inevitable dark places in life. Poems become material for healing work in writing circles, to explore with your therapist, to share with a trusted friend or to reflect upon within your own heart.

Giving attention and care to your fragility and resilience will nurture your ability to make healing poems. When fragility and

Especially in this time of managed care, more emphasis seems to be placed upon medication and the quick amelioration of symptoms, short-term work and privatized, profit-making clinics, than upon the lovely and mysterious alchemy that comprises the cords between people, the cords that soothe some terrors and help us heal.

                              —*Lauren Slater*

resilience are joined together, you give birth to a form of sensitivity that is rooted in lifeforce. Look at the way wildflowers can kiss their way through glacial ice.

Respect for your vulnerability *and* courage will help turn your sensitivity from a weakness to an ally. When you write with this kind of sensitivity, your poetry can help ensure a safer journey through dark experiences.

Like a trowel that digs the dark, compacted, wintered earth to prepare it for spring planting, hearing or writing a poem works upon your life so something new can grow. A poem allows the air of new thoughts into your mind, the moisture of feeling into your heart, and a joyful current of energy comes alive in your body.

Inside the condensed words of a poem, possibilities not yet considered are revealed. Writing holds the potential for comfort and insight to come out of your difficult or painful experiences. Writing, especially about painful topics, may sometimes be impossible. At the very least it may feel scary, like entering unknown terrain on a dark night. Yet the time will come when we walk forward, even one step forward, in the dark.

Truly, the work is not only reading or writing a poem, it is in living on: living on through heartaches of loss and disappointment, flourishing in spite of your "rough seasons." But *how* do you choose to live on? One way is by expressing the "good singing" of poetry. Make room for your cry of pain in a poem. Speak of the place you are glued together. Find yeast in words so your poems will become like "fresh bread on the table." The yeast of your poetic speech will leaven intuitive understanding in your heart and a resilient, liberating, even joyful knowing in your bones.

The time will come when you will write, while walking in the dark—and instead of banging your shins once again, something unexpected and transformative will happen.

Appreciating poetry is probably like appreciating anything else. It means having the generosity to let a thing be what it is, the patience to know it, a sense of the mystery in all living things, and a joy in new experience.

—M. C. Richards

CHAPTER TWO

THE SAME RIVER TWICE

Merging the Healing and Creative Processes

The very fact that a thing—anything—can be fitted into a meaning built up of words, small black words, that can be written with one hand and the stub of a pencil, means it is not big enough to be overwhelming. It is the vast, formless, unknown and unknowable things we fear. Anything which can be brought to a common point—a focus within our understanding— can be dealt with.

—Lara Jefferson

THE HEALING AND
CREATIVE PROCESSES:
STEPPING INTO THE
SAME RIVER TWICE

I wake to sleep, and take my waking slow.
I feel my fate in what I cannot fear.
I learn by going where I have to go.

We think by feeling. What is there to know?
I hear my being dance from ear to ear.
I wake to sleep, and take my waking slow.
                                        —*Theodore Roethke*

As we saw in Chapter One, poem-making became a way for Noel, Cathy and Joe to "think by feeling." Their heads and hearts spoke together. Something in their lives impelled them, called them or moved them into action; to "learn by going where [they had] to go." Their poetry embodied their experience, their pain, their insight, their stories, the precious and passionate act of living.

This chapter will look at different ways to enter the healing and creative processes. We will look at how these companion processes are seen as separate. Too often our heavily scientific approach to health care reverses Theodore Roethke's lovely insight so that we try to "feel by thinking." Going in that direction, human beings get lost in the shuffle. We'll see how poem-making invites us to renew feeling so that creativity and healing can merge in our lives.

Whether your path includes meditation, therapy, reaching out to others or just living the best you can in a tough world—or all of these—we all want lives that are meaningful. You may

I think writing poetry is a matter of agreeing that you have these two people inside: every day you set aside time to be with the subtle person, who has funny little ideas, who is probably in touch with retarded children, and who can say surprising things.

—Robert Bly

*

be trying to make your way to success through a career that demands huge amounts of your time or by following some more unconventional route—but it seems for each of us, there is an increasing need for meaning-making in our daily lives.

Struggling with difficult personal problems or the challenges of daily life in the world, where we are now and where we are going is often strongly influenced by where we have been. How we relate to our past experience affects where we go from here.

Whatever form of therapy fits your particular temperament, *externalizing your experience* by *creatively expressing* it on paper, and if possible sharing it with someone who listens well, is a way to state how things are, release old hurts, set healthy directions and develop potentials that make destructive past behavior or experience more and more a thing of the past.

> *If you don't know the kind of person I am*
> *and I don't know the kind of person you are*
> *a pattern that others made may prevail in the world*
> *and following the wrong god home we may miss our star.*
>
> *For there is many a small betrayal in the mind,*
> *a shrug that lets the fragile sequence break*
> *sending with shouts the horrible errors of childhood*
> *storming out to play through the broken dyke. . . .*
> —*William Stafford*

Spiritual traditions and practices also address ways to relate to and heal painful experiences. Some emphasize prayer, service, confession, forgiveness, and God's redemptive power. Some teach living with clear awareness in the present moment and forming a deeper relationship to the earth. Each of these pathways are intended to help an individual feel more of their intrinsic connection with the Tao or Spirit, with the unfolding process of their life experience and soul journey.

A spiritual practice may instruct you to sit and observe your breath, returning to the flow of the in-breath and out-breath each time the mind wanders—gently returning to your breath,

Perhaps the truth depends on a walk around the lake.

—*Wallace Stevens*

noticing each unfolding moment with keen attention. Concentration opens you to awareness and insight. Meditation allows you to develop a calmer center so that you may view problems from a fresh perspective.

> I have lived on the lip
> of insanity, wanting to know reasons,
> knocking on the door. It opens.
> I've been knocking from the inside!
>
> —Rumi

Whatever spiritual path you walk, to refine your understanding of healing and how you respond to suffering and joy, you must ask questions that are appropriate for you, intuit the guidance that is right for you and feel more sensitively for how to apply the healing process specifically to your life. Creativity is a key to unlock each of these three things and it is natural to us. Enter poetry and poem-making.

Poem-making allows us to make profound discoveries about ourselves. It can become a beacon during our dark times; it can even "cure anguish and cause joy."

The greatest thing about religious practice is it makes life large—and literature did the same thing for me.
—*Robert Haas*

> *Poetry is not a form of entertainment, and in a certain sense not even a form of art, but our anthropological, genetic goal, our linguistic, evolutionary beacon. We seem to sense this as children, when we absorb and remember verse in order to master language. As adults, however, we abandon this pursuit, convinced that we've mastered it. Yet what we've mastered is but an idiom, good enough perhaps to outfox an enemy, to sell a product, to get laid, to earn a promotion, but certainly not good enough to cure anguish or cause joy.*
>
> —*Joseph Brodsky*

BETWEEN THE LINES
OF YOUR STORY

Your story is important to tell. Tell it too linearly or literally, however, and you may not catch important underlying feelings, images, bodily sensations and postures, or metaphors that would surprise you and create growth were you to listen closely to what is written between your story's lines.

Lucille Clifton shows the connections between significant periods throughout her life in a very simple way. A few images emerge in her poem to hold the essence:

> i am running into a new year
> and the old years blow back
> like a wind
> that I catch in my hair
> like strong fingers like
> all my old promises and
> it will be hard to let go
> of what I said to myself
> about myself
> when I was sixteen and
> twentysix and thirtysix
> even thirtysix but
> i am running into a new year
> and i beg what i love and
> i leave to forgive me

Lucille Clifton uses the image/sensation of "old year" blowing through her hair like the wind to succinctly express her desire to break free of the past. Image/sensations are an important element in poetry. They put you in direct contact with the flow of living in the present moment. They become a contact place to feel your process and make the poem live. An image/sensation allows a story to condense and hold years of telling and deep feeling. One powerful image/sensation can reveal in a moment paragraphs of writing and hours of talking. Out of your simple image/sensation, your deep voice may feel and speak.

Poetic elements of sensation and image tell your unique story more tangibly than literal explanations. Image and sensation make your story felt; what you express becomes a *bodily felt*

You must give birth to your images. They are the future waiting to be born . . .

—Rainer Maria Rilke

sensation. You will more easily be able to picture and feel what you are writing or speaking of. This combination will give greater focus to sustain and energize your process of healing. Instead of saying "I feel a sense of loss" you might say:

> *I wake up at the far edge of autumn,*
> *frightened, cold, drifting down, alone.*

Or instead of expressing a desire for "a deeper relationship with nature" you might write:

> *I want to stand and feel a thick summer breeze*
> *flow warm over my naked sovereign self,*
> *my essence borne into the breathing of an entire landscape*
> *and the incomprehensible language of living things.*

Let your images and sensations of experience and reverie find a place on the page in the following exercise.

EXERCISE
Capturing Images

> *The secret of sailing is to sail on solar wind. Hone and spread your*
> *spirit till you yourself are a sail, whetted, translucent, broadside to the*
> *merest puff.*
>
> —Annie Dillard

Focus on a physical sensation/image to connect with your creative and healing process. For instance, what does the sound of water at the shore bring up for you? If you close your eyes and hear those waves lapping, where does your mind go? What connections and/or images come? A friend was ill with the flu and in thinking of this man who has a beautiful heart, lying in bed there in his home, I thought of these lines to express a sense of comfort and well-being:

Your arrival occurs at night
to a deep, safe harbor,
where the only sound
is closeness to home.

The subtle sound/image of waves in a harbor held the feeling of "closeness to home" for me. Imagine your experience of water along the shore. Does it look like the Atlantic or Pacific shore—do different feelings inhabit those places? Or is there another body of water altogether in your imagination? What insights blossom in your awareness through this sensory contact? Feel sensation/insight directly through your body.

Langston Hughes wrote this poem about the dry dusty land wanting him to come back to rich sensory experience, to come back to life. Hughes includes a few strong sensory images:

DUST BOWL

The land wants me to come back
To a handful of dust in autumn,
To a raindrop
In the palm of my hand
In spring.
The land wants me to come back
To a broken song in October,
To a snowbird on the wing.
The land wants me to come back.
                    —Langston Hughes

Use the following physical sensations/images to serve as catalysts to awaken your imagination and to recall life experiences. If you can't experience these things directly, imagine that you can—or find your own. See what arises! Write everything you can about the connections sparked by these images and sensations:

* walking barefoot on a hot city sidewalk
* listening to the wail of sirens and rush of vehicles
* standing naked under a waterfall
* tasting snowflakes for the first time
* holding someone in your arms
* smelling and tasting food from a different country
* petting your cat or dog
* hearing thunder when you were a child
* watching fog roll in over the hills

THREE STORIES OF HEALING AND CREATIVITY: NOEL, JODIE AND SUSANNE

Noel: "A Creative Collaboration Between Myself and Something Other than Me"

Poem-making helped Noel overcome grief about the loss of her athletic ability. Noel was an extraordinary long-distance runner. Running was her way of diving into the flow of life. But when she reached forty, her knees and hips developed arthritis. Bone spurs formed in her spine from the repetitive motion of striding and caused her a great deal of pain. Noel had to give up running and, more importantly, the freedom she felt in the act of running. What could possibly replace this freedom?

I would find myself sitting in a chair crying and crying. I had tremendous grief but nowhere to put it. My body was aching for the place that could move me beyond myself into a connection with everything.

What I loved about running wasn't so much hammering the ground with my feet but being in this flow where things felt alive around and within me. Being in the presence of nature, running through the hills: that space where it is timeless. Losing that timelessness was a cause for my grief. I started to give my grief words and gradually began to discover something: I could touch into this same place when I wrote.

I find that when I write, I am deeply concentrated and connected to life. This connection comes about through an intense concentration joined with receptivity. It is so much like the flow of running. I lose all sense of time when I write and move through infinitely varied terrain—just as I did when running.

I have no doubt poetry is the best caretaker of my soul that I ever found. It steers me in the right direction. I've never missed with a poem. My poems teach me about how to see Jake, my teenage son. How to love Jake. Poems teach me how to love my husband, how to appreciate who he is. Poetry is teaching me how to exist with the pain and the love of my family. To hold the love and pain at the same time.

I can't say this is all my wisdom. It is something of a collaboration between myself and something other than me. My poem says to me: this is how to do housework as if it could be a blessing. Poetry is teaching me to be kind.

For Noel, writing poetry became a way to have a creative relationship with life. Through her inner work of dealing with the nature of promises, of change and loss, she discovered an even greater promise: a way to relate to the joy of the present.

Creativity is, foremost, being in the world soulfully, for the only thing we truly make, whether in the arts, in culture, or at home, is soul.

—Thomas Moore

Listen.
The new grass stands
upon a podium of dirt,
promising Earth her spring.
Listen, and you will hear
everything promising something:
The planets their fidelity
To Sun, Moon her loyal tending
of the tides.
Listen, and on a still night
you will hear your own breath
make a shy but certain promise to Life;
listen well, and Life will
promise herself to you
like an eager bride.

—Noel Beitler

The promise Noel made to herself is to collaborate with life. With that promise, she is dedicated to uniting the inner processes of creativity and healing.

EXERCISE
Listening Well

What does listening tell you about relationships? What does listening have to teach you about being close to your creativity and healing process?

Practice listening. For instance, listen to the sounds of your child or children at play and when they speak to you. Not just their words and the meaning of their words, but the sound of their voice. Listen to the sounds you hear from your kitchen window, around your home or when you go to the market in your town or city. Listen to emotionally charged sounds like a baby crying and people arguing, as well as the sounds of machines, like motorcycles revving or sirens roaring. Listen for birdsong and the wind. Listen carefully to all of these and write about your experience.

Find some particular place where you really want to spend time listening. What do you hear? What kind of relationship is formed from your listening? Find a language to show this.

Listening creates holy silence.
Listening is like the rain.
    —Rachel Naomi Remen

Jodie: "Do Not Wipe Your Tears Away"

This shaking keeps me steady. I should know.
What falls away is always. And is near.
I wake to sleep, and take my waking slow.
I learn by going where I have to go.
            —Theodore Roethke

Being responsive to your feelings and needs will help keep you in touch with your creative process. To reclaim our feelings we must be able not only to know what we feel but to find a language for those feelings. Writing poetry, even as a beginner,

*

may give you just what you need to tap into that place where you "think by feeling," and "take [your] waking slow."

One afternoon during a four-day workshop, students wrote poems related to their grief experiences. Grief poems came about naturally. The opportunity presented itself for us to reveal what is usually kept under pleasant wraps. Within the safety of the circle, fine poems of loss spilled out and hearts opened. (What drew these forward was keen open-hearted attention rather than probing analysis.)

A man read his poem, and as he did, he cried. Others cried with him. Someone approached him with a box of Kleenex, but Jodie motioned "no" to the person. Jodie knew what he needed and that was to cry. The box of Kleenex was set aside. About a half hour later, Jodie asked if he could read a poem he'd just written:

It is easier in our society to be naked physically than to be naked psychologically or spiritually— easier to share our body than to share our fantasies, hopes, fears, and aspirations, which are felt to be more personal and the sharing of which is experienced as making us more vulnerable.

—Rollo May

DO NOT WIPE YOUR TEARS AWAY

Do not wipe your tears away.
Let them flow down your cheek.
Let them create a stream on your face
to allow the healing waters to flow.

Let the waters cleanse your skin
and wash your face with silk.
Let them caress you lightly
and reveal to you, your heart.

Let the water fall to the earth,
and a tree will grow from it.
Let your tears flow from their depths
and they will release the seeds of your soul.

Do not be careful
Do not be contained
or proper or polite.
Do not wipe your tears away.

Taste them on your lips
and know that you have graced yourself today.
                                        —Jodie Senkyrik

This is what Jodie had to say about his poem:

Ever since I was a young boy the message I got was to not cry. So I
didn't and consequently I stopped being open to my life and feelings.
What I've discovered is that openness includes allowing myself to feel
pain. I had stepped out of a river of healing by not being open to crying.

Now I see crying as a way to enter back into the river of healing.
To cry is to flow with the river. I've seen people who stop crying in a
support/healing group and how they step out of the river. They stop
their process. Kleenex gets passed around and we lose the thread with
our immediate feelings. We put the mask back on. We screw the lid back
on. We apologize for making a scene.

My line "Taste them on your lips" is a way for me to know that by
tasting my tears, I'm in the river. I can be glad about the taste of tears
even if I'm sad, because tears taste all right. More than anything else,
I always thought I needed to be contained and in control. But I've
decided that letting tears flow is all right because I am here to heal.

The river flows towards new life. It allows me to move from one
place to another in my life. Writing this poem helped me to share with
others my process of healing.

EXERCISE
Reclaiming Feelings

Consider those times when you shut off your feelings of sadness
in order to appear "fine," either to others or to yourself. (Or, if
your tendency is to inhibit feelings of joy and delight, write about
that process.) What image or metaphor describes the experience
of suppressing your feelings? What image or metaphor could illustrate giving those feelings more room? Without allowing the
emotion to overwhelm you, what would giving your feelings
more room in your life look like? Make a poem about this.

*

Let the young rain of tears come.
Let the calm hands of grief come.
It's not all as evil as you think.
                                        —Rolf Jacobsen

Susanne: Entering the Dark Places with Innocence

Teach me, Oh Great One,
to enter now the dark places
with innocence.
Cause, I pray you,
the words I encounter there
to stick fiercely to my toes, my sinews,
my throat, my hair, my soul,
that I may return with them
to the world of communication among humans.
                                        —Susanne Petermann

When we are suffering from a serious illness, we may feel as if we've been flung down hard by some yet unknown force. In a kind of daze, we wonder desperately what can help us. We don't want to be swept away by the swift emotional and physical undercurrent of illness but that current can be extremely rough.

Poem-making can help you to steady yourself so that gradually it is possible to respond *to* your illness rather than react *from* it or become totally lost in it. Writing in your poetic voice can give dimension and creative power to your difficult and confusing experience. The process of making a poem can put us in contact with our spiritual roots and creative muse, from which we can draw strength and guidance.

Only when you express the struggle and uncertainty of illness—your anger and sadness and fear—can you respond to it. Responding to your illness opens the way for you to become more aware of how to best attend to the process of healing. Su-

The quest for certainty blocks the search for meaning. Uncertainty is the very condition to impel man to unfold his powers.

                                        —Erich Fromm

sanne tells her story of having breast cancer and how writing
poetry helped:

*
* *I moved up to northern California to attend university in January of*
* *1995 and began studying psychology. It was late summer when the tu-*
* *mor was discovered in my right breast. I found images and metaphors*
* *that helped me to express my fears, the anxiety, everything that went*
* *with the experience. I would write a poem, in order to firmly place that*
* *experience into my story and in my memory.*
*

> *Because a skeleton speaks to me daily*
> *I cannot ignore how lovely*
> *the fur of an animal I find on a roadside*
> *or in the hollow of my armpit.*

*
* *The poems came from unexpected places. I turned the doctor's notes from*
* *the radiology test that first indicated the possibility of cancer into a*
* *poem. I read the report and what surprised me was the rhythmical na-*
* *ture of this very technical report. The report had colorful words and in-*
* *teresting syllabic cadences. The words almost seemed to be a style of*
* *architecture.*
*

RADIOLOGY REPORT

> *Routine*
> *medio*
> *lateral o-*
> *blique and*
> *cranio-*
> *caudad*
> *views were per-*
> *formed. A suggestion of a*
> *mass.*
> >   *A suggestion of a*
> *mass*
> *in the lower right*
> *breast corre-*

sponds to the
palpable
lump.   *This*
nonspecific
finding is most
likely be-
nign, however
ultrasound
demonstrates a
well-defined
echo   a
well-defined
echo   at
ap-
proximately
5 o'
clock.
                    —*Susanne Petermann*

I think the meaning of this poem is still evolving for me. All I know is that the reactions that I receive from people when I read it to them are long silences, and then they start slowly nodding their heads with the sort of weight of how grim this report sounds, given the fact that tumor turned out to be malignant.

Making the poem slowed down this matter of fact, stark informa-tion, written on preprinted forms in a medical report, so that I became aware these words are talking about ME. The words "likely benign" are belied by the phrase "well-defined echo." The report leaves the out-come of my life all very ambivalent in a very cold, detached way.

The poem points to a certain part of me that is bitter and resentful and very anti-medical. It expresses the way that the medical system can be so cold and my surprise about that, feeling like a laboratory animal. This poem is pointed and stark, there is nothing soft about it. But that is so much of my experience of our medical system.

I think what we lack isn't science but poetry that reveals what the heart is ready to recognize.

—*Joseph Campbell*

The act of writing gave Susanne back a sense of her soul. She let her imagination infuse her experience and start to transform it. Writing became the process through which she would not let herself be lost in the depersonalized environment of medicine. The following is a journal piece that takes the form of a prose poem:

Tomorrow I go to surgery; this is the last evening I will be spending with a part of my body, my right breast . . . But tonight the atmosphere is thick with present tenses. I find myself so deeply rooted in my house slippers that I can feel seeds sprouting in the ground under my feet under my house, and in the ancient eyes of my friends who are arriving for a ceremony. The gray-blue corners of the room hold a hush, a watery silence. I will light more candles, lest we drown.

Drumming begins to rattle the edges of my consciousness, each woman with a drum, each round head of each drum as round as the circle we form. There, someone dressed in black velvet. My eyes go out, then come back again: there in my private hell, a surgeon cracks my shoulders apart like a thigh from a drum stick.

THE JAZZMEN OF POETRY LET LOOSE: RECLAIMING A LANGUAGE OF LIFE

> The media are excellently equipped to pose enormous questions followed by puny answers. For enormous answers we have always turned to poetry, whether it is by Isaiah, Sophocles, Tu Fu, Shakespeare, Whitman, Neruda, or Allen Ginsberg, though even in poetry the answers are grassy hills compared to the vast and gloomy Everest of the question.
>
> —Jim Harrison

Finding an authentic language to enjoy in your healing poems can be difficult, because, while our culture values freedom of speech, it does little to help us discover a language of depth and honesty and feeling. Mass media tend to cultivate conflict rather than dialogue in public discourse. Most radio talk shows sharpen the blade of the language of intolerance.

As consumers we're forced to live on a diet of cardboard box words. Commercials, though occasionally entertaining, are basically contrived poetry, sexy but empty words and images with no nutritional value.

The slick phrases used in advertising and TV and films lull us into believing that life's complexities can be adequately explained with neat cliches and simplistic slogans. Life is rarely portrayed as a sheer wonder, a mystery.

Unless we have the language to express the richness of our experience, we don't feel whole, and discovering our innate wholeness is what healing is all about. Poem-making can be your lifeline to a more genuine existence. Passionate language can be a way to reconnect with your humanity.

I wrote a poem to stand against our culture's onslaught of rootless words. One evening, I heard a woman read her poetry. Her passionate love for the earth and for speaking truth inspired this poem:

Poetry, in the past, was the center of our society, but with modernity it has retreated to the outskirts. I think the exile of poetry is also the exile of the best of humankind.

—*Octavio Paz*

CRAZY JANEL WANTS TO HEAR
THE JAZZMEN OF POETRY LET LOOSE

Pale gardeners of flat and moveless hot-house poems
have fast-food eyes for merely words arranged in soil
paper thin, the ash-gray agribusiness of their minds.

They pull the roots of music from the very breath and mouth
that creates Life's organic blossoming
into rhythm, into sound, vibrations of the word.

Oh, for creatures drunk on juicy light of lyric breath
and incandescent wailing of Earth's dark and fecund mouth,
that magnificent jazz of which we all are made.

★

EXERCISE
Writing with Passion

> *Dear children, you must try to say*
> *Something when you are in need.*
> *Don't confuse hunger with greed;*
> *And don't wait until you are dead.*
> —*Ruth Stone*

Writing with depth and passion intensifies the creative and healing processes. Experiment in the following ways: 1. Free write about something in nature that inspires *your* passion. What metaphor, image, sensation, sound "captures" that natural entity? Use one or two of these poetic elements as a magnet to attract your words. 2. Write something—a love poem or an outraged rant—that manifests your strong desire to reclaim a language of feeling for yourself. 3. Speak out passionately about your fear, anger, sadness or loss. Picture this feeling with a concrete image such as a wall, a fire, a wild animal, falling flower petals or ice. Let that image represent your feeling or give it a voice for that feeling.

Writing is an arm, a hand to touch reality. It was like trying to scratch an itch I couldn't reach. But it wasn't an itch, it was a whole world. The writing helped me to be in that place. It was where my experience was alive.
—*Glo Lamson*

LEARNING TO SPEAK: MAKING POEMS TO RELEASE EMOTION

Learning to speak with clear intention and feeling is possible to do. You may not yet have access to a language that can place your emotions onto the page. Marge Piercy writes in her poem *Unlearning to Not Speak:*

> *She must learn again to speak*
> *starting with I*
> *Starting with We*
> *starting as the infant does*

*

with her own true hunger
and pleasure
and rage.
　　　　　　　　　—Marge Piercy

Marge Piercy names simple words: hunger, pleasure, rage. Yet these words hold a tremendous life force. Why should they be difficult to speak? What is inside of them?

The following exercises should be done with care. If you want to explore issues like fear and anger, it is a good idea to have adequate support from a counselor, or to share your writing in confidence with a trusted friend. Share your writing with someone who knows how to hear you.

Onie Kriegler is an educator in holistic health and does therapeutic body work. She wrote a poem about her experience of losing her voice to fear, and then gradually reclaiming it:

Fear snatched my voice away
and I have been bargaining with him ever since.
Fear entered my life like a relative planning to stay for a long time.
He had good reason to come more than enough reasons to stay.
Little girl makes her way
no life more precious than this,
no spirit more delicately rendered.
Thick tights, short dress, hand knitted sweater, solid buckled shoes,
she is dark and sturdy made for movement,
a stranger to language, she moves sure footed on the bleak terrain.
Fear came to rest on her, a bird of prey perched on too small shoulders,
she bore him into her adolescence as a toughness,
an I need you not aloofness,
quickly interpreted she was left alone.
Desires stilled in tightly corked bottles of tears
opened privately only in the presence of dreams.
Girlwoman banks her fires
bargains once more for a fragment of her voice
to move her on.

　　　　　　　　　—Onie Kriegler

Onie had this to say about her poem:

The issues I write about often relate to finding my voice. If I lose my voice, I come back around to gaining it again if I write. By writing, I develop that skill of seeing when I lose contact with myself and also saying what I need to say. Both happen simultaneously.

Writing is especially helpful at those times when I don't have words for how I feel. Those times when there is no language to match my feelings. It's not like the feeling is beyond words—it's that I go mute. I silence myself. When I silence myself I lose contact with experience in my body. As a result of that, whatever experience I am having is not able to be named.

It has to do with being afraid to speak for fear of what might happen to me. Not speaking is forsaking my integrity in order to appear noncontroversial or unconfrontational.

That self-abandonment is very painful, and it is when I lose my voice. Fear of not being liked, being left, being judged. As women, we are taught to be pleasing. Fear of standing strongly with a voice that could get us labeled a bitch is a big part of our conditioning.

When writing a poem I give myself permission to speak. Poetry's open form almost invites it. I get to see and hear myself. I get to place myself in front of me as I speak. I externalize a relationship with this very passionate aspect of myself. That relationship is the transformative piece for me.

EXERCISE
Releasing Emotions

Read Onie's poem again. Is there an emotion or circumstance in your own life which has suppressed your voice? What images arise? Write these on paper. Let your words flow. Don't erase or worry about spelling. Paint freely with your own words. Don't hesitate to use the powerful images, sounds, bodily sensations or vibrant words from your word-flow.

Use the words that accurately name what must be named. Use details, your direct experience, metaphor and imagery, your imagination and the holiness of your heart to tell the story of:

* how your inner voice was discouraged or suppressed.

_____

_____

_____

* when your inner voice grew quiet.

_____

_____

_____

* how you handled that loss.

_____

_____

_____

* how you found your way in the world without that voice.

_____

_____

_____

* what inner poet-qualities you want to regain.

_____

_____

_____

* what dreams and desires you want to reclaim.

_____

_____

_____

* what passion you will bring to this process of reclaiming your desires and dreams.

_____

_____

_____

★ your reclaimed creative self (paint an image of it).

_____

_____

_____

★ how you will move back into the world, changed in this way, and maintain this new voice.

_____

_____

_____

Develop a poem from your response to these questions and suggestions. Name what may have hidden, discouraged or suppressed your voice. Work with the images, feeling and sounds— any response that feels potent. Allow yourself to write more, to go off in an entirely different direction. If nothing comes to you now, go run, meditate, play and come back to the exercise at a different time.

If you feel like you need more help in gaining access to raw material for the exercise above, write at the top of a blank page one word which names your feeling, such as: fear, rage, grief, loneliness. It could also be a short phrase, such as: _I'm Not Seen or Heard, My Broken Dreams, I Am Hurting._

Use images, sounds, and rhythm to form a poem based on the word or phrase you've chosen—but do not use the actual word or phrase in your poem.

WEAVING TOGETHER THE PERSONAL AND UNIVERSAL PROCESS

> Poetry is the art of letting the primordial word resound through the common word.
>
> —Gerhart Hauptmann

The creative process can connect us with both our uniquely personal stories and with the universal. But when sorrow or serious problems press heavily upon us, we may forget the larger picture for a while. The most powerful way to reconnect with the world outside yourself is to tap into your sense of relationship and community.

The AIDS quilt comes to mind. Sponsored by The Names Project, the AIDS Quilt memorializes the lives of those who have died from AIDS. It is made of thousands upon thousands of brightly colored quilted panels. Each panel represents a person. Panels are made by a loved one of the person who has died from AIDS.

The quilt has the elements of poetry: panels are made of color, texture, shapes, images, symbols and language. The panels contain links and connections of those who are being remembered and those who remember. There are both biographical facts and stories of the heart. Eight panels are sewn together as one. The entire quilt of well over 33,000 panels has been displayed many times in Washington, D.C., and throughout the country.

The quilt resurrects memory. It honors individuals and outlasts death by joining lives together in the creative process. *Each quilt is part of something loving, grieving, personal, beautiful, and universal.*

A woman talks about the process of making a quilt for her son and all the people she felt connected to in the process:

As I began to design Mike's panel and lay out the pieces, I felt as though it was the saddest and most beautiful experience of my life—somehow the pain of burying my son in October of 1986 and the joy of giving birth to him thirty-seven years ago merged.

Then, when I took the pieces to my daughter-in-law's house to sew them together I felt this experience—creating the panel—truly became an all-family project. And I knew it was a joint family effort that would have pleased Mike very much . . .

. . . All across America there are other mothers like me, as well as fathers, grandparents, sisters, brothers, sons, daughters, nieces, nephews, lovers, friends, who have found themselves—or soon will—drawn to the Quilt by the immense power of its hope and humanity . . .

I did it for two reasons—for Mike and for all the others who've been lost to AIDS, and for myself and all the others who've lost them.

—Sue Caves

Remembering how we fit into a much larger context can help us to expand beyond ourselves. Released from preoccupation solely with ourselves we can *feel* for the larger community and creative process that we are a part of—even as we attend to our most private and personal issues.

Poetic language makes the link between personal and universal realities more tangible. The turn of seasons, the rounds of the moon, the ebb and flow of tides can be shown to mirror experiences and changes in our personal lives. Feeling these connections helps us to understand our relationship to a larger spectrum of life. By discovering, through poem-making, the connection between our own life and what exists beyond us, we recognize how we are related to each other, to all of creation, to the unknown. And knowing this will help us heal.

EXERCISE
Connecting the Personal with the Universal

1. Write about an experience, object, place, time in your life, or person toward whom you feel a deep personal relationship. Using metaphor, simile or another poetic device, allow your perception of that connection to expand in a way that links you and what you are writing about with something beyond yourself, something larger.

I feel that appreciation with others in creating a way of life that would give all of us respect, and the joy of creativity in all senses, need not be a burden.

—*Adrienne Rich*

IMAGE OF MYSELF 3

my sons and daughters are like the first twinkling of the stars
eternally embedded in beauty like their mother the sky Goddess
i watch them grow each day with wide and watchful eyes
their lives glowing like moons caressed by my darkness
as the world blindly asks me if i am sensitive
i silently answer as i spin on my own axis
wrapping my arms around my children and kissing them
they become the universe

—*Ira B. Jones*

*

2. Look at an experience that is painful in your life—loss of a loved one, loss of a place you loved, the loss of someone's friendship and esteem, your feelings about suffering or social injustice in the world—and make a "poetic panel" to represent your connection to that person, experience or circumstance in the world. Make your panel in the same way The Names Project Quilt represents the connection between the quilt-makers and those who have died. Use magazine clippings, photographs, poems, pieces of cloth, phrases, poems or words. Create your own poetic collage to connect you with a wider circle of humanity.

CHAPTER THREE

POETIC TOOLS FOR YOUR HEALING JOURNEY

Creating with the Elements of Poetry

Half on the Earth, half in the heart,
the remedies for all the things
which grieve us wait for those who know
the words to use to find them.

Penobscott people use to make
a medicine for cancer from Mayapple
and South American people knew
the quinine cure for malaria
a thousand years ago.

But it is not just in the roots,
the stems, the leaves,
the thousand flowers
that healing lies.
Half of it lives within the words
the healer speaks.

And when the final time has come
for one to leave this Earth
there are no cures,
for Death is only
part of Life, not a disease.

Half on the Earth, half in the heart,
the remedies for all our pains
wait for the songs of healing.
                                —Joseph Bruchac

GETTING STARTED:
APPLYING POETIC TOOLS

> Everything I do in this odd business of writing poetry is
> based on intuition. I have no rules, only patterns that I fall
> into. Most of my reasons for doing what I do, craftwise, can
> be answered, "Because it felt right at the time."
>
> —Judith Minty

I have a good friend who will tell me what a Petrarchan sonnet and a palinode are, which is helpful because otherwise
I'd have to look it up! Detailed knowledge about poetic forms is
fascinating and helpful, but it's not required for writing poetry.

There are certain basics, however, that every poet should be
familiar with. In this chapter we will focus on five poetic tools
and how to use them. You will learn how to *apply* these ingredients as you engage in the art of poem-making for healing and
growth. The raw materials for poem-making include:

✳ *simile* ✳ *metaphor* ✳ *image* ✳ *line breaks* ✳ *word choice*

Most poets *discover* through the process of writing what the essential elements of poetry are and how they work. Although I
am going to give you some fundamental information about poetic devices, I'm sure that, like most poets, you will find out for
yourself what tools work best for you. Everyone's creative
process is unique, and each of us employs a unique combination
of poetic elements to accurately and passionately express what
we want to say. You'll also find that one set of tools will suffice
for one particular poem, but then you'll want new ones for a different kind of poem, or when you are in a different mood or
frame of mind.

✴

In this chapter you will learn how to move between spontaneity in your poetic expression and applied knowledge about poetic tools. A child once defined creative experience as finding "answers to questions you didn't know." Willingness to explore unknown territory will help you learn to use poetic tools—and the exercises in this chapter will provide you with the opportunity to experiment.

Treat poetic tools and words like clay, color or musical notes. Use them to put language into action like a pitcher might throw a strike with a baseball. Mix them as paints. Integrate them into a whole system like your brain, heart, lungs and other organs work together to make your body alive and healthy.

Galway Kinnell defined poetry as "making something physical out of words." Healing words do not come from the intellect but from your gut, your heart. A poem made in this way is a thing of action; it is *alive*.

SIMILE: DISCOVERING CONNECTIONS

Similes—making a comparison between two very different things using the words "like" or "as"—allow you to surprise yourself when you write.

Here are a few examples of simile. James Wright, writing about walking toward Indian ponies in a field, startles us with this unusual comparison:

> *They bow shyly as wet swans*

Emily Dickinson wrote this delicious simile comparing books and poetry to boats and horses:

> *There is no Frigate like a Book*
> *To take us Lands away*
> *Nor any Coursers like a Page*
> *Of prancing Poetry—*

William Shakespeare surprises us by reversing what we might expect in a simile describing a lover when he writes in one of his sonnets:

My mistress' eyes are nothing like the sun

The rest of the poem continues to make fun of (through various poetic devices) typical clichés about the qualities of a lover, yet by the end of the sonnet what we have is an expression of true love.

You may use simile sparingly, but as a device it helps to show the relationships between one thing and making the creative tension between two seemingly different things compelling and vivid.

One day I gave a group of fifth-grade children words from which to make a poem. To my surprise, Carolyn came up to me with her word on a piece of paper and asked, "What does this word mean?" Her word was *rivulet.* She had never heard that word before! She was meeting it fresh. I sensed something magical could happen. Carolyn was right in her "beginner's mind." I told her it was a tiny stream of water, something she could jump across. A short while later she came back with a poem about friendship.

FRIENDSHIP

Friendship is eternity,
Like two little rivulets that flow side-by-side forever
Between the two, lies the vision of sweetly being.
And when ashamed they release,
and flow down different sides of the mountain.
But then again, slowly but surely,
you can see them side-by-side again.
        —Carolyn Keane

Carolyn used both metaphor and simile in her poem. We'll explore the use of metaphor soon, but let's focus on her use of sim-

We must learn to see the world anew.

—Albert Einstein

✳

Children have their active subconscious mind which, like the tree, has the power to draw food from the surrounding atmosphere. For them the atmosphere is a great deal more important than rules and methods, equipment, text-book lessons . . . But in our educational organizations we behave like miners, digging only for things and not like the tillers of the earth whose work is a perfect collaboration with nature.

—Rabindranath Tagore

ile. A simile uses the words *like* or *as* to indicate a comparison: "Friendship is like two little rivulets." I hadn't spoken much to the class about similes but Carolyn got a picture of one in her mind by feeling this brand-new word—and suddenly, it connected with her innate sense of the hardship found at times in deep friendships. Her fresh response to a single word was more important for making her poem than a definition. She "got it" on her own. That's not to say definitions aren't worth knowing.

I'm only encouraging you to trust a spontaneous sense with your poem-making. Feeling and playfulness are catalysts for poem-making rarely taught in school; yet joy, heartache and whimsy reveal your truth and unique voice. Expressed in a poem they can have a healing effect. Like Carolyn, being receptive to your experience, to your wealth of feeling, is a deep resource of "knowledge" that can guide your writing.

It is not just words that will surprise us when we approach them with a fresh mind and attitude. The "stuff" of everyday life can awaken our surprise, new perception and understanding. Common things can provide a link between our inner and outer worlds. Let's look at another poem that employs simile. This poem is about a bar of soap—imagine seeing soap like this!

The bar of soap
is so much more
than it appears
to be. The little
package washes
you clean, like
a dream, the
slightest sound
can wash it
away.
Its shape and
size make all
the difference.
It has no
outer shell.

Just smooth
white slippery
solid. Dreams
do not require
a shell. Nothing
protects them.
There is nothing
to break through.
You fall asleep
dreams are there,
you pour the
water over
it, the soap
substance
is there.
It appears
so little yet
does so
much.
        —*Elizabeth Bolton,*
              eleven years old

Making connections between the cleansing and ephemeral nature of soap and dreams, Elizabeth tunes us into images and insights that are wise and refreshing. Her short line breaks give
her poem a compact energy, the very image of a bar of soap.
They give a crispness to her simple idea. Strengthened by these
poetic choices, her poem is able *to contain* surprise for us. It
draws out our interest and evokes our delight.

As adults we do not have to lose touch with the fresh perceptions Elizabeth expresses about everyday things. The world
of meaning and wonder that children, artists and poets frequent
is a world you visit as well, perhaps without being aware of it.

You go there in nighttime dreams and daytime reveries. You
go there when you do work you value or when you play. You go
there in sorrow and love. You go there with a single kiss. You go
there walking through a forest with a friend or riding on the

The more poetic, the more real.
                —*Novalis*

lonely subway. You may visit this place if you wake trembling and isolated in your bedroom at two a.m., thinking of a loved one you've lost or a relationship that is breaking up. You enter this creative world when beauty, passion and the sacred move you to feel at one with life.

E X E R C I S E
Simile—Making Connections in Your Daily Life

Just as Elizabeth compared a bar of soap with a dream, use a simile to help you explore something in your life that is in need of healing. Consider any troubled aspect of your life at the moment: your health, work, family, friendships, community.

M E T A P H O R S :
A N   A L C H E M I C A L   B O N D
O F   L A N G U A G E

> *Music—*
> *A naked woman*
> *running mad through the pure night!*
> —Juan Ramón Jiménez

Metaphor is an alchemical bond of words that unites two different things. This occurs in various ways. In some metaphor, the correspondence between two things is precise and exact:

> *I am water rushing to the well-head*
> *filling the pitcher until it spills . . .*
> —Jane Kenyon

> *My rage is a cloud of flame.*
> —Marge Piercy

*

In other forms of metaphor the connection is not an exact equation but something more implicit. Jimenez' metaphor *relates* the word *music* to a "naked woman / running mad." More than either an exact equation or an implicit relationship between different things, metaphors compose entire realities. Rather than words strung together in a logical and linear way to explain a point of view or describe something, metaphor *instantaneously* presents *a complete picture.*

A metaphor may be strong and direct yet ask us to perceive subtle, unusual connections. Metaphoric language challenges us to perceive interplay between the unexpected notion and direct statement. Our understanding of this interplay can be instantaneous if, as Theodore Roethke suggested, we "think by feeling."

Metaphors engage our ability to perceive connections; connections made between something particular and a larger reality. Metaphors show relationships between outer experience and inner feeling. Metaphors are intended to satisfy head and heart; they enable a sense of psychological and spiritual balance; they open communication between the known and unknown parts of our lives; they foster integration between our everyday self and our potential self.

Metaphors are best understood intuitively. Metaphor-making will help you to recognize, develop, use and express your intuitive knowing.

For all of these reasons metaphors offer great healing power.

A metaphor does not usually make literal sense but it makes intuitive sense. It expresses a truth that exists beyond the rational mind, giving a broader meaning to life.

My imagination is pre-linguistic.
—*Gary Snyder*

HEART OF WATER

When I was a baby my heart
was a tiny fish swimming
in a gargantuan sea of things to come

*

When I was a toddler my heart
was a trout in a large lake of
thoughts and feeling

Now my heart is becoming
a salmon ready to go to the sea
of the troubles I will have to face

When I am old my heart
will be a whale swimming
in a sea of memories

When I die God will become
a whaler.
—Orion Misciagna, eleven years old

What a marvel that an eleven-year-old can appreciate his life with such creative perception! Orion's startling self-awareness and faith is revealed in the last stanza; we can feel it as a rush in our spines, as the hairs on the back of our necks tingle. Soul speaks in this poem, through the inventive yet simple "sea life" metaphors.

You too can use metaphors to broaden your expressive powers. When intuitive knowing connects deeply with the meaning of a single metaphor, it is often more useful in healing your pain than a thousand words or psychological theories.

METAPHORS FOR SELF: "THE ANCIENT ENDURING WELL IS ME"

Mary Kay Turner, M.D., works in general surgery and on a trauma unit in an Indianapolis hospital. She sees most people heal and leave the hospital, but she also sees catastrophic injuries for which there are few good answers and a lot of painful questions. Mary Kay writes poetry to take care of herself in such intense circumstances and to deepen her sense of spirituality. She wrote this poem in a workshop:

THE WELL

I am a well
ancient, enduring
even in the stark
and arid times
I have never gone
completely dry.
Send your bucket down
my deep recesses
have much to give.
Send the rain down,
my mouth is open
to this gift from the wide sky.
Send the storm down
though my weathered mortar
cracks, and the stones shift
I remain standing still.
                    —Mary Kay Turner

Mary Kay comments on how this metaphor connects with her life:

For a long time I identified totally with being a wife and a surgeon. I was wrapped up in doing those roles. But it wasn't enough. When work went badly I felt horrible. Something about this approach to my life began to feel spiritually bankrupt.

I wanted to look at who I really am. That led me into therapy and recovery. Much of my recovery work includes valuing my creativity and writing. The ancient, enduring well is me. The image and voice of a well reminds me I am more than what I do. I want to be in touch with that inward place. There is something about writing that is part of going to the well—of coming back to myself. It's vital if I am to do the work I do and be the woman I am.

Writing poetry gives me a place to rest when things are rough. When people are dying around me, or I am concerned that I need to do something differently and don't have any good answers, poetry helps me find my source and a new perspective.

This "well" is a place in me, but it also reminds me of a place in my patients. The well says that there is something more, something eternal, something within us that is renewed through human experience. This is my impression of what God is: a part of all of us that survives rain and storm and even death.

My poem tells me that I can handle whatever comes up if I am willing to go down into my depths. To do that, I need to be myself—not just identified as a doctor. There is something very poetic and feminine about this image for me. On a rough day, I'll descend down and just be there for a while. I'll come back up and enter into life.

EXERCISE
The Power of Healing Metaphors

1. Think of an area in your life where you need sustenance. At work? At home with family? Taking care of an aging parent? In a relationship? Make two columns. Jot down that area of stress in the left column. Include a few notes on that stress: difficult memories or circumstances, how your body feels in that place or circumstance, qualities of relationships, etc. For instance: *work past dinner time, furrowed brow, deadlines on my desk, competitive co-workers.* In the second column write words—images and metaphors—that nourish you. Take words from each of these columns and link them together in a poem. How can the nourishing words be applied to ease the stressful ones?

2. Use the words below (or ones you think of yourself) to express metaphorically aspects of yourself, something in your life, or someone you know:

wind	prison	moon	house	knife	fountain
jasmine	mask	island	well	ashes	ghetto
hurricane	jaguar	dolphin	peach	stone	glove

THE HEALING POWER
OF IMAGES

> A morning glory at my window satisfies me more than the
> metaphysics of books.
>
> —Walt Whitman

Images are drawn from sensory experience and help us *to feel*
what the writer or speaker is communicating. Whitman is more
satisfied by the morning glory because it is real and alive, it
communicates something to him about reality that is particular,
clear and unmistakable. Images offer us direct experience. They
can show themselves to us through any of the senses.

I ask people to imagine themselves standing at a busy inter-
section in their town or city—or to recall any other place of activity that is part of their daily routine. As they settle into
imagining this street corner (or whatever place they have chosen) I invite them to describe, as precisely as they can, the images and direct sensations they experience.

People begin to speak. Some voices are strong, others cau-
tious. Unique rhythm and sound is heard in each voice, in a
chorus of sense and sound:

I never find words right away.
Poems for me always begin with
images and rhythms, shapes, feelings,
forms, dances in the back of my mind.
—Gary Snyder

*The smell of new fallen rain glimmering upon the leaves of wan city
trees. The dark rumbling sound of trucks. The persistent wings of pigeons. Vibrations trilling in the soles of my feet. A frail and disoriented
man bent over in ragged brown, baggy clothes pushing a Safeway
shopping cart stuffed full of blue plastic bags. People swooping by him.
Steam rising lazy and hot through a grate on the busy sidewalk. A
balding, short, worried-looking man in a rumpled business suit, impa-
tient for the stoplight to change, grasping at a Styrofoam cup of
steaming coffee. Announcement flyers, colors running, stapled around a
rutted telephone pole. A freckled energetic and happy redheaded high
school girl in a plaid Catholic school uniform with a W on her tight
sweater holding a load of books in her arms. The sound of a revving
bus engine, exhaust rising in a billowing black veil of odor, the brief,*

* cool leftward glance of the hefty bus driver as he pulls into traffic. Sun-
* light glints diamondlike off an older woman's fancy sunglasses as she
* sits in her red sports car at the stoplight.

Voices call out in spontaneous, improvised impressions. This is a start. The street corner in our mind's eye is thus brought into focus; it teems with life and holds our interest. Seeing and listening—a sense of touch, even smelling attentively—gives you the raw material with which to create an image that can then represent a particular place or person or feeling or idea.

How does recalling images and sensations on a street corner relate to healing your personal wounds? Learning to focus your attention in the midst of your daily life enables you to perceive, in detail, the richness and complexity of every place, every person, every moment. This mindful concentration is a skill that will help you make images for your healing poems.

The wide dispersion of brain areas involved in imagery—especially visual imagery—indicates the importance of imagery to the survival of the species.

—*Jeanne Actherberg*

* Millions of people, unseeing, joyless, bluster through life in their half
* sleep, hitting, kicking, and killing what they have barely perceived.
* They have never learned to SEE or they have forgotten that man has
* eyes to SEE, to experience.

—*Frederick Franck, artist*

A new light is thrown upon mundane experiences when we begin to take notice of the myriad images that constantly surround us. We can feel them resonate in the body.

In his poem *Hymn*, Jack Kerouac's image of people slipping on ice while walking to work leads him to recall his family history. Eventually the poem becomes an expression of his own yearning:

> And when you showed me Brooklyn Bridge
>   in the morning,
>   Ah God,
> And the people slipping in the ice in the street,
> twice,
>   twice,

two different people
came over, goin to work,
so earnest and tryful,
clutching their pitiful
morning Daily News
slip on the ice & fall
both inside 5 minutes
and I cried I cried
That's when you taught me tears, Ah
  God in the morning,
    Ah Thee
And me leaning on the lamppost wiping
eyes,
  eyes,
    nobody'd know I'd cried

or woulda cared anyway
    but O I saw my father
    and my grandfather's mother
    and the long lines of chairs
    and tear-sitters and dead,
        Ah me, I knew God You
        had better plans than that
So whatever plan you have for me
Splitter of majesty
Make it short
  brief
Make it snappy
  bring me home to the Eternal Mother
  today
At your service anyway,
  (and until)

What is Kerouac's attitude toward the workers he's describing?
What does he feel for them? The evocative images he comes up
with ("goin to work, / so earnest and tryful," "clutching their
pitiful / morning Daily News," "the long lines of chairs / and

tear-sitters and dead") reveal very specific perceptions and emotions.

Kerouac observes human struggle in a way that moves him and us to profound feeling. Noticing daily life with the alert and receptive eyes of a poet is one of the most essential elements in creating your own poetic medicine.

E X E R C I S E
Turning On to What You See

> See a peach bend
> the branch and strain the stem until
> it snaps.
>
> —Li-Young Lee

Visualize a place where you tend to function on "autopilot." Perhaps you are at work or at the market, perhaps at the kitchen table where you read the newspaper or go over plans for the day, perhaps in your living room watching TV. Now pretend you have just landed in a new world. Write down the images/ sensations of everything you experience being in that place for the first time. Catch the details.

_____

_____

_____

Draw from your list one image—the one that holds more energy and feeling than the others. Write more about this image. Include details and nuances about that image which reveal more about being in that place. What feelings does that image evoke in you? How does this image relate to your life?

EXERCISE
Capturing Images

This exercise reveals the threefold healing potential of image-making: the power of an image to evoke creative response; the capacity of images to serve as containers of feeling; and the capacity of images to inspire a voice for your feelings.

> *How the days went*
> *while you were blooming within me*
> *I remember each upon each—*
> *the swelling changed planes of my body*
> *and how you first fluttered, then jumped*
> *and I thought it was my heart.*
> —Audre Lorde

Step One: Remembering Childhood Images

Make a list of images you remember from childhood or youth. Among the images that arise, choose those that hold positive memories. Let your images appear effortlessly in your mind's eye. Treat them like snapshots you might look through after many years. Start with simple images.

We will work with more painful and difficult images later on in the chapter. The purpose of this exercise is to use images to awaken creativity and tune in to the feelings about your life.

What sensations do you experience recalling your image? Recall your sensations at the moment of experience: smell, taste, touch, sight, hearing. Absorb the image into your body— feel as if you are reliving that remembered image. Focus your image in your mind's eye; "catch it" whole. *Describe your experience quickly, let words flow, give detail.* Here is an example:

*   *Opening a large box in our backyard apple orchard . . . bright sun*
*   *shines down, the blue jay with the hurt wing is inside. I fed and cared*
*   *for it . . . now will it fly away? Box is layered with grass, sticks and*

shriveled leaves of lettuce. I am five years old. I am standing close to an apple tree in summer. Dense narrow branches wind up to the sky. The apple tree is small but I am smaller. Talons of the nervous blue jay scratch jittering sounds on the cardboard. I open the large and wobbly box and wait. The blue sky is also waiting for the large blue jay to fly—and she does—into the apple tree.

_____

_____

Step Two: Feelings Through Images

Reflect further upon your childhood images and write down emotions associated with them. For example:

Wonder about flight, love and sadness for the hurt of a creature, hope for freedom.

_____

_____

Step Three: Making a Poem Using Image, Feeling, Voice

Write a poem using material gathered from the first two steps. Stay in touch with your senses as you focus on your image; listen for the voice of the image; and then express the feeling drawn from your primary image. Here is my poem:

> *childhood is a wobbly cardboard box,*
> *opened for a broken-winged blue jay healing*
> *inside, and inside healing*
> *are apple trees, wet summer grass,*
> *large sky, flight of wings, and inside flight*
> *is longing for home and and the chance to sing.*

Present your images as clearly as possible in your poem so that you *show* the feeling rather than label it with a word like *sad* or *happy*. Let the image *reveal* your feeling rather than tell about it.

We need to allow and trust the voices of the unconscious which speak to us in dreams, or through the body, while at the same time using all our faculties of thought and reason and discrimination, all our knowledge, all our strength and delicacy of feeling, all our practical good sense and fineness of intuition with which we may be gifted.

—Irene Claremont de Castillejo

_____

_____

_____

_____

USING IMAGES
TO EXPRESS
PAINFUL FEELINGS

The purpose of some poems is to unload blocks to your well-
being so you can move on. Like a good crying jag, these poems
are written to give room to your emotions. You allow strong
emotion to flow in tough poems like this; you write in whatever
form allows you to best speak your truth. You can feel cleansed
after writing a poem like this and it may open the way for healing.

This next poem is a clear example of combining image and
emotion. It is almost entirely comprised of one powerful image:
a pile of dirty laundry!

JAMMED/CRAMMED/DAMNED

Emotions piled in a corner
One on top of another
Stuffed in
Crammed
Jammed
Heaped high
Overlooked
Too busy to get to
Like days' old—or is it years' old—laundry
in a too-small hamper.
Smelly
Soiled
Discarded
Embarrassing
A blight in an otherwise well-ordered room.

The lid won't shut.
I cram them in.
A few spill onto the floor
    A stray grey
    A raging red
    A simmering burnt orange
    A withholding white

Don't mix the colors with the whites.
Wash in cold water.
Do not add bleach.
Warranted to reveal manufacturer's defects.

Emotions, mostly contained, put away.
Waiting. Over there. In the corner.
                    —Anne Harrington

All of our senses are engaged in this poem. Color, smell, texture, temperature—all of these sensations merge with emotion. Anne's "color selections" to represent her emotions deepen the connection with this image of dirty laundry in a hamper.

Anne talks about her poem:

I've written from an analytical point of view for years but recently discovered that I needed to write about feelings. A turning point came when I visited an AIDS facility and was inspired by the spirituality of that place. I wrote about the art and panels of client photographs. I wrote about a unique memorial in the meditation room—a suspended tree branch weighted down with objects commemorating people who died there. As I wrote the article and thought about the visit, I wept. At that moment, I realized that there was a part of me that wasn't getting expressed in my writing.

Another event that made me more aware of feelings and how I deal with them has been an extended marital separation. The separation period has been a time of enormous grief. It has also stirred memories of other losses. I found little that could help me adequately express the level of grief and conflicting emotions that I felt. I also noticed that I couldn't control or predict what (or how) I was going to feel next. For a rational-logical person, that was very unsettling.

"Jammed/Crammed/Damned" was a unique experience for me. It was one of the first poems I'd ever written and was the first to capture a glimpse of the private side of me. It helped me think about how I repress or avoid difficult feelings. By owning these feelings, writing them down, speaking them out loud to a group, and hearing members of the group affirm the truth of these words in their lives, I felt the therapeutic power of the poem. I felt that by the end of the process, I was already a little different. After the workshop was over, I wrote a sequel to the "Jammed" poem called "Hanging Out the Laundry in the Back Yard Before Dawn."

One of the things that surprises me about poetry is that it can help me access deeper levels of understanding and awareness. While this doesn't happen all the time, I may write down some word or phrase or line that provides an insight I wasn't conscious of. Poetry is part of my life now.

EXERCISE
Images of Painful Feelings

Notice how Anne's poem gets its power from equating painful emotions with dirty laundry. She creates the image of painful emotions stuffed in a hamper by stacking short lines on top of one another. What image might you create to represent your painful feelings? Try this: 1. Choose one strong image that holds positive or negative emotion for you; 2. Visualize and feel that image; 3. Write a poem that illustrates your emotion by describing the image you have chosen.

*

IMAGES THAT EVOKE
MIXED FEELINGS

You may think you know with certainty what a particular image in your poem means, only to find out, days or months later, that your understanding of it has changed.

Poems layered with meaning, the ones whose significance tends to shift or expand after many readings, are especially beneficial in dealing with powerful emotions. You can return to them many times, and they will continue to speak to you in new ways. You will learn from them long after they've been written.

Some images may evoke both harshness and tenderness. You might be surprised that harsh and tender feelings can coexist in the same poem. Such disparate feelings might drive one crazy in a more rational context, but a poem has the ability to hold mixed feelings, which makes it a unique vehicle for helping us understand difficult or painful issues in our lives.

The images you need to express your present struggle will come up spontaneously. Your work is to *receive* them. Pay attention to what you dream at night. Or allow yourself to mindlessly "daydream." What images arise? Catch the images that come to you like a sail catches the wind. Carole Oles writes of a poignant and painful image of standing on a city street as a child:

In poetry many things are going on at the same time and these layers of time and density of language make the poem uniquely poetic.

—Donald Hall

MOTHER AND CHILD

No, I said, and stood.
It was summer.
You were tired and hot
on Steinway Street,
your feet swollen.
Your eighth month
floating the boy
who would die.

No I screamed
and ladies passing
tut-tutted.
When I looked around
you were gone.
I was marooned,
thirsty among the tall people,
my hands full of August.

Years later you told
how you'd hidden in a doorway
watching fear
turn me supple.
You rushed over
when enough was enough.

Mother.
I am out in this street
with no hat on.
The pavement shimmers
and writhes, lovers pass
with their smiles in their pockets.
Mother, be in the doorway
ready to rain.

—Carole Oles

Oles' image of a frightened child alone in the doorway speaks
of abandonment; the image of this same child now in her
adulthood standing on the busy street "with no hat on" carries
a message of how past abandonment continues to make itself felt.

Sharp images are created in such words and phrases as:

"floating the boy / who would die"
"marooned"
"thirsty among the tall people"
"watching fear / turn me supple"

*

"the pavement . . . writhes"
"smiles in their pockets"

These words provide emotional "clues" that can be felt with your senses. They communicate Oles' mixed feelings about a psychologically complex relationship with her mother.

EXERCISE
Healing the Past by Revisiting Images

The first three stanzas of Oles' poem are in past tense. She *recalls* experience. In the fourth and last stanza, Oles' voice shifts to present tense. She asks for what she could not ask for as a child.

Just as you did in "Capturing Images," allow images to arise in your mind. Choose one image that holds a negative emotional charge. Start with an image you are able to work on safely.

Using the Oles poem as a model, make a poem that recalls your own troubling circumstances. Draw upon aspects of image-making you've already experimented with—feeling and voice. State your experience in the past tense. Toward the end of your poem shift to present tense. Use your poem to tell your past story; give voice to what you have not yet said in response to that experience; and retell your story by telling yourself what you would most like to hear.

LINE LENGTHS: CRAFTING YOUR LINE TO THE TUNE OF YOUR HEALING

Line lengths and layout construct the images of a poem just as atoms unite to form a stoneware mug, a pouting lover or a grizzly bear. Atoms arrange themselves to make it possible for you to drink your morning coffee, decide to stand very still or recognize one of the many faces of your lover.

Lines, similarly, compose the structure, or the gestalt, of a poem. The word *gestalt* literally means *shape, form* or *arrangement, structure.* Line lengths and breaks create the unique shape of your poem and help determine its meaning. New experiments with poetic lines over the past one hundred and fifty years are an indication of the evolution of poetry but also reflect changes in our understanding of how the world and universe work.

Dramatic changes in the line structure of poems began to appear in the poetry of Walt Whitman, Gerard Manley Hopkins and Emily Dickinson in the mid–nineteenth century. Even more radical experiments with line breaks were made by twentieth-century poets William Carlos Williams, e. e. cummings, Denise Levertov, Allen Ginsberg and many others.

These changes opened poetry up and allowed it to breathe more on the page. Less encumbered with specific meters (though not altogether rid of them either) the poet could have more freedom to shape the poem so it could express movement and feeling. This change in the structure of a poem reflected a desire to write diversely without being limited by conventional forms of verse.

Interestingly, these changes in Western poetry occurred at the same time as the discovery of the application of electricity and Einstein's development of relativity theory. It wasn't a coincidence!

We learned physical form is not solid as it appears; *everything* is made of energy. Electricity and relativity theory changed our concepts of what matter is, our relationship to it, how we could create with it, and what we could speak about. So, too, changes in poetic form radically altered possibilities of what a poem is and how a reader and writer interact with it on the page.

Modern poetry's experiments with where a line breaks on the page allow a synthesis of spontaneity and structure, an integration of raw emotion with an *organizing principle.* Einstein's relativity theory is not about anarchy or pure unpredictability; it reflects the combination of spontaneity and structure. This same inspired structure can also be used when making a healing poem.

Allen Ginsberg's *Howl* broke from the grip of academic reserve; the poet's wild, passionate voice is heard:

I had my little student read David Wagoner's poem "Lost." He said to me, "These sentences are all funny." I said, "Yes, it's poetry!"

—*Kimberley Nelson*

Breakthroughs! over the river! flips and crucifixions! gone down
the flood! Highs! Epiphanies! Despairs! Ten years' animal screams and
suicides! Minds! New loves! Mad generation! down on the rocks to
Time!
Real holy laughter in the river! They saw it all! the wild eyes! the
holy yells! They bade farewell! They jumped off the roof! to solitude!
waving! carrying flowers! Down to the river! into the street!

How the lines in a poem are made on a page can help open up our access to the poet's consciousness—and to our own. We literally give ourselves more space with a creative use of line breaks and lengths. We are able to perceive not just the meaning or message of a poem but enter into the creative process and the be-ing of that poem. It is more possible to walk into a free verse poem as we write or read it, and as it were, look around. More formal verse can be very clear but it is more solid and dense, allowing us only to stand outside to appreciate it.

Here are two poem fragments that show how line lengths influence the emotional impact of a poem and its capacity to allow us inside to experience it directly. The first poem is by William Wordsworth (1770–1850):

> *Our birth is but a sleep and a forgetting:*
> *The Soul that rises with us, our life's Star,*
> *   Hath had elsewhere its setting,*
> *   And cometh from afar:*
> *   Not in entire forgetfulness,*
> *   And not in utter nakedness,*
> *But trailing clouds of glory do we come*
> *   From God, who is our home:*
> *Heaven lies about us in our infancy!*
> *— from Ode: Intimations of Immortality*

The following fragment is by Allen Ginsberg from his poem *Wales Visitation.*

White fog lifting & falling on mountain-brow
　　　Trees moving in rivers of wind
　　　　　　　The clouds rise
on a wave, gigantic eddy lifting mist
　　above seeming ferns exquisitely swayed
　　　　　　　　along a green crag
　　glimpsed thru mullioned glass in a valley raine—

Wordsworth writes in perfect compact lines. He communicates a truth through images that are steady and in language that is direct. His lines conform to the same rhythm and express a certain predictability. Wordsworth's meaning is thus explicit. Ginsberg opens up the body of the poem, allowing "white space" on the page to indicate shades of feeling. He translates the inner pulse of his vision by radically changing the line length and word placement on the page. Ginsberg's poem is more implicit in the meaning we might draw from it. Wordsworth may be telling us a truth we might discover or intuit if we looked through the window of Ginsberg's poem with enough longing. Yet both men are expressing something exquisite.

HOW LINE BREAKS AND LINE LENGTH EXPRESS EMOTION AND MEANING

The length of a line of poetry and where it breaks affect the meaning and emotional impact. Various line lengths and breaks can communicate some of the following:

✳ *Rhythms* of thought and feeling

Robert Frost wrote these lines:

　　　Love at the lips was touch
　　　As sweet as I could bear;
　　　And once that seemed too much;
　　　I lived on air

*

> *That crossed me from sweet things,*
> *The flow of—was it musk*
> *From hidden grapevine springs*
> *Downhill at dusk?*

This regular metric pattern, dactylic dimeter, provides automatic emphasis on the fourth line as providing a climax, conclusion or commentary.

* Exact representations of the mind's moment-by-moment movement; the lines indicating the poem's "breath"

Elsa Weiner, a workshop student, writes about preparing food in a busy retreat kitchen:

> *busy place and bright*
> *flashing silver*
> *chopping vegetables*
> *pressing tofu*
> *loud talking*
> *one hundred pounds of salmon*

Elsa's lines show exactly what is happening; her quick thought/breath lines are like the chopping of vegetables!

* Flow of natural speech

New Blues from a Brown Baby is a good example of natural speech:

> *Some of my loneliest hours have been with you.*
> *But now I know what I have to do.*
> *Got to stop being your mother.*
> *Stop looking down at you.*
> *Got to stop being your teacher.*
> *You'll learn for yourself what is true.*
> *—Saundra Sharp*

These lines represent the cadence of conversation. This way of "speaking" allows for rhyme to occur naturally, unobtrusively, whereas the Frost poem relied on a specific meter to carry the intentional rhyme scheme.

✳ Enjambment

> *The cat sleeping on the fence is famous to the birds*
> *watching him from the birdhouse.*
>   *—Naomi Shihab Nye*

Enjambment is a folding over of words and sense from one line to another. The break of your lines is essentially done by feel— what feels right. Enjambment is about providing a sense of movement to your poem. Enjambment also occurs in more radical line placements on the page. John Dooley writes about walking on the earth:

> *i went to walk upon*
> *Her face, and She,*
> *content, kind, truthful,*
> *   gifting, patient,*
> *offered me places in the*
> *   curves of Her nose,*
> *   upon Her forehead, in Her*
> *   earlobes so that*
> *i may feel Her breath*
> *   as She kissed the top*
> *   of my feet with air,*
> *a gift placed with care*
> *in the cupped hands of my heart.*

The lines flow with the sensations of the poet's bare feet. The brevity of each line seems precious, seems to hold the reverence Dooley feels toward the earth.

E X E R C I S E
Playing with Line Breaks and Line Lengths

1. Practice different line breaks and lengths in your poems by trying some of the examples in this chapter.

2. Experiment with putting different emotions into poetic lines. Anger, delight, and sadness: how would they look on the page? Do a free write in paragraph form focusing on one emotion and an incident that evoked it. Don't think so much about the content of your writing right now. Next, break your free write piece up into the shape of sadness. Focus on the feeling—what shape does the feeling of your sadness have in poetic lines? How does it move? Where do the lines break? Go back and develop the content of your feeling poem when you have found a shape that feels right.

3. Read a number of different poems by different poets out loud—and notice the feelings and movement of the lines. Apply what you discover to your own writing.

M A K I N G   W O R D   C H O I C E S (O R   N O T   L E T T I N G   T H E G O O D   O N E S   G E T   A W A Y)

Line lengths are the structural component of a poem, they give it shape on the page. But your word choices particularize an image. Words you choose create the unique texture for the images in your poem. Finding the right word may come to you naturally after you've written several drafts of your poem. Rather than thinking of this process as "correcting" your writing, think of it as an adventure in word discovery. Discovering the best possible word or words for your poem is one of the most exciting parts of the poem-making process, one you will come to appreciate and enjoy.

Giving attention to the words you choose and how you combine them is another way using poetic language has alchemical, healing powers.

✳

Words with spark, words that surprise, make a poem potent. Words that are "on target" capture our attention in the context of the poem. But here is an important point: it is not necessary or even desirable that each word have an electric charge. Simple words will ring true. We begin to lose freshness in poems, however, when we retreat for too long into vocabulary that is expected.

The process of finding the right word to energize a particular place in a poem is akin to putting a precise spin on a tennis ball or placing an emotional color on a phrase when you sing. One word can make all the difference.

Some simple guides will help. Read your poem out loud. How does a word, phrase or line sound to your ear? How does a word, a phrase or a line take shape in your mouth when you speak it? What do you feel when hearing this word or line? Be receptive to the movement, shape, textures and tonalities words possess beyond just their meaning. Experiment using words you don't usually use. What words make your poem come alive?

This excerpt from Jane Hirshfield's poem *The Gift* reflects the search for just the right word to describe her experience of a horse eating a pear:

> . . . *and he is careful even in greed,*
>
> *even in the undignity*
> *of his foolish—no, it must be*
> *named true—his entirely goofy adoration*
> *and long-tongued worship of pears;*
> *when he knows what is pear,*
> *what is hand, when he looks*
> *in my face as he chews and the crush*
> *slobbers out and foams as bright as spent happiness*
> *onto my foot, onto my sleeve . . .*

Hirshfield moves from greed, to undignity, to foolish, and finally, to goofy. Each word brings her a little closer to what she means but it is when she says "entirely *goofy* adoration" we know

In a poem the word should be as pleasing to the ear as the meaning is to the mind.

—Marianne Moore

*

Once you begin to see and hear, the life in language ignites, and almost anything can strike you as poetry. The sparks are released, the light shines, the word sounds.

—M. C. Richards

she's found it. It took a leap of faith to see a horse as being goofy, but the poem demanded that word be found.

Besides the search for a word that "names something true" there are other things to consider when making word choices for your poem:

* repetition of words or sounds
* how words relate to one another
* aliveness, freshness, flow

Repetition of a sound, word or a phrase enhances emotional impact. Repetition can also provide a foundation on which to build other words in the poem. Its use is similar to hearing the bass note supporting the melody of a song.

Samuel Taylor Coleridge's poem *The Rime of the Ancient Mariner* is well known for a variety of phrases and word repetitions that enhance the hypnotic tale:

> *The ice was here, the ice was there,*
> *The ice was all around:*
> *It cracked and growled, and roared and howled,*
> *Like noises in a swound!*

and

> *Alone, alone, all, all alone,*
> *Alone on a wide wide sea!*

We can see how *repetition* of the "s" sound in the following lines from the poem *Fern Hill* by Dylan Thomas gives the line its flow. *How words relate to one another* and *freshness* also work together in these lines:

> *And the sabbath rang slowly*
> *In the pebbles of the holy streams.*

Thomas' word choice involved going beyond logic to instill an inanimate concept like "sabbath" with qualities of sound ("rang") and motion ("slowly"). The sabbath is not just a day but has the ability to ring like a bell: "the sabbath rang slowly . . ." And with the phrase "holy streams," Thomas stuns us with the unexpected poignancy of how "holy" and "streams" relate to each other.

EXERCISE
Making Word Choices
(Or Not Letting the Good Ones Get Away)

1. Keep a running list in a notebook of words that you like.

2. My friend Susanne Petermann likes to read her poems, line by line, backward. She wants to experience the poem not just for what she thinks she means but to hear the words/lines alone as separate from sense. The sound of each line comes into high relief and she experiences how that sound sings in the poem. Try this out with your poem!

3. When the words you've chosen contain a lot of consonants, you may sense the texture of your poems as being more solid. Consonants make statements. They pounce on things like a cat upon a rubber ball. Vowels, on the other hand, may be like opening a door or leaving more breathing room in your poem. Strong vowels in a word can be expansive and indicate something more might happen. Here are a list of words that are strong in both consonants and vowels. Do a free write using these words and experiment how you could use them in poems.

If You Praise A Word, It Turns Into A Poem.

—*Caitlan Weber*

rainbow	break	seeds	horn	brass
fat	odor	dry	frail	munch
freeze	delight	stamp	ridge	spillway

*

AFFIRMATIONS

> Poetry is available to all of us and it can save the dreamer in us all.
>
> —Erica Jong

I feel that in the future many many poets will blossom forth—the poetic spirit will spread and reach toward all . . .

—Gregory Corso

Affirmations loosen the hard, compressed soil of subconscious resistance to growth. Picture your mind like a garden: affirmations are not the vegetation of your garden, but act as "amendments" for the soil. A gardener provides amendments to restructure the soil for new growth.

Affirmations are statements of intention, statements of action, statements of faith. Use affirmations to catalyze something much more mysterious and wise in yourself than "positive thinking" encompasses. Say these affirmations out loud to yourself, slowly and with care:

Reclaiming my creative imagination . . .

> *I am creative.*
>
> *I value the healing power of language.*
>
> *I write from my gut and heart.*
>
> *I trust humor and sensitivity.*
>
> *I honor the language of my feelings.*
>
> *I give voice to the wild and joyous parts of myself.*
>
> *I give voice to the stormy and grieving parts of myself.*
>
> *I am compassionate toward myself.*
>
> *I make a place for mystery and the creative in my life.*
>
> *I hold close to myself that which is dear to me.*
>
> *I am safe writing on the page.*
>
> *I make my home a place to write.*

Write the affirmations that you like best on a large card and put that card where you can read it often. Write your own affirmations about the value of your creative imagination. Use your own words to say your truth.

Reclaiming my creative imagination . . .

_____

_____

_____

_____

_____

To write poetry is to be alive.

—Rainer Maria Rilke

CHAPTER FOUR

THE FRAGILE BOND

Expressing Poems of Pain and Love

Between Parent and Child

There is a craving in children to receive images—to take from the world its many and varied pictures of itself. But just as they are willing acceptors, so too do they crave to give, to project onto the world their images, to bring those pictures of their minds to the companionship of someone who can receive and is able to acknowledge their gifts of images, who can help at the birth of that trust which enables the imagining self to communicate because it knows it belongs in the world and to the world, making and taking the world, its fullness.

—Richard Lewis

We did not come to remain whole.
We came to lose our leaves like the trees,
The trees that are broken
And start again, drawing up from the great roots.

—Robert Bly

"I HAD NO IDEA MY CHILD THOUGHT THAT WAY . . ."

> Oh, Mama, just look at me one minute as though you really saw me.
>
> —Emily, from *Our Town* by Thornton Wilder

Working with children and their poetry is a fascinating part of my job that teaches me a lot about healing work with adults. Much of what a child knows instinctively about expressing creativity we try to rediscover as adults.

Children will often present a poetry reading for parents following our sessions. Some parents tell me afterward: "I *had no idea my child thought that way.*" It is a powerful statement for a parent to make. I invite them to tell their son or daughter. Children who feel they've been heard on a deep level gain faith in themselves. A parent's acknowledgment is much more than giving approval; it is a recognition of mystery in that child.

Writing poetry helps children to blend their imagination and language skills together as both are blossoming. It gives them a way to explore and manifest their sensitivity, which is so often abandoned in the process of growing up, and poetry allows a child's natural curiosity to come alive in the form of language.

If more people would listen to children's poems, it could be an antidote for our troubled world. Children's poems remind adults of things we have forgotten; an imaginative, fresh view of life we want to feel again:

A child is the privacy of the universe learning to talk to itself.
—*Richard Lewis*

✳

Inside a bubble
there's a sea of petals
and a wind of water.
                    —Greta Weiss, first grade

WAITING IN LINE

When you listen you reach
into dark corners and
pull out your wonders.
When you listen your
ideas come in and out
like they are waiting in line.
Your ears don't always listen.
It can be your brain, your
fingers, your toes.
You can listen anywhere.
Your mind might not want to go.
If you can listen you can find
answers to questions you didn't know.
If you have listened, truly
listened, you don't find your
self alone.
                    —Nick Penna, fifth grade

I am not young enough to know
everything.

                    —J. M. Barrie

THE LOVER

The winds whisper
lavender, sandalwood
jasmine, gardenia.
The earth's soil,
the moon's attraction to the sea.
        —Veronica Paz Olalla, eleventh grade

Many parents become more aware of their child's imagination, insight, and distinct "otherness" through poetic language. Assumptions and fixed perceptions are released as they open to a sense of surprise about who that child is. Surprise is a gateway through which parents reminds themselves—or learn for the first time—that their children are on a unique adventure, with stories to tell about their journey.

For the child, knowing that he or she is genuinely seen and heard is an incomparable gift. For the parent, satisfaction comes in seeing their child shine, through their ability to communicate on other levels.

Being open to what your child thinks and feels indicates a willingness to allow them to emerge as a creative individual. This is what we want for ourselves. The statement *"I had no idea my child thought that way"* is exactly what many adults wanted to hear from their own parents but didn't.

Adult workshop participants will say the same thing after getting started on a poem: *"I had no idea I thought that way!"* That sense of freshness and surprise need not come to you only through your children when they are very young; it can continue throughout your life as you discover your own poetic voice.

The poems of e. e. cummings often show that this childlike wonder exists within us as adults. It is our innate sense of awe that draws out the poet in us all.

I threw my cup away when I saw a child drinking from his hands at the trough.

—Diogenes

It takes a long time to become young.

—Pablo Picasso

> who are you,little i
>
> (five or six years old)
> peering from some high
>
> window;at the gold
>
> of november sunset
>
> (and feeling:that if day
> has to become night
>
> this is a beautiful way)
>   —e. e. cummings

✻

Opening to the Way Your Child Is

1. Notice things your child says which reveal his or her uniqueness. Notice nonverbal details about your child. Watch how they create and explore their world. Watch their joy or sadness or curiosity or concern. See if you can *feel* their experience just as you feel your own. Look beyond preconceived notions about them. Let evaluative ways of looking go. Don't play the critical parent! Naturally, you may have frustrations and genuine concerns about your child, but in this exercise emphasize your love simply for their existence in your life. Question yourself: am I seeing this child with fresh eyes? Let them surprise you! Free write what you notice about your child. (Note: If you are not a parent, choose a child you feel close to.)

Drawing from your free write, condense and distill one, two, or three specific qualities about him or her and a single central image and/or action. Include details associated with that image, action and qualities. One woman gave this response about her six-year-old son, Adam:

> *Bits of masking tape stick to the rug,*
> *slivers of cardboard, pencils, scissors*
> *lie unperturbed in the aftermath of flight.*

> *Adam holds the belly of his new plane,*
> *the light in his eyes a wingspan of possibility.*
> *Poised at the runway of my attention*
> *he readies his craft for takeoff.*

> *Folded around a hollow body of air,*
> *this wizardry of cardboard and calling and faith*
> *finds a cushion of air and its purpose.*
> *Grounded in the engine of my own dark mood*
> *I see Adam smile the whole distance*
> *from incredible to flight.*

2. The best way to get to know a child is to ask open-ended questions. Your questions are an invitation to the child to share his or her thoughts with you; there are no right or wrong answers. Questions can be about their feelings, their opinions, nature, everyday events in their lives. Your question could be an offer to do something together. Try asking your child the following questions or think of your own. For instance:

What do you think the stars see when they look down on us?

What makes the grass grow?

What interested you today in school and on the playground?

What imaginative story would you like to write and tell?

What made you feel the best about yourself today?

What would you like us to do together for the next twenty minutes?

Let your child's response to any of these questions and/or your reflections on what they have said condense and distill into a poem.

POEMS ABOUT PARENTS:
FRUSTRATION, ANGER
AND RESOLUTION

There is apparently a fragile bridge between expecting nothing and wanting everything.

—Jim Harrison

We may spend a lot of time as adults going back and forth over that fragile bridge, traversing between hope and frustration, love and anger in our relationship with a parent. We may resolve to give up our expectations about how we want a parent to respond to us only to find ourselves, on a visit home for the

*

holidays, hoping that this time they'll treat us differently. Or may feel we've put family conflicts behind us, but when we're with a parent for any length of time, the heaviness of the past sets in.

Woven through this inner emotional tension, connected by this swaying bridge between relinquishing expectation and wanting love, are the family and individual stories that make the landscapes of our lives. All the details and circumstances found in those stories—the good and bad times—whether joined tightly together or torn apart—these can be materials for your poem-making.

The times of difficulty and challenge, of love expressed and stony silence. The way a parent responded to your creativity. The time you handed a poem to your mother and she only corrected your spelling. Times your father didn't have time to listen to you tell a story. Times they cared for you or you cared for them. Times when no one seemed interested in how the other felt. Times when doubt held more power than faith. The impact of illness, death and other catastrophes—things that no one had any control over. Times you've broken through into new understandings about life and your parents didn't recognize this change. Times you were too angry to understand the problems your parents had to deal with.

It is not easy to give closeness and freedom, safety plus danger.
—*Florida Scott Maxwell*

What you want to find is a language that will contain anger and love and give it boundaries, a place to store the intensities of your ambivalence. You want to communicate these feelings in a form that will hold together and not slip away unsaid into the back of your mind.

Expressing your feelings in a poem, you not only have the opportunity to be emotionally honest, you can also reflect back on the poem later, and observe those feelings from a more distanced perspective. When you allow poetry to give your experience and feelings a particular shape, you gain a deeper understanding of those experiences and feelings.

Stories of growing up and relating with our parents flicker in images, sense impressions, landscapes of feeling and memory.

You can follow a single thread to begin a poem about your relationship with a parent. What feeling and image is strongest right now?

You may want to write things that are unpleasant and harsh. That's all right. You may feel your parents would be hurt if they read or heard your poem. That may be true, but that doesn't mean you shouldn't write such a poem. They do not have to read it. David Budbill wrote a poem about a disturbing scene he witnessed between a parent and a child.

Poetry allows one to speak with a power that is not granted by our culture.

—Linda McCarriston

WHAT I HEARD IN A DISCOUNT DEPARTMENT STORE

Don't touch that. And stop your whining too.
Stop it. I mean it. You know I do.
If you don't stop, I'll give you fucking something
to cry about right here
and don't you think I won't either.

And so she did. She slapped him across the face.
And you could hear the snap of flesh against the flesh
halfway across the store. Then he wasn't whining anymore.
Instead, he wept. His little body heaved and shivered and wept.
He was seven or eight. She was maybe thirty.
Above her left breast, the pin said: Nurse's Aide.

Now they walk hand in hand down the aisle
between the tables piled with tennis shoes
and underpants and plastic bags of socks.

I told you I would. You knew I would.
You can't get away with shit like that with me,
you know you can't.
You're not in school anymore.
You're with your mother now.
You can get away with fucking murder there,
but you can't get away with shit like that with me.

*

Stop crying now I say
or I'll give you another little something
like I did before.
Stop that now. You'd better stop.

That's better. That's a whole lot better.
You know you can't do that with me.
You're with your mother now.

It's okay to write what you need to say. You don't have to lash back, but you can speak your anger and hurt. You can say what happened. Such a poem may not be the last thing you need to say, but it might ignite your creative fuel for getting started on the path to healing.

You may choose to share your poem with no one but yourself, or perhaps a confidante you trust. Whether you share it or not, write it first for you. Allow something unexpected to happen. You must take the chance and let your voice come forward.

What shrinks inside us, these stones
that rattle in our throats
tell us only
to go on getting older.

But the eyes want, the fingers, the emptiness
of the mouth
wants something to speak to, some lost
born of a mouth with its unpredictable answers.
                                              —*Chana Bloch*

When I was young, to make something in language, a poem that was all a piece, a poem that could stand for what I was at the time— that seemed the most miraculous thing in the world.

                    —*Theodore Roethke*

Elsa Weiner is twenty-two and has written poetry since she was fifteen. Elsa has tried therapy to deal with her relationship with her mother but felt resistance to it; she says being alone with words lets her feel more fully. Poetry provides a way to find her own direction. Her poem contains longing and angry indignation, hurt and resolve.

MOTHER—EYES CAST DOWN

You should not be so ashamed
you should hold me.
I am yours to hold.
I am your birthright.
I want to feel the heat of your gaze,
know you are alive.

I want the palm of your hand
to curve around my ribs
and hold that small space like a shrine
or an animal.

You pull on your hat,
fidget in your seat,
you want to leave me.

Lost moments are piling in doorways.
Either you walk through that door or I do.
It doesn't matter anymore who does the leaving.
The silence is easier to bear
than your double-edged words
and your imperfections.

I don't want it to be made up to me.
I'm not looking for excuses or apologies.
I'm looking for people I can trust.
I'm looking for actions that speak as loud as love
and never slow down,
never leave and come back,
and never ever cease.

Elsa names that sacred place around her ribs where she wants a
mother's touch, that place in the doorway of never meeting, the
empty place of not being received.

At first, I felt uncomfortable writing a poem about my mother that is angry or contains feelings that may hurt her, but I wrote it all down anyway. By doing that I got more space around that anger. I also gained an ability to listen for new feelings. I want to have enough clarity about my anger to be freed from it rather than stuck with or in it. Making this poem and others is where I began dealing with anger. It's helping me move into a new way of interacting with my mother that isn't so dependent on those feelings.

My voice is getting much stronger. I feel more distance from my mother because of the writing I've done. This poem clears a pathway for focusing on my needs. I am figuring out: What do I want? How are the people in my life helpful to my growth? How are they not helpful? Who am I going to let in and not let in? How am I going to decide that? My poem says I want people I can trust. People who prove themselves to me. There are times when I feel disgusting and unlovable, and times when I shine. I want people who will be there for both. My poem is about learning to trust.

Poems of anger can give way to poems of acceptance, but you can't force yourself to accept a difficult parental relationship. What you can do is pay attention. Writing will help you to see what is possible. There may be improved communication with your father or mother while they are alive, and this interaction may encourage new insight. It is also possible that the death of a parent may push you in the direction of acceptance. The healing work you do concerning your relationship with them may be highlighted by feelings of grief, abandonment, the need to become more true to yourself, or perhaps, a desire to know your parent with a deeper sense of connection.

RITUAL

For seven days after my mother died,
I slept in her bed and sipped her wine.
Her long black dress fit me, so I wore it.

*I patted my cheeks with her makeup
and smeared red lipstick on my mouth
like a child playing dress-up.*

*After seven days, I scattered her ashes
and returned to my house,
surprised to find her face in my mirror.*
                    —Donna Kennedy

The kind of healing process and acceptance we're speaking of is often more difficult for men. Mark Henry is forty-two and began writing poetry in his mid-thirties. He attended a workshop I gave many years ago. During the workshop and for a while afterwards, Mark wrote angry poems about his father. They provided a useful cathartic force but did not stop his inner war. Persistence helped him find a deeper resolution; and so did Mark's wife, who offered genuine support rather than a critical attitude about how he dealt with his emotions. Recently, Mark sent me this poem; it signified a breakthrough:

SECOND ANNIVERSARY

*I dumped on
You
dumped on
Me.
I wondered today,
what about your Jesus years,
of birth and babyhood.
Laughter and illness,
TB and bassoon band,
traveling quiet man,
the literal original thin man
gone bald, to potbelly.
Basketball coach, teacher,
traveling book salesman,
king of the World Book encyclopedia,*

*

LA Times reader and *Bonanza* watcher.
Your warm, comforting stomach and heartbeat
soothing my brewing storms to sleep
for a night.
The Chevrolet, or was it the Ford sedan that burned?
The VW bus and the blue van,
the pickup truck and the compact Nissan.
From hillsides to desert and across the country,
educator of students and sons.
Ulcer, cancer, growth, depression, junkyard home.
Cries of lost love, lost wife, lost wonder.
Persevering all those angry, dumping years.
Fears and television joined in living, married bliss.
You called me "stupe."
I resented the shit out of you.
You dumped on me you loved me.
I dumped on you I loved you.
You died two years ago today, dad.

—Mark Henry

Tumbling sounds and images, lists of cars, careers and illnesses, concrete details and honest emotions—all of these elements help Mark express who his father was and what their relationship was like. In remembering the real stuff of his childhood, Mark is able to create a vivid portrait of his father.

Looking back and recognizing the struggles in his life, this poem helps me accept my father. Seeing how he dealt with his tuberculosis, the illnesses he endured, the loss of his wife (my mom) to cancer which basically sent him into a depression for thirty-three years. I know those are some of the reasons why he wasn't there for me, which for years I was angry about.

The lines "soothing my brewing storms to sleep/for a night" reminds me there were moments of tenderness between us interspersed with those days and months of loneliness. The cars represent the trips we took across the United States. Dad wanted us to gain a love for our country, the environment, and history. It was in trying to have a dialogue

* *with him about these things after his death that this poem came out. It is*
* *also a poem to forgive myself for the way I treated him.*

EXERCISE
Poem of Want and Poem of Acceptance

Explore both or one of these exercises depending on where you
are now in your relationship with your parent.

1. Make a list of what you wanted in a relationship with
your parent(s) but didn't get. Make another list of what you
have come to feel is valuable that you received from them. Be
particular. Take the most potent things from both lists and
shape them into a poem.

2. Think about your parent(s) and what their lives were/are
like. Not just the cold facts and "red-letter dates" but . . . what
they enjoy(ed), what they accomplished, how they are (were)
uniquely themselves, how they interact(ed) with you, their way
of teaching or loving you. What are the particulars of their individual and family history that seem most significant? Let the
specific images that come up help you create a poem which
deals with accepting your parent(s) for the real persons they
are/were.

PARENTS, CHILDREN AND THE PASSAGE OF TIME

> Put this in your notebooks:
> All verse is occasional verse.
>
> —Ellen Bryant Voigt

Time has profound implications for parent and child. Time is to
relationship what wind is to the maple tree. You can't really see

Children can turn anything into anything. For this gift we call them magical, born alchemists of the spirit. But they are more than this: they are the first real inventors—and each child in her own time invents the world all over again, as if it had never been made before.

—Richard Lewis

the wind, but without it, maple trees would not be as beautiful. Time is more than money; it may be this wind of love.

Poems in this section deal with the use and passage of time between parent and child. Time well spent will nourish and encourage your child's creativity and give the same support to yourself. But what about having enough time to make a living, fulfill other responsibilities and peruse personal interests, especially for single mothers or fathers and families where both parents work? How difficult it is!

Looking back as adults on their time spent together, parent and child might wonder: Was there enough time between us? A parent with young children might ask: Is there time for me? Is there time for my child? When a child leaves home or a parent ages they both might ask: Where did the time go?

Vesela Simic is the mother of a spirited three-year-old girl. She helps her husband with his start-up business in solar energy systems. Finding time in her day or evening for writing is an infrequent luxury. Vesela wrote in her journal about her child, her personal struggles, her family, the unpredictable way her days go and her longing to find time to write:

Every day is a good day. A good mantra. Yesterday morning I brooded; there was no time to write. Jasmine woke up with me. David set off for work. Jasmine needed breakfast . . . buttered wheat toast with blackberry jam . . . and milk. I needed a shower. Jasmine joined me. These showers take much longer than a shower alone . . . shampooing my hair and Jasmine's, careful not to let any soap in her eyes, careful to massage her head, not scrub it, so that she learns to massage herself, not scrub. Soaping my body . . . soaping Jasmine, patient with her exuberant skating on the bar of soap . . . waiting again until she washes me, her hands gently gliding about my back, arms, chest, her face smiling fully engaged in me. There was no time to write. She wanted me to read to her. In her stories everything works out . . . in my story I could not shake the inertia, the dullness infecting me. No time alone to face myself on the page. I could not make pesto for dinner, clean the basement, clear out the garden. Every day is a good day because David comes home and understands how some days are like this and he takes

us out for a Chinese meal and even when I order the Long Life Tofu and
halfway through grow tired of its taste and wish I'd ordered Kung Pao
Chicken, Jasmine says to me, "I liked my noodles, Daddy liked his
tofu, tell the man you didn't like your food," so Jasmine and David
have satisfied my hunger . . . we go to bed, our family bed with Jasmine
in the middle, and I am warm and the night is cold and windy. I did
not write. Still every day is a good day.

Although Vesela's gentle lament is that she has little time to write, her journal entry is filled with her life: she *notices* details, she *recognizes* her feelings, she *responds to* her family experience. She is aware of how much LIFE is found in simple things: toast, soap, children's books and Long Life Tofu. Being open and responsive to our daily lives will help to keep our sensitivity primed even when we cannot write.

Adriana Paredes was born in Mexico City. She moved to the United States with her twelve-year-old son Rodrigo a few years ago. It wasn't easy to leave her native country behind, but writing and reading poetry helps her to bridge cultural and language differences. Adriana writes in both Spanish and English, holding to her roots yet extending herself into her new land. She feels poetry is a language that transcends barriers. Its essence is connected to her son, and she only needs a moment to realize this:

My child, Rodrigo, brings poetry into my life. From the moment he
was conceived I was aware of his presence. My awareness of every-
thing became more and more acute. Any incident in my life that stirs
deep emotion becomes a deep silence. And from this silence emerges some-
thing that is like a fierce child who wants to be born onto the paper.

"Unbroken Promise" was born at a time in my life when I was so
wrapped up in demanding social events that there was no time to see my
child. One Sunday morning as I walked into my living room I looked
at him. My son was curling his long and lean body in front of the TV.
An overwhelming recognition hit me: through all the changes in our life
together, all the movements, he is the most important gift I have ever re-
ceived from life. Writing the poem was my way to let him know that in

spite of my busyness this was my promise and it is unbreakable. Rodrigo received the poem with a smile.

UNBROKEN PROMISE

I see him playing
from the corner of my life
A life that feels too full
to have time to watch.

I sigh and try to keep up
with the details.

What color are the flowers?
Is the address right?
Where is the place to meet the ocean?
Is the music an old waltz or a slow dance?

In the midst of all this creation
we need to find a place to live
And I breathe, because I want a home for him.
Where he can grow taller than I am.

He sits and plays
writing codes that allow him to enter
into deeper challenges and new worlds.
I move around
the challenges life brings.

And for brief moments,
our eyes meet.
I reach to touch
his face, and hug his dancing body.

Any resistance
melts away, when I whisper
in his ear, I love you.
     He is my child and I his mother
     No matter what other songs I sing.
          —Adriana Paredes

PROMESA SIN ROMPER

Lo veo jugando
desde un rincón de mi vida
Una vida que se siente muy llena
para tener tiempo de mirar

Suspiro y trato de seguir
con los detalles

De que color son las flores?
Es la dirección correcta?
Donde es el lugar para
     encontrarnos con el oceano?
Es la canción, un viejo vals a una danza suave?

En la neblina de esta creación
Necesitamos encontrar un lugar donde vivir.
Y respiro porque quiero un hogar para el
Donde pueda crecer mas alto que yo.

El se sienta a jugar
escribiendo claves que le permiten acceso
a retos mas profundos y nuevos mundos.
Yo me muevo alrededor
de los retos que la vida me brinda.

★

Y por breves instantes
nuestras miradas se cruzan.
Extiendo mi ser para tocar
su cara, y abrazar su cuerpo que danza.

Cualquier resistencia
se derrite, cuando susurro
en su oido, Te amo.
El es mi niño y yo su madre.
No importa que otras canciones cante.

When children grow up and leave home, it is a time of transition for parents. As they reflect on the past and experience new beginnings, parents can give voice to this poignant time of life by making poems.

Robert Evans raised his daughter, Phoebe, on his own. The sledding incident described in the poem below happened many years ago, when Bob had not yet developed an interest in poetry. It was only much later when attempting to convey to friends an adventure he had in the Pacific Northwest that he realized he was trying to write poetry! Phoebe went away to college at this same time, and her absence from his life on a daily basis had a strong emotional effect on him, contributing to his interest in creativity and self-expression.

Bob made this time in his life important. He attended a writing workshop at a local community college and has written poetry ever since. He founded a once-a-month gathering of local poets which has been thriving now for seventeen years. This is one of Bob's early poems.

ON RUNNERS

When my daughter was two
we set out to go sledding;
first layers of sweaters and snowsuits
until she was a small spherical bundle,
then sanding the rust off runners,
then the thermos of cocoa for later.

At the crest of Deadman's Hill
I put my darling aboard. Hold on tight
I said, I'll have my legs around you
and steer with my feet. *She giggled.*

As I bent to tie my bootlace the sled
and Phoebe slid silently away.
All the memories and hopes I had
for her rose in a lump to my throat
as I stood rooted there
watching her descent. She picked up
terrific speed, became airborne
at every bump, whizzed across the bow
of an eight-man toboggan, side-swiped
a larger sled, never let go, never fell,
diminished to a dot, finally still.
Then I could run to her.

Well she made it, and I
made it through being a father,
but what I'll remember is
how she slipped away.
                    —Robert Evans

This poem is sharp like runners on a sled. We are very close to
what happens on that hill.

A poem is a way of capturing a moment.
                    —Nikki Giovanni

I wrote this poem about sixteen years after the sledding incident. I de-
scribed the scene as precisely and detailed as I could. I kept coming back
to the image: she slid away silently. I was a long way from being able
to help her.
   I knew something at that moment deep inside when she was two, al-
though I would not have been able to articulate it at the time. My soul
had a moment of insight but it took my mind a while to express and un-
derstand it. Phoebe on the sled was a profound metaphor for the separa-
tion I felt when she left home.

I wrote this poem around another major transition in my relationship with her. I drove Phoebe with her stuff in our old station wagon to Los Angeles to attend college. We unloaded her things and were about to say goodbye. Suddenly we burst into tears. I saw it: the sled had actually slid away again with her on it.

Phoebe struggled to survive on her own. From the day she started walking, my instinct was to reach over to keep her from falling on her face. But I had to pull back because she needed to walk on her own. The awful truth of the parent: to be terrified about the risks your children are taking when you aren't there, when they have to decide for themselves what to do. Phoebe made it. Like her ride on that hillside, she seems to have grown up silently and so quickly.

EXERCISE
Time Well Spent—Writing Poems About Parenthood, Writing Poems to Your Child, Writing Poems with Your Child

1. If you have children, how do you feel about the time you spend with them—is it time well spent? Do you take the time to notice how they are growing? How your relationship to them is changing? Write a poem about this. Write also about making time for yourself and how you would best spend it.

2. Take some time to stop and consider what you want to give your child or children. Write a poem of promise or love to your child.

3. Write poems with your child! You can start out by making a "word bowl" together. Think of words together—gather them from books or magazines or just pull them out of your head. Do this while you are spending time together, driving, or hanging out at home. Write these words down on cardstock paper and put them in a bowl. Pick twenty words out of the bowl and make poems out of them. Come up with your own ways to make poems together—and have fun! Adjust exercises from this book or *Finding What You Didn't Lose* to fit your needs. See my suggested reading list for other books on poem-making for children.

WRITING POEMS TO
HEAL THE WOUNDS OF
CHILDHOOD ABUSE

Children have exquisite imaginations, but they also write frankly about their pain and the problems they have. Children listen closely to what adults ignore or pretend does not exist. It is important to listen to children when they write about painful things. During classes I taught in a high school, a girl handed me this poem:

TERRIBLY LOUD SCREAMING KEPT THE HOUSE AWAKE

Why was he so cruel?
She would wait night, after night, after night.
Waiting for his face or a phone call.
Half asleep, worried in bed, the keys
*   would unlock the door.*
The keys would unlock her fury.
She would race to the hall, screaming with anger.
The children fast asleep for hours would
*   awake to a war of horrid words.*
Doors slamming, glass shattering, and
*   terribly loud screaming kept the house awake.*
Her tears take over her fury.
He sleeps on the couch.
She runs to her room, cries herself to sleep.
The children, hold each other for comfort, and
They, too, cry themselves to sleep.
                                    —Lisa, *eleventh grade*

The impact of Lisa's poem is powerful and raw. She writes with clarity about her broken family circumstances. She is learning to "think by feeling." Her lines "Her tears take over her fury. / He sleeps on the couch" reflect compassion for her mother and father. That I am able to receive and listen to her poem helps to validate her courage to write these truths about her life.

She can call on this feeling and insight when making choices about her own life.

When a child is abused or is witness to abuse or violence, it may act as a lock on the gateway to the good they deserve in life. The garden of childhood just beyond that gate may never be claimed and instead grow full of weeds. Adults who never visited their own garden in childhood often carry that lock with them and, unfortunately, bestow it upon their own children. Writing strong feelings on paper may help to unlock that gateway and give you the opportunity to recreate a place for your garden to flourish again or even for the first time. Breaking the lock of violence and abuse with the truth may make it possible for current relationships and circumstances to gradually take root in healthy ground, so that you can grow from what Robert Bly called "your own great roots."

Writing poems about an abusive family history does not magically "heal" the past. Allowing pain to surface, struggling with it, threshing out the weeds in the garden of your childhood—this takes time. Poem-making is part of a larger process of recovery that includes learning to take care of oneself physically, psychologically and spiritually.

You may only write painful fragments, intense journal entries, harsh and angry rants to release your feelings. You might want to burn these poison poems or bury them in a ritual ceremony. On the other hand, you may want to keep these poems so that you can look at them from time to time with the intent of honoring your truth-telling so that you no longer disown yourself. These difficult poems may help you to notice your understanding as it develops, allowing you to see how you've grown. The best approach will be something to experiment with and feel for yourself. Your poems will serve as a container for your feelings and insights so that you can work with them in whatever way is best for you.

It is the *action* of writing poems that is important, especially when shared or spoken out loud with a counselor or support group. Writing and giving voice to your experience of abuse with others present helps to dispel the secrecy maintained around these issues. Simply to have someone listen to your truths will give a gathering power to your healing process and to your commitment to no longer harm yourself or others.

Anything you write about these issues is worthwhile. Some poems may mark major breakthrough points in your healing and go to the heart of your painful experiences.

What follows is a poem by Reverend Ellen Grace O'Brian about the anger of her father, his abuse, how she coped with it as a young child, and what it means to her now as an adult. Ellen's words arise from both innocence and experience: she remembers the actions and feelings of the little girl she used to be, but she also uses the insight she has gained as an adult. If you listen closely (her poem is available on tape recording—see my suggested reading list), you will hear the lonely innocence of a betrayed childhood and, just behind the words, an honest loving of self that is so crucial in the process of healing.

Wounds of childhood which we carry into adult life make it clear: everything in life is related. Although the process of writing these poems about abuse is often focused on releasing the past, your writing can also act as a bridge of understanding to those you have relationships with in the present.

We can consciously tell our stories of the past *in the present* so that what happened in our past will be less apt to unconsciously repeat itself. We speak and write these poems so that in the present and future we can know and be aware of our shadows, but not be misled by them. *Burying the Gold* is a gift from a wife to her husband so that he will know the frightened-child part of her.

Ellen is the Senior Minister of the Center for Spiritual Enlightenment in San Jose, California. She is the mother of a son and a daughter, and resides in Santa Cruz with her husband and stepdaughter.

BURYING THE GOLD/A STORY FOR MY HUSBAND

The small girl,
awakened by her drunken father
that night, learned this:
She could not win.

*

He was disturbed,
disturbed past anger.
Coming home walking through
the kitchen
there was a feeling
he did not like, or
perhaps it was a sound.
Someone spilled juice on the floor
and didn't clean it up right.
It left a residue.
A sticky residue of something.
Something that stopped him
when he came in
in the middle of the night.
Maybe that sticky feeling
said something to him,
maybe he heard right out loud,
"Things are out of control here!" or,
"No one cares!"
Who knows.
The walls actually said those things
all the time there
but he played loud music
when he came home at night
so he didn't hear them.
Maybe that sticky residue
just made it impossible for him to imagine
on such a night that he slipped silently
past them all, sleeping.

She had long ago learned
to sleep with one eye open,
scanning the horizon
for his return.

He said he wanted the truth.
The truth would be all that mattered.

Did she do it?
If she said no,
he would keep her up all night interrogating her,
if she said yes,
he would beat her.
She said no. Then,
when she got too tired,
she said yes.
She spoke that yes
with the only power she could find.
Like a silent star falling in the sky
she said inside I will not feel.
And she didn't.
The sting of his hand on
her bare flesh was dull, and
there was no sound.
No sound and no feeling.
Just a falling sensation,
falling inside, in slow motion.
When it was over
she walked to her room
and there were no tears.
There was only that slight tremor
at her chin, the falling away inside and
her own knowing: she had become his daughter.

The next morning she set out
on her own
taking what she cared most about
and feared to leave behind:
A small doll carriage
packed with two baby dolls and their clothes.
She would not leave them there.
She took her souvenir from the fieldtrip
to the lost goldmine,
a small vial filled with water and tiny flecks of gold.
She knew the gold was valuable

✳

and it wasn't safe in that house.
What she didn't know was:
it was already lost.
She walked, pushing the carriage,
the dolls and their clothes,
and the vial.
She walked past all of the houses on the street.
She walked past the school.
Past the corner store where she sometimes took
her pennies to buy sweets
to change a bitter day.
She walked to the orchards
at the edge of what she knew.
She didn't discuss the predicament with the dolls,
so as not to worry them.
She pretended that she didn't already know what she would do.
She pretended that she had options.

Before she went back
she dug a hole in the orchard
and buried the gold.
She planned to return for it when it was time.
She didn't really think about the gold again
until the day she saw the tractors
digging up the earth in the old orchard
making foundations for the new homes.
The dolls had long since passed on
losing hair and limbs along the way to
the forgetting of their names.
The trees now down
the orchard turned over and she
so much older feared:
something was lost that cannot be recovered.
There was no real pain in this
the pain was that of a phantom limb
long ago cut away,

sending signals
out into empty space.

> *And so I tell you this story for her*
> *because I think you should know*
> *when you give her the gold necklace*
> *on her birthday*
> *the bracelet as a valentine*
> *the ring at the wedding.*
> *The small girl,*
> *still sleeping with one eye open,*
> *looks to see:*
> *Has it returned?*

The healing force of creativity is alive in Ellen as a young child. The dolls, the vial of gold, and the apple orchard show how she created meaning in the midst of violence. The poem reveals her caring concern for her dolls and the empathy that often develops as a result of suffering. She instinctively knows the natural world of the orchard to be a safe place. Ellen's protection of things valuable to her is a symbolic expression of how her psychological immune system responded to her father's anger. The "T-cells" of our psychological immune system can also manifest as poetic medicines: symbol and image, rhythm and feeling.

The poem is made even more potent by the fact that at the conclusion, Ellen recognizes the "small girl still sleeping with one eye open" still resides within her. Healing from painful past experiences doesn't mean our fears and our hurts disappear. But instead of looming in the foreground and preventing us from experiencing life in the present, such fears and hurts, if they are dealt with and understood, can be placed in their proper context—as part of our life's "story." The understanding of another person who loves you helps to remind you of this. Ellen tells about writing her poem:

* *The poem began with the image of the gold vial. I wrote it on Valen-*
** *tine's Day as a gift for my husband. I worked on the poem all day and*
*

it was well past dark when I finally gave it to him. He didn't get any dinner but he got the poem! It turns out to be a love poem. When I gave it to Michael, he cried. We cried together. We recognized this fragile bond of our relationship and he thought it was beautiful.

I asked my father if he would be willing to read it. He replied, "Yes." That experience opened up the conversation about my childhood which we had never been able to have. I had done a lot of healing work by myself and in therapy prior to being able to invite my father to read the poem. I wanted a relationship with him, but I was aware of my lack of willingness to show up completely and tell my truth. In writing this poem I found I was able to say very uncomfortable things. The poem made it possible to say them in a way that softened the experience for both of us. Prior to the poem it was a very different experience—a stony wall of resistance would always go up.

When dad read the poem, I felt he sensed my childhood reality. He said to me, "So you felt I was an ogre to you?" I said, "Yes, I did." He didn't try to deny or negate my reality. In fact, he affirmed for me that he knew he had been drunk many times and wasn't always aware of his actions.

Sharing the poem with my father came out of a very strong intention I had to either make a real relationship with him or let it go. It wasn't possible for me to continue to relate on the surface with someone who I love very deeply. Because I was not able to speak and be heard about my childhood reality, I carried a lot of anger and resentment. So I only saw him as that ogre. Since a bridge has been made with the poem, I have been blessed with being able to see his strengths and his gifts.

This poem deepens my relationship with my husband by making it all right for him to know what is vulnerable in me. He sees that in me anyway, and I want him to understand that I know it exists. I don't have to pretend otherwise. Making that child known, making room for that child, is important to a loving, whole relationship for us.

These exercises might prove especially helpful if they are done while working with a therapist, counselor or minister.

EXERCISE
Special Objects and Places of Childhood

For Ellen, the vial with gold flecks and her dolls were important objects in her childhood, symbolizing a connection with her urge to protect and love herself. These were talismans—catalysts for her poem and the process of healing. The orchard was her place of safety. Consider objects and places from your childhood that gave you comfort or were important in some way.

Was there a special object you had to soothe the storms of your childhood? It could be anything: a toy, a stuffed animal, mitt and ball, a cap, household objects or a pet. What place did you feel a sense of safety—a window you looked out of, a spot in nature, a structure or building other than your home?

Ellen says, "I didn't know the meaning of the gold vial until I wrote about it." Find those things in your childhood memory that have resonance, and explore the meaning that is held in them. If you still have that object, hold it in your hands. Or find an old photograph of it. Let these things and places speak to you. Feel them through your memory of childhood. Use your memories and sensory recollections of these objects and places.

Only when I make room for the child's voice within me do I feel genuine and creative.

—Alice Miller

EXERCISE
Your Childhood Voice and Qualities

Do this next exercise with the help of a willing partner or close friend. Ask your friend to notice your childlike qualities. He or she may witness subtle shifts of your body language, nonverbal clues and moods that express your child-self. Ask him or her to tell you about that child. In what circumstances does he or she most frequently appear—even if just for a moment? This information is not based on the opinions of the "critical parent" but a loving friend. What is seen in the face of that child? As your friend offers you specific information, feelings and impressions,

✳

make note of these and watch for these clues yourself. Watch over a period of weeks, take time to pay attention to those moments when your child-self emerges. What does this child have to say to you? Write down the impressions that come to you and shape them into a poem.

CHAPTER FIVE

ANDSCAPES OF RELATIONSHIP

Reflecting on Intimacy, Marriage and Longing

*T*here are many disciplines that strengthen one's athleticism for love. It takes all one's strength. And yet it takes all one's weakness too. Sometimes it is only by having all one's so-called strength pulverized that one is weak enough, strong enough, to yield. It takes that power of nature in one which is neither strength nor weakness but closer perhaps to virtu, person, personalized energy. Do not speak about strength and weakness, manliness and womanliness, aggressiveness and submissiveness. Look at this flower. Look at this child. Look at this rock with lichen growing on it. Listen to this gull scream as he drops through the air to gobble the bread I throw and clumsily rights himself in the wind. Bear ye one another's burdens, the Lord said, and he was talking law.

*L*ove is not a doctrine, Peace is not an international agreement. Love and Peace are beings who live as possibilities in us.

—M. C. Richards

CULTIVATING INTIMACY:
SURPRISE, DISCOVERY
AND TENDERNESS

> The heart is a place of tenderness. The cultivated heart re-
> ceives intensification towards tenderness.
>
> —Robert Bly

There are innumerable books and teachers that present techniques to improve the quality of your marriage or other significant relationships. These books and teachers offer a wide variety of value systems, useful facts and creative options, with varying degrees of emphasis on the spiritual, physical and emotional parts of relationship. Many provide excellent maps for helping us to understand where we are and where we want to go.

Such maps can serve as superb guides, but they may not help you to directly perceive lessons particular to your life and your relationship. It's one thing to recognize that yes, generally speaking, men are from Mars and women are from Venus, but since *your* arrival on Earth, have you had the courage to explore your own voice—your never-heard-before-in-the-history-of-the-world voice?

And have you spoken to your partner in this voice? Have you written the poems only you can write—the poems expressing your fears, frustrations and joys as you attempt to join your life with another's? The insights of a particular teacher or psychologist may be helpful as you struggle to make your relationship more fulfilling and loving, but drawing from your own creative resources has a uniquely important impact.

Using your poetic voice can help you to understand yourself

and your relationship to your partner in a way no outside authority can do for you.

Poem-making can be a way to bridge differences and be more personal in your communication with a mate. We make poems not only as men and women who come from "different planets" but as unique individuals whose origins are richly complex and whose destinations are yet to be realized. Because poem-making almost always reveals something we didn't previously know, poems about our relationship can surprise us with truths about ourselves, our mates and the lives we have together.

The self-discovery and surprise that come to you when you express yourself through poem-making are the result of the poem revealing to you who you truly are. There is the sudden recognition after writing your poem, "Yes, this is who I am." You feel yourself relinquishing the static, clichéd view of yourself, and becoming reacquainted with what is essential in your heart and spirit. That sense of self-discovery can lead to your being more authentic in your relationship, more emotionally honest with your partner, and more open to who they truly are.

When you can relate to someone close to you with the openness and the capacity for surprise and change, it can breathe freshness into your relationship.

Marge Piercy's poem *To Have Without Holding* expresses what it might look like to bring intensity and openness into a relationship. Within that openness is the opportunity to see someone as themselves, not as we would like them to be or as we define them to be. Nothing is harder! Here is the first stanza of the poem:

> *Learning to love differently is hard,*
> *love with the hands wide open, love*
> *with the doors banging on their hinges,*
> *the cupboard unlocked, the wind*
> *roaring and whipping in the rooms*
> *rustling the sheets and snapping the blinds*
> *that thwack like rubber bands*
> *in an open palm.*
>
> *—Marge Piercy*

It is difficult for many of us to express our feelings to those we're closest to. Men often find it especially hard. A decision by a man to include creativity as a part of his relationship with a partner can help change this.

Men sometimes have the mistaken notion that poetry is insubstantial. That's not true. Making a poem is not unlike building a house. A poem is a structure in which to house your thoughts and feelings on the page.

A poem is a place where you can grapple with what is important to you. The courage to feel and speak from gut and heart is the challenge that awaits anyone who works at poem-making. Feeling from your heart and gut can be uncomfortable. It may take time to adjust to not necessarily having answers but rather a whole range of changing feelings. The mind likes to categorize and know things for certain. But it is unlikely that anything self-revealing and intimate will happen when you are entirely certain of things.

Jack Winkle is forty years old and has been married for ten years. A book he read had inspired him to try a particular practice of being honest with his feelings. Jack didn't think he was making much progress, but one evening going home from work on the train, this poem poured out:

> Tell me a tale, I'll tell you a tale
> A story of scats of cats, and moles of holes.
> Tell me the TRUTH—
> I'll tell you the truth
> Of miles of files, of places I've seen,
> Of means of things, but where's that TRUTH?
> OK, I lied, that wasn't the truth.
> I'm really a bugger bear, I swear.
> No shit, I AM!
> You thought me a man, a really nice man.
> I was taught to scam, to plan, to filter, and hide.
> I am darker than I look. No, not a tan, a Shadow—
> with bags of gooky, sticky, putrid hidings.
> You see my baggage, will you run? RUN!

★

> *I don't blame you*
> *Scares me so bad.*
> *That tale can wait another day.*

Jack's fine image, "I am darker than I look. No, not a tan, a Shadow," is courageous and self-revealing. Jack says that his tough self-analysis was helped by the fact that a creative door opened to him in the process of writing.

> *I felt very happy writing this poem. It was a dark subject, but I wrote it*
> *down in pencil and didn't futz with it much. I am not used to having*
> *the creative juices flow. I felt almost giddy! I wrote it just for me, but I*
> *read it to my wife and then to a men's group and everyone thought it*
> *was great. I felt it helped the group go deeper. Saying this in a nonlogi-*
> *cal way was very freeing. I wanted to make it nice at the end of the*
> *poem, but that's not how it is so I didn't do it. The poem is about hiding.*
> *I just wanted to say that emotionally that's what I do, I hide.*

Riding that train home, Jack wrote his way into new emotional territory. The process is like flushing out old, stagnant water and allowing fresh water to come in. He has written other po- ems since which remove logical filters to reveal more personal feelings. Exploring a fuller range of feeling, Jack is gaining ap- preciation for his many strengths, as well as for his shadow.

"ALL MARRIAGES ARE MIXED"

Susan Dion is the author of an excellent booklet entitled *Write Now: Maintaining a Creative Spirit While Homebound and Ill* (see my suggested reading list). She has been ill with a chronic debili- tating illness since 1989. In an earlier phase of her life, Susan was a dynamic college history professor and administrator. She continues to write about and participate in family life. Susan wrote the following poem in the early stages of contemplating remarriage about twelve years ago.

*

ALL MARRIAGES ARE MIXED

Do not merely consider the differences of
  race
  class
  education
  religion
  age
  previous marriages
  children already born

Contemplate two people
  one woman
  one man

With unique understandings
  calcified habits
  complicated visions, feelings, and rationales
  individualized histories and cultures

Mixed voices
  attempting a voluntary association
  of intimacy, love and giving
  coupled with the residue of everyday life
    bad breath in the morning
    scrubbing the hairs out of the tub
    dealing with garbage

One woman, one man
  hoping to sustain a fragile experiment
  knowing quite clearly

All marriages are mixed.
                                —Susan Dion

Rather than offering herself solutions, Susan names the complex layers that are created when two people bring their lives

*

Freedom in the mere sense of independence is meaningless. Perfect freedom lies in the harmony of relationship which we realize not through knowing but in being.

—*Rabindranath Tagore*

together. She invites all of these aspects into the place of the poem. She weaves them together in a simple and straightforward way. Instead of trying to figure it out or make one aspect of marriage stand out above the rest, she figures everything *in*, she *in*-cludes.

Susan touches on the blessings, uncertainties, insights and pressures that cause relationships to break up or hold together—everything is out front and on the table. Something in the texture of the poem knits these disparate parts together and permits us to look at the varied elements of a marriage relationship. By the end of this poem we may have a sense that this "fragile experiment" of marriage is worthy of our time and has an honest chance to succeed if our eyes are open and our hearts willing to do the work.

Susan writes that marriage is "attempting a voluntary association / of intimacy, loving and giving / coupled with the residue of everyday life." What words stand out in your mind as you read this line? I strongly hear: voluntary association, intimate, residue of everyday. Each of these phrases feels like a very separate thing. Yet in the context of marriage—clarified by Susan's ability to experiment with them in her poem-writing—they have the opportunity to establish a relationship with one another.

Marriage and other intimate relationships are potentially capable of providing a place to frame the many facets of who you are and a process through which you can learn and grow.

Consider this: In your relationship, this "voluntary association," how do you respond to your partner's longing and needs and also ask for the space and consideration you need to maintain intimacy over an extended period of time?

How do you nurture both your own personal growth and closeness with your partner so that a relationship remains an opportunity rather than a trap?

When it comes to love—to romantic love and sexual love and married love—we have to learn again, with difficulty, how to let go of all kinds of expectations.

—*Judith Viorst*

How can the intimate aspects of a relationship remain fresh and authentic, so that they do not slip into expectations and possessiveness and turn what is voluntarily given into a joyless obligation?

In every longstanding intimate relationship, what is "intimate" must learn to coexist with "everyday residue" (dirty dishes, bad breath, toothpaste squeezed-from-the-middle, etc.). At some point, most of us wonder whether this "voluntary association" was such a good idea to begin with!

Reflection on what a marriage contains and how we place these various elements in relationship to one another, as Susan Dion does in her poem, may help deepen our perception of what it means to love someone.

Susan reflects on how her poem came to be:

This poem came to me when Tom and I were considering marriage after dismal previous marriages. My eyes were more open to all the complex issues that come up when two people decide to commit. I was looking at two individuals—a man and a woman—Tom and I—and recognizing all the baggage we bring. Writing this poem moved on thoughts about the bravery and courage and deep love it takes to make that commitment.

Tom and I met in 1985 and had a four-year courtship, including two years of long-distance love between the Philadelphia area and northern Wisconsin! So we've been married for almost eight years now, shared a household for ten years, and together and in love for almost twelve years.

What compelled me to write this poem was a desire to see clearly the potential pain and misinterpretations that can occur even in a relationship where two people love each other very much. I may have known all of this on an intellectual level but living it included facing all those daily roommate issues! I've had to use a lot of self-talk to accept our differences without being annoyed and angry. I had to allow us to mature and grow and give—companionship and intimacy, sexual performance and raising a family—all these are part of that growth.

I don't know how I had the guts to enter into a third commitment. That is the true miracle! Adjustment is a big word. Adjustment to something profound and new can take years and lots of effort. My training is in history, so I do take the long view. Our expectations for marriage are time-bound by our culture and are especially high in the twentieth

* century. *Writing has helped me to be aware of a larger context for my*
* *relationship with my husband.*

Poems reveal where you are right now, and the process of writing them also helps you discover what you are becoming. Your perceptions of what it is like to be in a relationship can be made more clear to you through making poems. The poem is *a place* to express the fear, uncertainty, delight, warmth, ambiguity and paradox of relationship—and it is also *a process* by which you learn from all of these.

EXERCISE
Integrating Disparate Elements in Your Relationship

The healing of our present woundedness may lie in recognizing and reclaiming the capacity we all have to heal each other, the enormous power in the simplest of human relationships: the strength of touch, the blessing of forgiveness, the grace of someone else taking you as you are and finding in you an unexpected goodness.

—Rachel Naomi Remen, M.D.

Explore conflicting elements in your marriage or other intimate relationship. You can consider either a past, present or imagined future relationship. Make two columns and label them: "Intimacy" and "Everyday Residue." Free write about both of these—include your attitudes, feelings, experience and longing.

1. What aspects of your relationship are voluntary? Why did you *choose* to marry? What have you volunteered for? Taking out the garbage . . . raising children . . . dealing with the unexpected . . . attending the same meditation classes . . . working through problems?

2. What aspects of your relationship are intimate? What do intimacy and love mean to you? Sexual closeness . . . being comfortably silent together . . . a capacity to accept imperfections . . . a willingness to confide and share?

3. What aspects do you consider part of the "everyday residue"? A bad habit that never changes . . . dirty dishes . . . nagging? Do intimacy and everyday residue remain separate, or do they sometimes interrelate in your relationship? Shape your free write into a poem.

★

4. Explore any phrase from "All Marriages Are Mixed" and find out what it means for you by free writing your personal associations and then shaping these into a poem.

RECOGNIZING THE ESSENCE OF SOMEONE YOU LOVE

> In wise love each divines the high secret self of the other and refusing to believe in the mere daily self creates a mirror where the lover or the beloved sees an image to copy in daily life, for love also creates the mask.
>
> —William Butler Yeats

Yeats' advice about "wise love" may sound unrealistic when one must deal with the challenging day-to-day circumstances that arise in intimate relationships. But appreciation of a beloved's best and deepest qualities, of their "secret self," reminds you of what you most love about that person and helps anchor your relationship.

These could be qualities that first caused you to fall in love or that you recognized much later as your bond deepened.

This attention to your partner's best qualities is not sentimental but rather a way to place something sacred and alive at the center of your relationship. Poem-making offers a way to explore what you appreciate, value, or admire about your partner—what fascinates you, what endears them to you, what makes you feel closest to them. Making your perceptions of your beloved visible in a poem is to love and celebrate that person.

If you choose, you can share your poem with your partner. Your poems can be given as gifts to mark birthdays or anniversaries. Writing and sharing your poetry will honor these special dates in your partner's life and your life together.

Someone who loves us can often see our soul potential more clearly than we can ourselves. When this happens, it has a catalytic effect, it invites and encourages the dormant, undeveloped part of us to come forth and find expression.

—John Welwood

✳

The highest purpose of art is to inspire. What else can you do? What else can you do for anyone but inspire them?

—Bob Dylan

Writing poems can also bring ritual to your sexual experience with a partner. Just as we engage our aesthetic talents to create a pleasant atmosphere for a fine dinner, with table arrangements, candlelight and music, so our artfulness and creativity can bring ritual to making love.

Certainly an important experience like sex deserves thoughtful planning too. You could set a date to make love and plan to write poems for one another ahead of time. You could read them to each other as part of your love-making date, or perhaps, a little earlier in the day, you could leave the poem you've written for your partner in a special place. They could find, read and reflect on your poem in private before you meet. Your poem could be an appetizer to whet your lover's hunger and evoke a soul connection to enhance your love-making.

Whether love-making or a birthday is the inspiration for writing your poem, expressing the essence of what your partner means to you is a way to enrich your relationship.

Judy Grahn's poem *Paris and Helen* invokes luxurious attributes to describe how two lovers feel about one another. This naming of attributes is a kind of natural praise—not praise for the accomplishments that the world usually gives recognition to but for those attributes that show a person's soulfulness.

PARIS AND HELEN

He called her: golden dawn
She called him: the wind whistles
He called her: heart of the sky
She called him: message bringer

He called her: mother of pearl,
    barley woman, rice provider,
    miller basket, corn maid,
    flax princess, all-maker, weef

She called him: fawn, roebuck,
    stag, courage, thunderman,

*

all-in-green, mountain strider,
keeper of forests, my-love-rides

He called her: the tree is
She called him: bird dancing

He called her: who stands,
has stood, will always stand
She called him: arriver

He called her: the heart and the womb
are similar
She called him: arrow in my heart.
— Judy Grahn

Praise for your partner can also be expressed through description of natural landscapes, spiritual and erotic qualities, animal names and attributes and archetypal identities that illustrate what your partner brings into your life and to the world.

You might find metaphors to describe your loved one by taking time to contemplate their activities, qualities, interests, gifts and responsibilities. Follow the roots of these everyday things back to something that is reflected in natural or universal processes.

What if someone is understated, eloquent and clear in his thinking? What if someone is passionate—rich and dynamic in her feeling? Perhaps these images: *clear reflection on the lake* and *lover in red shoes of dusk.*

Grahn weaves metaphors with great balance as the "he" and "she" of the poem speak back and forth. Metaphors within each stanza relate to one another:

Beauty is everlasting
And dust is for a time
— Marianne Moore

He called her: the tree is
She called him: bird dancing

He called her: who stands,
has stood, will always stand
She called him: arriver

✳

A tree is steadfastness, the capacity to stand steadily through time. A dancing bird is delight and the freshness of something new arriving.

Your imagination is a place where metaphor, simile, rhythm, words and images of praise for your beloved may come to you if you are receptive and attentive. This process may not be easy if your relationship is going through a difficult period. That "mere daily self" is often very hard to look past!

Writing a poem of praise for a partner may prove worthwhile even if there are many difficulties in your relationship. I am not talking about writing this poem as a way to deny abuse, ignore intolerable circumstances or avoid difficult decisions and realities. I am suggesting that writing a praise poem may help you across those arid and turbulent landscapes that occur in any marriage or relationship that is vital enough to have intense times.

It's usually easier to remember the occasions when things don't go as you plan, when your partner messes up, is unable to meet your expectations or satisfy your longing. It can be difficult to step out of the critic role in which your partner's mistakes are so apparent and see instead what is lastingly good in them. It's a challenge to see beyond a person's time-bound self and recognize the enduring soul qualities of another.

Your capacity for creativity, however, can help you write your praise poem. Take one strong thread of what you know about your partner—perhaps they are stalwart or have a sense of beauty—and stay with that thread. Feel your core thought. Take time to allow its meaning to speak to you. Write that down.

Writing this celebration poem may help you establish longer rhythms in your relationship—as if the poem were like the sun that inevitably shines following a week of fierce storms. A relentless hard rain within moments becomes clear drops that shimmer in the sun and illuminate vibrant green. If you write this poem it will be there for you when the storm clears. It may be of benefit to you in ways that you cannot imagine at the time of writing it.

The challenge and difficulty of relationships is nothing if not humbling. A strong relationship that holds promise and even bears fruit for years may suddenly flounder and eventually end. The result can be shattered hearts and disillusionment.

Making an effort to see beyond your partner's frailties and record your loving perceptions of them may serve as a preventative medicine against the bitterness and hurt that can occur with separation or divorce. What that loving poem offers to your healing may not be apparent until long after you write it.

This may not happen for some time after a relationship ends. Your poem may help you remember what was essentially good—and this can assist you as you let go of the relationship and move forward.

After working in therapy with my loss, confusion and anger following my divorce, the poems I had written about my wife during our marriage were a key part in my ability to retain a strong awareness of her soulfulness. This awareness is directly related to the kindness and respect we extend to one another now.

> *BELOVED, SING, AND DEEP RIVERS BEND*
> *for Susan Montana*
>
> *Beloved, sing, and deep rivers bend*
> *to hear themselves resound in you;*
>
> *feel your words become smooth and clean as a riverbed*
> *fresh made by the unhurried housekeeping of stars*
>
> *that speak freely amongst themselves*
> *old languages of lovemaking and dreamless rest,*
>
> *the same ease from whence the awakened currents*
> *of your life descend darkbright mountain solitudes*
>
> *single silent wintry voice to the joining sound*
> *that springtimes heard and unheard smiling choirs sing.*

The poem captures my appreciation for Susan that is not limited or diminished by having let our marriage go. It evokes some sadness in me now because it speaks of a promise yet to be fulfilled in my life, but the poem does not make me despair about what was.

Such praise poems leave me with the sense that "seeing" someone deeply is a gift that requires attention; it is not a mere consequence of living together.

I needed to write other difficult poems specifically about the breakup of my marriage, but the poems I had written to appreciate Susan also played a significant part in my healing.

EXERCISE
Recognizing the Essence of Your Partner

Take time to think about your husband, wife, lover or anyone who is beloved by you. Contemplate their qualities and what they most enjoy about life. What do they bring to your relationship through their essential traits and gifts? How does their presence in your life affect how you experience the world around you? Engage your imagination when you think about your partner and describe them from a wider, metaphoric perspective.

INTIMACY AND VULNERABILITY

> At the very point of vulnerability is where the surrender takes place—that is where the god enters. The god comes through the wound.
> —Marion Woodman

We are not taught that intimacy between people could include embracing—deeply, lovingly—our vulnerabilities. What we are vulnerable about may feel *unacceptable* to bring into our relationship, because it somehow signifies that we are not satisfying an imagined standard of perfection.

We strive to show only our "best side" in an intimate relationship but that can't last long. The best possible light that shines on at "noon" on any partner in a relationship will descend and eventually cast shadows on their personal landscape. It is usually this place of shadow and half-light where our wounds and vulnerabilities are found.

We need to become more aware of our shadowed regions and reveal them to our partners if we want to cultivate a deeper intimacy. The landscape where light and shadow exist is a good one to plumb for healing images and metaphor. Dusk and dawn are not just times of lengthening shadows; they expose the subtle beauty of changing light, reflection and silhouette.

Intimacy does not come by maintaining your "best side" at all costs. Intimacy is a willingness to share the *many sides* of oneself. Singer Joni Mitchell's popular tune from the early seventies "Both Sides Now" lyrically expressed the inevitable heartache of showing ourselves from one side only and captured her longing to no longer hold back emotional honesty: "Tears and fears and feeling proud / To say I love you right out loud."

Mitchell's romantic song shows us how youthful pride that hides vulnerability is an impediment to being intimate. The fear of sharing "both sides" is not limited to young people!

The necessity to express who you are may pull at you more profoundly as you grow older. What happens to loving and intimacy as the body ages? The denial of aging as a part of life may actually deny us our self-respect, creativity, wisdom and life-force. Writing a poem to explore your feelings about aging may help you value and integrate something real and lasting within you. Your poem may also reveal vital truths in your understanding of relationship and purpose in life.

We are healed to the extent that we love ourselves as we are right now— blemishes, vulnerabilities and all— not as we wish we will be at some time in the distant future.

—Marsha Sinetar

✴

REACHING TOWARD BEAUTY

Your love declines. You, thinking little lines
around my eyes are fallen lashes, try
to brush them off. I do exfoliate.
In this autumn of my being, parts of me
fly, like tossed and wintry-blasted leaves.
I don't regret their passing. I must work
to make a clean and crystal-perfect form.
I, alchemist, and I, philosopher's stone,
have sacrificed the fat, and froth, and fur
of youth, to walk through fire, leap in the dark,
swim inward rivers, pray at a wailing wall.
The wrinkles, sags, the graying hair are earned.
You mourn like a child over a broken doll.
Only the core of this crone was ever real.

—Hyacinthe Hill

William Butler Yeats returned again and again in his later poems to themes of aging, passion in relationships, pride and taking the good with the bad in life. Yeats' Crazy Jane character is the voice of a "wise crone" who is still connected to the deep-rooted energies of Eros. She will not allow any outside authority (the churchmen in this poem) to compromise her truth or deny the erotic roots that feed her life even as she ages. Crazy Jane knows life must include the messy, the lowly and the dark if love is to find full expression:

CRAZY JANE TALKS WITH THE BISHOP

I met the Bishop on the road
And much said he and I.
'Those breasts are flat and fallen now
Those veins must soon be dry;
Live in a heavenly mansion,
Not in some foul sty.'

'Fair and foul are near of kin,
And fair needs foul,' I cried.
'My friends are gone, but that's a truth
Nor grave nor bed denied,
Learned in bodily lowliness
and in the heart's pride.

'A woman can be proud and stiff
When on love intent;
But Love has pitched his mansion in
The place of excrement;
For nothing can be sole or whole
That has not been rent.'

Crazy Jane insists on *living* as much as possible rather than withdrawing to die. She does not buy the Bishop's judgment of appropriate behavior for a woman "her age"—a recommendation made so he will not be uncomfortable with her eccentricities, wildness and strong voice!

The last four lines of Yeats' poem are startlingly spiritual *and* erotic. Whether you take the image of "the place of excrement" as a stable where the Christ baby lay in a manger amidst animals, or where human sexuality and bodily functions occur where "fair and foul" indeed are "near of kin," Crazy Jane's message remains the same: she will find wholeness and spiritual connection through her relationships, her honesty, her brokenness and her ecstasy.

Love does not come to us because we are perfect or because we've made safe decisions based on dogma. No matter what our age, love can enter the place where we feel shitty and broken.

It may not be physical wounds or aging, but a more internal "imperfection" that needs a healing touch. It may be our human hearts' struggle to reconcile fair and foul within us that needs a listening ear. Inevitably, we will bring *something* wounded with us into our relationship.

Through poem-making we can gently share our vulnerabilities with a receptive partner and find understanding shelter.

✳

MOONBEAMS

The pale moonbeams carry us into
    a deeper place within our
    night.
Somehow,
Somehow,
        we find love in the
        coves and in the
        paleness.

Please do not leave me when my moods
    make me a burden to you. I
    need to be heard and to be
    loved. Stay next to me and
    give me what I have never had.
                    —*Elizabeth I. Roberts*

Again, healing love is shared in places unexpected and hidden away: "within our night" and "coves and in the / paleness." This poem is beautiful because it shows that it is a strength to ask for what you need. Poetic language may express your vulnerabilities in such a way that they can be heard by the heart of another.

But here is an important consideration about intimacy that is much easier said than done: We must be willing to accept *nonacceptance* if we want to be intimate with someone. Your partner may not want to hear what you need to say. Still, you must be willing to go just beyond the edge of what I think is safe to share with my partner if they are going to know something new about me.

Intimacy, when it comes, can be a magic that transforms a relationship into something joyful, life-affirming and sacred. Deep love can touch our wounds and transform us.

Susan Dion wrote the following poem about her husband, Tom Francis. She lovingly considers the vulnerability of their bodies and celebrates the erotic pleasure of their relationship.

JUNE HEAT

You come to me in daylight
The children are gone
The air is dense, hot

Dark hairs flecked with silver
Cover your strong, large chest
Solid

Residual markings in sculpted hollow
Between straight lines of collar bones, base of throat
Old punctures, tracheotomy, worn intrusions

Hidden for a lover
Are thumb-sized depressions
identifying locations, chest tube traumas

Tracing thin scars, center
Surgical site, open heart
Guiding, beating, whispering, confiding, pleasing

Brown red skin entangled with
Pale thin legs,
Arms, fingers, blonde hair

There is cause for celebration
The children are gone
The air is dense, hot.

—Susan Dion

A soul connection is a resonance between two people who respond to the essential beauty of each other's individual natures, behind their facades, who connect on this deeper level. This kind of mutual recognition provides the catalyst for a potent alchemy.

—John Welwood

June Heat traces more than just a constellation of scars and the history of two bodies. The acceptance these two lovers express for one another reveals the contours of love and shows sexual desire present even when there is illness and physical imperfection. Susan comments:

Tom was honest and open with me about his heart operation when we started to see one another. He had served in the Peace Corps in West Africa in his twenties and had become deathly ill. He had a severe tropical parasite. Every body system was failing, but they were able to save him. In his thirties, as a result of this parasitic illness, Tom developed congestive heart problems and had to undergo open-heart surgery. He received a new valve and pacemaker. One doesn't realize the kind of scarring that chest tubes will make! I can feel the pacemaker in his body. It is a part of his life and our intimate connection. In this poem I am able to express my awareness of his past scars as we make love to one another.

This is my love poem to Tom but I am in this poem, too:

> Pale thin legs,
> Arms, fingers, blonde hair

I have been sick with multiple health problems since 1989. I hate the pain, sickness and limits imposed by my illness. I do not have symptom-free days, although I do experience some days with less oppressive sickness. However, exertion—even "light" exertion—exacerbates the intensity and debilitation of flu, weakness, fatigue, and pain. Given these harsh parameters, I've chosen to maintain a desired sexual relationship with my dear partner. Indeed, despite awful illness which cruelly robs significant areas of my life, I benefit greatly from our love and its sexual intimacies.

It may not be physical problems or illness you want to write about in terms of vulnerability and intimacy. It could be about anything you have difficulty accepting about yourself and sharing with the person you love. Allow your words to touch those less visible scars. Use your words to speak what is true and to uncover the transformative magic of acceptance.

EXERCISE
Writing and Ritual—A Salve for Your Wounds

In Chapter One, I spoke about strewing rose petals on my stump as a way of healing the pain associated with losing my right leg. Create such a ritual for yourself. You can do this for either a physical or an emotional scar. Perhaps your scar arose out of a broken relationship. Possibly it is a more visible physical disability that limits you compared with "normal" people. Your ritual might include enjoying a specially prepared bath, a visit to a favorite place in nature, invoking healing spirits through ceremony. When you feel ready, invite a partner to take part with you in this healing ritual—perhaps you could make love and consciously notice and include whatever imperfection has gone unattended or unloved. Let these experiences seep into you and when the time is right, write a poem to hold your experience.

EXERCISE
Writing the Vulnerable Thing You Didn't Say

Think of a time when you had something to say to your partner and didn't say it—something that made you feel vulnerable, or insecure, or would have revealed your desperate need for love, for a touch. Let that memory of your hushed voice and your churning heart form the seed of the poem you will write now to celebrate the soft, yielding, weak, precious parts of yourself that you once cast aside as too shameful or too insignificant to show.

EXERCISE
"When I Am Old I Shall Wear Purple . . ."

Imagine who you will be as you grow older. Write a poem about your passage to eighty or ninety or one hundred years old.

How will you get there? How will intimacy be a part of who you are? What hurdles did you encounter along the way? How will you make your journey and relationships rich with meaning and magic?

EXERCISE
Writing a Love-Making Poem

Take some time to consider an intimate experience in love-making and then write. Include a full range of feeling, all of your senses. Let your poem express the attentiveness of loving, as Susan Dion's poem does. Be bold like Crazy Jane. Bring your beloved's body and heart into your poem. Bring your own as well.

THE SEASONS OF MARRIAGE

Like nature's landscape—which changes with the influence of weather, environment, natural disasters, and seasons—a couple's relationship also undergoes constant change. Sometimes the shifts take place over a long period of time, sometimes within the space of a day or a moment.

Storms and bright days may occur within the course of different seasons, which are in turn enfolded into longer rhythms of yearly cycles. Such changes mirror our physical, emotional and spiritual lives. Soaked to the bone by rain or warmed to sublime relaxation by the sun, we may forget that what is happening now will change.

The seasons of our relationship touch us in different ways, and we may better understand them when we can perceive a larger context. The poet's eye particularly sees that the love two people bear for one another connects them to something more universal.

Sing fair the Lady and her knight.
Sing the two friends, brothers or lovers,
   who keep troth.
And praise, praise,
   the man and the woman
   naked betrothed
who give green to the earth
   and by their love
raise the day's light!

These things we sing fair
   from the earliest time
burnt leaf of november and green of may
   the change of the year,
   the rounds of the moon,
we sing in our measures and
   return with our rime.

For our Lady   waxeth and waneth.
   Joan grows sullen
   and Joan delights.
burnt leaf of november and green of may

These things we number
   among our delights:
burnt leaf of november and green of may
   the replenishing work
   and play we devote
to the troth we keep with the source of light
   that is right, right,
as the stars in their courses
   bind the dark.

For our Lord   has awakened our hearts.
   John has known grief
   and John's known joy,
burnt leaf of november and green of may.
            —*Robert Duncan*
       from *A Song of the Old Order*

Robert Duncan's poem (it is actually sung) shows a natural correspondence between the universal processes and relationship. We cannot predict what our seasons hold for us, but we can notice the larger patterns and longer rhythms we are part of. Writing is a way to record and recognize these longer rhythms.

Laurel and Pete Lagoni both grew up in Iowa. They met at Iowa State University in their freshman year and started to date. At the beginning of their senior year, they married.

After three years things were bad for them. They fought. Each struggled to find purpose and direction. They drank and engaged in destructive behavior. Both became disillusioned. Here is what Laurel had to say about the problems they had early in their marriage:

> *My husband Pete and I have been married for twenty-one years, literally half our lives. We married quite young and, during the early years, we had numerous problems. Unfortunately, we worked them out in fairly unhealthy ways—affairs, alcohol, and separations that came about due to destructive arguments rather than constructive time apart to ponder what we both wanted in our lives.*

Written by Laurel in the early years of her marriage, this poem describes both love and conflict:

MARRIAGE

Sleeping was touching.
*   Like forks in a tray, we matched tine for tine.*
Your bent legs pocketed my knees,
*   your rump pressed into my pelvis.*
My arm looped through your arm like a neck through a noose.

Then we shared one pillow.
*   My cheek nested in the hollow of your neck.*
My blonde hair intertwined with your brown.
*   On one pillow, our dreams mingled.*
The intimacy woke us to mutual panic.

We tried sleeping back-to-back
  like Mexicans during siesta.
Shoulder to shoulder, spines aligned, legs entwined,
  but the noose tightened,
And I left our bed to again have private dreams.
                    —*Laurel Lagoni*
        originally written 1979; revised 1996

The push and pull of their relationship, the restlessness, the sweet overtures, nagging constrictions and eventual destructive retreats from intimacy—all these are in this poem. Laurel talked about the insight she gleaned from reading her early poems about marriage:

When I read through my early poems I wrote about our marriage (or more accurately the relationships I was involved with outside my marriage!), I feel sad. I wish Pete and I would have known then what we know now. Yet, those days gave us our current marriage. We know how good we have it because we also know how bad it can get. Today we appreciate rather than scorn the kinks and quirks of each other's personalities.

Laurel wrote this next poem twenty years after *Marriage.* Notice there is a more integrated and inclusive quality in the images and structure of her poem compared to the first. More joy and clarity permeate the images of a natural landscape that describes her relationship with Pete.

WATERFALL

Rushing water fans over the wide, sloping mountainside
like a lacy, white, full-skirted wedding gown.
The she-water, cloaked forever in ceremonial garb,
marries herself over and over to the
dark granite bulk beneath her.

*Fifty visits in thirty years and they are all but the same.
There is a narrow, new tributary and two more fully-grown
    trees beside them, but
he—that rock—stays and supports her and
she—that water—dances, leaps and bustles over him,
for all eternity, the bride.*

                                                    —Laurel Lagoni

I used to see Pete's stability as boring. I perceived it as a problem in our relationship. I am more like water. I change quickly and that made him uncomfortable. We were constantly bumping up against each other. But after a lot of work in therapy together and persistence, he likes that I stretch him, and I appreciate how he is so steady and cuts through to the core of an issue.

When I read my early poems I see how painful it was for us. I am grateful to have both old and new poems because it is clear how far we've come. We know where we've been and we know each other's shameful secrets. Like two old friends, we find comfort and genuine pleasure in one another's company.

There are subtle changes in our outward appearances and children have certainly changed the "landscape" of our lives together, but Pete— that rock—provides consistency and stability and I—that water— keep rushing and dancing through life; ever-changing, but changing now within the context of my own familiar riverbed.

EXERCISE
Seasons of Love

Changes in Pete and Laurel's relationship are recorded in poems that range over twenty years. But changes occur in marriage or any intimate relationship over much shorter spans of time. A relationship can change dramatically in three months—especially the first three months! Changes happen moment-to-moment. Relationships have their own seasons. How would you describe the seasons of your relationship? What experiences in your relationship might the images of Spring, Summer, Fall and Winter signify? What is new in your relationship? What is green and flourishing? What is it time to let go of? What is cold or asks for solitude and waiting? Verbally sketch material that describes the different seasons of your relationship and shape this material into poems.

THE HEART OF LONGING: RETURNING TO YOURSELF

It is possible your partner is emotionally unavailable to you on levels you wish were shared. No amount of wishing may change this fact. This can be very painful. Your partner may not hear what you have to say, or recognize how you change and evolve, or welcome your desire to live from your truth rather than habit.

Your thwarted desire for communication in your relationship could move you toward despair or anger or resign you to live that "life of quiet desperation" Thoreau wrote about. Or lack of communication may evoke a profound longing in you for *something more.*

In this section, two poems describe different kinds of longing. Both are concerned with meaning in relationship. Consider the word "longing" with its connotation of *stretching.* When we long for something it usually means we are willing to stretch for it. Stretching emotionally may relieve tightness or cause temporary strains, it may move us past limitations or force us to examine why we make certain choices to being with. Longing is not a bad thing. It is a part of life. We need to stretch. Longing enlarges our perspective and engages our heart.

Longing draws our attention to the dangling carrot—whether it be a relationship we don't have or a desire for healing in a relationship we do have. This can be a critical juncture for coping with your heart's desire. What does your longing have to teach you about yourself? How do you live with your longing? What does longing do to you, what do you do with it?

Loneliness does not come from having no people about one, but from being unable to communicate the things that seem important to oneself.

—Carl Jung

*

To fall in love is easy, even to remain in it is not difficult, our human loneliness is cause enough. But it is a hard quest worth making to find a comrade through whose steady presence one becomes steadily the person one desires to be.

—*Anna Louise Strona*

Writing words that speak what matters to you—what you long for—may be your ultimate responsibility in tending consciously to your life.

It seems that healthy longing has more to do with activating oneself rather than passively pining for something to drop into our laps. We may not get what we long for, but our writing jumps into that place of longing and gives voice to it. We need not remain in quiet desperation. If we take the time to write about and integrate our longing, we will learn more about ourselves and be better able to live and speak for what we really believe.

Onie Kriegler writes that attention needs to be given to *loving* if a relationship is to remain healthy. Onie finds words deep in her body. She knows that when she is not breathing from deep inside, like anything that is alive and organic, what is living will rot.

Barely Breathing

There is nothing magical about love that is left untended.
It rots like scraps of vegetables lost in the bottom of the bin—forgotten
suddenly, after years of consumption there is no taste for them.
Turning out of form—insubstantial to something closer to dirt
limp to liquid it says:
begin again.

Magic is made in the between space of unknown, not quite
    and still ground.
It is made in flesh patterns and voice—
    and it takes all your guts to go there.

Love untended   is a supreme act of cowardice
all of human failing aligned thusly sounds out the chants of safety
bound bodies barely breathing hold together incomplete
    and shattered hearts.
Mind patterns lay grids of reason over circular dances
gripping down hard, we search blind for the way out
    for the place of rest

like Dorothy, we long to go home
praying at every altar
except the possibility in our own two feet.

Onie struggles to stand on her own feet and still make a clear
statement about the quality of relationship she wants. She says:

We seem to fail ourselves, and one another in relationships, out of fear
and habit. I think women and men both blame one another for what is
not happening. I ask myself: Am I making contact with my own re-
sources as I move into relationship? What do I bring to a relationship?
If I am not bringing my capacity for love, which is contingent on lov-
ing myself, then it's not going to happen.

But there is also frustration in this poem. I am saying, where are
you? I am saying if this love is going to grow, it needs conscious tending.

Many things may help you cope and still thrive in a relationship that does not nourish you in the way it might if your partner shared your intentions. You may need to pursue a variety of
strategies and self-care options in order not to abandon yourself
and your vitality.

Poetic medicines and the intuitive remedies they evoke in
you have the capacity to turn your resignation and sadness into
self-reliant energy and creative opportunity.

Longing may transform you even if you are in a relationship
that does not appear to be changing; this longing is not based
on hope for change in the other person but the courage to be
true to yourself. Such courage gives you permission to use your
anger and frustration as a creative flash point to stir your own
creativity and healthy behavior.

Your courage and creative acts do not involve blaming anyone; instead you live and write what is true for you. You do not
have to deny your hurt. Write of the respect you hold for yourself as you strengthen your ability to cope and perceive more
options. Your passion for how beauty heals and inspires you
does not need to be discarded because a partner does not share
the same passion.

There are no limits that language
cannot meet.

—Charles Bernstein

*

BIRD SONG

Here you go,
rushing off again
just as the tiny bird strums the air into music.
The bird hovers, its wings trilling,
its eyes taking me in slowly, as I approach,
almost without breath.
Here you are, binoculars in one hand,
the bird book under your arm.
You find the bird's ruby throat in the book,
its green neck that will never
find its way to your heart
in all its indescribable iridescence—reflecting flecks of jet,
or the color where the tiny green feathers
merge and mingle with the red.

You have an obsession for naming,
for possessing all that comes within your sphere.
You must think me lazy,
merely looking as I do,
content and unfamiliar with the song,
expectant to hear the notes for the first time,
shivery to feel the turbulent wings close to my ear.

I've seen, again and again,
how you conquer the birds,
how you flatten them against the sky.
Thrush and sparrow, lark and titmouse
more delicious on the tongue
than throbbing in the eye.

Do you find my arms too predictable?
My kisses so species bound?
Do you just have one name
for the colors of my hair,
or the wild song in my heart?

—"Marie"

Marie says:

> *"Bird Song" has a real time and a real place, in a long relationship*
> *with its share of ecstasies and agonies. I write poems like "Bird Song" in*
> *extremis. While ecstasy might at times flood me to the point of spilling*
> *over into a poem, agony often wants to weld itself to something, to at-*
> *tach to a presence larger and more powerful than itself—a poem. The*
> *poem is not the agony, but something more and something less. It is the*
> *place for my voice of longing to be heard. At the same time, it is a way*
> *to renew myself with the power and beauty of language that comes out*
> *of me even as song, even a plaintive one, may come from a bird.*

EXERCISE
Write a Poem of Longing

1. Write a poem about things you long for in your relationship. Perhaps you want more time to talk with a partner or
spend time in nature together, be alone with yourself, have
more physical intimacy and affection. Why do you want these
things—how do they awaken your longing? If you made them
a part of your life what would that experience be like?

2. Write a poem about your longing to your partner or dear
friend. You don't have to share it unless it is safe and appropriate. Be completely honest in this poem. Give your longings all
the room they need. What do you long for in your life, in this
relationship with your partner or friend, and with your world?
Tell yourself what you most want to hear.

> *Listen to the deep cello*
> *of autumn*
> *leaves descending*
> *like lovers go down*
> *into the unknown, with*
> *all their colorful ways*
> *and sad partings, they*
> *descend so slow as if*

✳

trying to push the ground away.
But no, they lie down
alone and stark
along the darkside of winter;
the only place to find
my next breath,
a never before;
to start again
the wet sound
of lithe and
flutelike spring.

—John Fox

CHAPTER SIX

HEN GOD SIGHS

Making Poems About Loss, Illness and Death

Poetry enacts our own losses so that we can share the notion that we all lose—and hold each other's hand, as it were, in losing.

—Donald Hall

WRITING THE WINTER
GARDENS OF GRIEF

*T*he stories and poems within this chapter are about experiences that ask us to go to deep places within ourselves; times when we have to make a journey through crisis, often with little light by which to see. Poem-making helps us move through grief, life transitions and illness by providing comfort and sustenance on this difficult journey.

For some, writing during an illness or deep grief may not seem possible. For others, poem-making will feel like a natural and essential part of getting through life's greatest challenges and stresses. It will be different for each of us. If writing is not possible just now, *reading poetry* during difficult times may be a great comfort. People have told me reading poetry was the only thing they could do to make it through the brambles of their grief. A woman told me that only poetry was pure enough to soothe her. Reading poems you enjoy may plant seeds for your own writing when the time is ripe.

At other times of loss and grief, your writing may be a necessity. Drawing from a well of feeling within your bones and soul, these words from within can help you cope in your daily life. You may discover your writing reveals a quality of sensitivity and compassion you've never known before. Like the wind that etches a rock face smooth, you can record your truth and loss with your words.

As the traditional medicine of many peoples demonstrates, disease can be treated with images. The patient, for her part, needs to see the images of her healing, just as any of us in distress might look for the stories and images wrapped in our complaints. But she shouldn't bring them too close to her, making them too personal, or they will break apart. We can only approach the gods through poetry, and if the disease is the disguise of the gods, then our medicine will be full of art and image.

—Thomas Moore

*

Dedee Rigg is a psychotherapist in practice in Connecticut. She made a collage-mask in a workshop to represent her "muse" and in doing this, her collage became a landscape of her grief over the death of her twenty-three-year-old son, Tyler, in a car accident. Dedee wrote this poem about her collage-mask:

THE MASK

Black descends down, falling
Are you my true self?
Is there some thing, anything
*   in your dark shapes*
that feels soft, comforting
The flower perhaps, the six petals of life
*   at the center—*
But no,
The hushed white rose speaks
Be fierce with reality
My nose was broken
It feels like my heart
shattered too that starless night
Perhaps that is music
dancing under my fish eye
or a kite flying from the notes,
bold sounds of the trumpet,
sacred to you
The tree bends
The mouth howls
Red leaves wither from the trees
The cracks move all the way through.

Creating a collage made it possible for Dedee's personal symbols and evocative images to come together in one place. Dedee then translated these nonverbal images into the lines of a poem. She says about her process and poem:

The blackness comes down from the top of my head. This is who I am now, black. Is there anything in this blackness that could feel soft or comforting? I drew the flower because I love flowers, and I had just walked the labyrinth modeled on the one at Chartres Cathedral where there are six petals at the center of the labyrinth. But no, it was not soft. Instead, the flowers were fierce. The therapist and novelist Florida Scott Maxwell talks about being fierce with reality and says it takes a lifetime to do that. When I don't express my feelings, I tend to numb myself. I wear a mask. It is painful to write these things down, but I don't have any other options.

The mask I made swirls with fierceness: red leaves that wither from the trees are blood, the mouth howls. It's my face too because I had my nose broken, splintered in many pieces in a car accident. The poem is about shattering—about the starless night on March 2nd, 1996, at 3:30 in the morning when Tyler died in a car accident. The music dancing under my fisheye, the bold sounds of the trumpet are Tyler who loved to play and listen to that instrument.

Many poems you write may come directly from your broken heart, filled with sadness and rage. Some poems may even break your heart open. You may uncover in that *breaking open* something that offers you hope or faith.

Writing may provide a resting place to ground you during times of grief and illness, so that you can treat yourself with understanding and comfort. Making a poem can be like taking a short rest, visiting a different place altogether than your hurt or illness—a place to put down your burden, even for just a short while.

Something nourishing may flow into your broken heart when you write from this resting place. What do you notice that soothes your torn heart?

Dedee touched that whisper of hope by writing about an experience with her grandnephew:

✻

FOR ISAAC

I heard the teakettle whistle,
You said it was sound.
Your pink finger pointed—
Rheingold, Settebello, Orient Express.
I said Andiamo Settebello.
You said Andiamo Dedee.
You are my hope.
Namasté.

A teakettle whistle inspires train names and sound play! Dedee delights in the sweetness of a little boy, and joins with him in a spirit of hope. It is almost more than hope. Dedee says "Namasté" to end her poem, which is the Sanskrit word for honoring the oneness one soul shares with another. She responds to Isaac's voice and love for trains. Dedee gently translates their tender relationship onto the page. This is a resting place, an important folding-in of hope into her life. This tenderness becomes part of the grieving process for Dedee as she lives through and writes the "winter garden" of grief.

THE WINTER GARDEN
for Tyler

Surrounded by silence, I sit alone.
No pale winter light appears through my window.
No hoary frost glistens on bare branches.
No sunlight breathes magic on snowy conical shapes.
In this season of the three Kings, I stare at the winter garden.

As in all seasons, my eye moves to one tree.
The graceful curved skeleton of the Japanese split-leaf,
great-grandmother to the one that weeps over your cold granite grave,
whispers time and memory and mourning, its naked trunk the
sacred anchor of your dark garden and mine, its wisdom
the impossible distant voice of my somber journey.

This winter my frigid garden is a copper world.
Braided in grey and silver green,
clumps of weeds and perennials hug the ground.
Forgotten flower stems stand like toy sentinels.
The pale rough bark of the cherry has begun to peel.
Yet the garden only pauses in momentary introspection.
It is my pewter soul that is stilled.

Inside my kitchen, I watch.
Like the winter garden, grief exposes its bare bones
    to the unrelenting cold.
Truths lie buried underground.
It is beginning to rain.

Ribbons of moisture weep down my window
(I'm told the Acacia Dealbata, a tree of great beauty,
flowers at the end of winter and has a scent on warm days).

Unlike the winter garden, I cannot see the possible springtime.
My numb heart only endures.
The wind penetrates my trunk.
This is the temperature of my life.

There is usually nothing that needs to be said to someone who writes a poem like this. What we can do is receive it and listen deeply. When we write such poems, we also should listen deeply to our own words. They will help us survive our time of grief.

What is to give light must endure burning.

—*Viktor Frankl*

A SENSE OF MYSTERY IN GRIEF: "SOMEONE TO HOLD UP ALL THIS FALLING"

The time of living through losses makes us prey for cynicism. Cynicism undermines our sense of mystery. Cynical attitudes

✳

would have us believe that bitter facts and doubt are more true-to-life than hope and the imagination that can help heal us. Cynicism considers uncertainty a weakness and would armour us instead with harsh judgments. Yet mystery and uncertainty keep our hearts open to something we don't yet know—to tenderness, healing and the sacred. Poem-making can be a good antidote to cynicism.

Rainer Maria Rilke's poetry shows us that the inevitability of loss does not mean we must negate the presence of mystery in our lives.

> *AUTUMN*
>
> *The leaves are falling, falling as if from far up,*
> *as if orchards were dying high in space.*
> *Each leaf falls as if it were motioning "no."*
>
> *And tonight the heavy earth is falling*
> *away from all other stars in the loneliness.*
>
> *We're all falling. This hand here is falling*
> *And look at the other one . . . It's in them all.*
>
> *And yet there is Someone, whose hands*
> *infinitely calm, hold up all this falling.*

Finding a way through your own writing to make room for both uncertainty and faith can help you come to terms with the losses in your life.

EXERCISE
Part I—Creating a Collage to Reveal Your Feelings

Kris Haas is a board-certified art therapist who currently works in the Behavioral Health Department at a hospital in California. Kris suggests the following collage exercise to help depict your grief or hope—or perhaps incorporate the two: "Do this exercise at a pace that's right for you. Go only as far as you feel comfortable. 1. Begin by going (in your mind) to the place where you feel creative and safe. Rest for a moment in that place and allow whatever feeling is strongest to come up with images to represent your pain. 2. Go through whatever magazines you have available. Rip pictures out—whatever grabs your attention, positively or negatively. Gather these together. They can be pictures, shapes, colors, phrases, anything at all. 3. Gather your collage images until you are ready to stop. It may take you fifteen minutes to gather these images. It may take a few days. You don't have to think about it—let your body tell you when you are done. Treat the process like eating—stop when it's enough. 4. Arrange your images on a large sheet of paper in a way that fits for you.

"Put your collage on just about anything: an opened-up paper bag, wrapping paper, newsprint. Use gluestick or tape to adhere your collage. This exercise is not about artistic standards. This is your own expression of pain, grief and hope. The collage, like your feelings, can change from minute to minute. You can express your feelings, change what you've expressed, learn from the process."

EXERCISE
Part II—Making a Poem from Images of Grief, Pain and Hope

Once you have created your collage, spend some time with it. You might put it up where you can see it easily during your day. Let it just be around for a while. View it from different angles. Don't search for words. Stay in touch with your sensory experience of making the collage and the feelings that come up when you look at it. Allow language to arise naturally as if the collage had a voice—or voices that speak to you about your experience and feelings.

EXERCISE
Finding Poems in the Resting Places of Your Healing Journey

Give yourself an opportunity to take a rest from the struggle. Imagine a peaceful and relaxing place, and go there in your mind. Or find an actual place in nature that soothes you. Watch for simple and miraculous things that speak to you of life. You could find these anywhere, as Dedee and her grandnephew did in the teakettle whistle.

EXERCISE
Opening to a Feeling of Solace and Spiritual Support

In Rilke's poem *Autumn*, he begins with the image of leaves falling to show the mood of loss, and then relates that to the earth "falling away" which becomes a human image of hands falling. Hands appear again in the poem, except this time it is "Someone, whose hands/infinitely calm, hold up all this falling." Write a poem about a loss in your life—but allow it to be something held up by "infinitely calm hands." Even if you cannot imagine that experience—can you describe it anyway?

HEALING BREAKTHROUGHS: THE GRACE OF POEM-MAKING

Bill Stephenson is a North Carolina writer and former professor. Bill was surprised to see how my suggestion to concentrate on something personally important to him, some thing he considered a "sacred object," could suddenly bring a poem into being. The object Bill chose was a little square black box—a keepsake remembrance from his wife who died. Bill says:

> *The poem just hit me as I walked from my cabin to the place where our writing workshop was meeting.*

SQUARE BLACK BOX

Square black box, tiny, lidded, empty,
Long-time companion, hard-edged in my pocket,
A gift remaining to me, though my wife has died who was its giver,
So long a companion the lid has scratched dim,
Hear me, relic and reliquary,
Holder of her memory even now,
Become my sacred vessel too.
Hold my inner emptiness in yours
And from your darkness bring me expanding vision
That emptiness is truly infinite space
Where all things are possible—
Where scratched and faded flowers
Blossom bright again,
And where lost love is to be found again
And held in a grasp as safe and close
As my fingers have when they hold tight
To your four corners

The poem came to Bill unexpectedly—as a gift—his voice is strong and clear as he "speaks" to the keepsake from his wife. Something comes alive in making that connection. The repetition of the words "hold" and "held" emphasize the constancy of Bill's love for his wife. Bill says:

After twenty-one years of marriage, my wife developed an illness that was sudden, severe, mysterious to doctors, and ultimately unstoppable. Her death left me in a devastation of loss and denial. But seven years later, in writing this poem, I realized suddenly that the black box I'd kept with me so long was a small, tangible means of summoning up the intangible. Looking into its dark interior was looking into the darkness of losing her, and finding how much I had not lost. The memories that time had dimmed were suddenly vivid again, just as imagination brought back the original colors of the flowers on the box lid. Memories of happy times of love came flooding back from depths I had thought to contain only pain and regret. The poem flowed onto my notebook page naturally and unstoppably from this gift of realization.

★

Your acceptance of a loved one's death may involve both a willingness to grieve and a resolve to nourish and deepen your love for that person. A poem can contain both of these; it can give voice to the "pain and regret" as well as the "vivid memories." The following poem by Dorian Kottler shows that poetry can also be a way to stay in loving contact with the one who has died.

LIST
(for my father)

Since you died I've been coming across
things that would interest you.

An article in Scientific American
about language, how it evolved
out of a nameless dark.

A gadget for making coffee
right in your car.

A poet whose lines
ring like cracks through ice

on a pond in March,
as yours do.

An all-Vivaldi concert
this coming Friday.

The list will grow longer.
Meanwhile I keep it
here at my desk, handy
on grief's tall spindle.
                                        —Dorian B. Kottler

At a certain point, your acceptance of the death of a loved one may be about a willingness letting go of trying to understand "why?," letting go of the past in order to open your heart to your loss. "Why?" may ferment and age into a kind of poignant wonder that offers you a deep, lasting connection with the person who has died. What did the relationship mean to you in its essence? Is it possible that in *letting go* of having someone we love, our love for them will remain?

Catherine Firpo, an artist and meditation teacher in Oakland, California, writes about the part memory plays in her acceptance of her father's death. Catherine's poem first appeared in a beautiful anthology of poetry about grief and healing, entitled *Voices of the Grieving Heart*:

Winter solitude—
In a world of one color
The sound of wind.
— *Basho*

ANDALUCIAN WOOD

the bits and pieces of paper i have gathered
paper that holds memory for me
holy cards imprinted with prayers to alleviate sorrow,
newspaper clippings in odd shapes skirt the inner
    landscape of my box of
Andalucian wood
long i have held memory here
long since the time of my recovery has this box
    embraced the forms of
events that have occurred in this new life
i wonder
do we hold onto the spirits of those we have loved,
    those we knew
i wonder
do we bind them to earth by refusing to let them go?
or is it a quality of being human that keeps us grasping at
    bits of paper, at
validation of memories and arms that no longer hold us
    in the moment's
dance

i wonder
do we trust ourselves so little that we hang on so tightly?
as if anyone really could erase the embers of our soul.

Catherine speaks about her father, her exploration of memory, and the poem she wrote:

My father died of a brain tumor within two months after he was diagnosed. It was a horrific whirlwind that seemed so surreal. Here was this wonderfully healthy robust man who in a matter of a few weeks was reduced to needing full care in every way possible.

There was a time I was in a bank with my father and mother early in this two-month period. Uncharacteristically, my mother was getting angry confronting a difficult problem at the bank. My father and I sat down together. He turned to me and asked, "What is it like on the other side?" I burst into tears. I was the only one at that time who would speak of his coming death. He wanted to know, feeling that I could help him. Those moments overwhelmed me. I told him that those who he really loved like his mother would be there for him as he crossed over. He had this great fascination with President Kennedy and asked me if he would be there and I told him yes. The more his life ebbed away I saw and felt his innocence and heart opening to an amazing fullness.

I brought this box of Andalucian wood home from Spain twenty-four years ago. There is a red cording inside that goes around the mirror on the underside of the lid. The interior of the box is red. Over the past seventeen years it has become a ritual container of memory for significant people and turning points in my life. I have various treasures housed there that are connected with my father. My dad was very Catholic and one day I was looking at the holy card with a painting and the prayer of St. Francis that had been printed at the time of his funeral. I looked at his photograph and it took on a whole new meaning—that's when I felt the box had a voice and that's when I started to ask many questions and my poem came into being.

It was difficult to let go. But creating ritual assists in the process. Planting trees on his birthday. Doing a rattle and chant at the Pomo Indian round-house. Keeping this box. Writing poems gives a voice to the memory.

EXERCISES
Sacred Object, List of Particulars, Container for Memory

1. Hold an object in your hands that connects you with someone who has died or passed out of your life in some way. Give yourself time to feel this object—remember its history and sense the essence, feel its weight and see what it looks like. Speak to it, as Bill did, and ask for a poem.

2. Use the idea from *List* of gathering the particulars of what the person you loved enjoyed in life and felt passionately about. Write a poem that expresses what you would put on "grief's tall spindle."

3. Find a special box or container in which you can place something special from the person who has died or something that represents that person. Perhaps it is a picture of them, a letter they wrote to you, or anything else. Over time, begin to place in that container other things that hold significance in your life.

SEEING BEYOND DEATH

Some of us may feel certainty about a person's spirit remaining after they have died. This possibility also exists with regard to animals. Eight-year-old Megan wrote a poem about her dog who had died. Her mother, Lisa, tells how this poem came about:

About a year ago, our dog, Sunny, a fleet and leaping animal, whom we'd rescued from cold and starvation in California, got hit by a car in Princeton. We felt loss and trauma. Sunny was a part of the rhythm of our lives and reminded me of my place among creatures. Megan carries a picture of her and Sunny around all the time. Last night she sat on the kitchen floor talking about Sunny and holding the picture. I suggested that maybe she'd like to write a poem about Sunny and she came up with this incredible piece—a way to mourn her loss and hold on to Sunny at the same time. As she sounded out some of the words and

phrases in the poem out loud, I could hear her touching the power of al-
literation, and watch her eyes move as if traveling through her imagery.
I think this poem presents an excellent example of how even a young
child can self-soothe through poetry, while enjoying the delicious plea-
sures of her own voice, and tasting the way words and images roll to-
gether with the animal passion of our dog, Sunny.

This is Megan's poem:

THE SPIRIT OF THE BLACK DOG

She is the black sky that shows all her stars at night,
when morning comes she goes down with the moon.
She is the black spirit flying south with the wild black geese.
She hides from the weird four-wheeled creatures.
One day one of the four-wheeled creatures came.
There.
She the black dog in the weird gray path.
When the creature was gone, she lying, the black dog, dead.
But only the dog was dead.
Not the wild great powerful spirit.
Her spirit is still with us forever.
Every morning she still goes down with the moon.
Every night she still shines.
                              —Megan Schulz, eight years old

Try the following exercise when the time is right for you.

E X E R C I S E
Seeing Beyond Death—"Her Spirit Is Still with Us Forever"

Imagine that after the death of a loved one, not only can there
be grief about your loss but the faith, or a glimmer of faith, that
spirit is able to express a deep and beautiful essence. What images of that essence come to you? What happens to a being af-

ter death? Shape both your feelings of loss and these images of
spiritual essence together into a poem.

POEM-MAKING, ILLNESS
AND THE HEALING
ENVIRONMENT

When we are seriously ill our vulnerability becomes more apparent in many ways. But our modern health care system's response
to that vulnerability is often lacking. The technology-laden atmosphere of hospital environments where we are supposed to
be healed is often at odds with our needs as human beings. In a
medical system that displaces human contact and sense of community with an intense reliance on machines and drugs, poem-
making can be a way to remember we are flesh and blood.

Roberta de Kay made poems to hold on to her humanness in
the midst of grueling chemotherapy treatments for cancer.

CANCER WARD—1990

The nurses' shadows run
along the hospital walls. They hurry
to us with a determined love,
these beings who can see death walking by yet
bring the aid of anti-nausea pills and inject shots

into our tubes. Yet up and down the hall,
the sound of gagging punctures their shadows
because even pills and shots
will not always stop our body's struggle to be free
of this medicine/poison.

In our rooms,
we watch the plastic tubes where
drops travel like slow rain
*   down and through the needle*
*   to the open vein. No one*

*

> counts or watches for long—
> we learned so soon
> to consider the bags as almost empty,
> to imagine our lives again
> as something more than dream, our heads
>
> as they once were with flowing hair.
> Yet in this same hour,
> we might be numb and out of our bodies
> or in tears, or sound asleep, or even
> gracefully swimming into a peace
>
> which dwells inside the flame
> of a prayer, a flaming prayer
> which will ignite,
> oh wonder of wonders,
> our next breath!
>
> —Roberta de Kay

Roberta's poem shows not just the facts of the situation but the complexity of human hope and experience that lives within the hearts of patients and nurses on the oncology ward of a hospital.

I wanted to leave a message about what I and others had gone through with the hope that it might be different in a few years. I've done significant rewriting of this poem trying to capture more. In an earlier version, I didn't fully show the dedication of the nurses. I also realized later that I had moved into a prayer of silence which became a profound resource. Today nausea during chemo is almost conquered and side effects are far better controlled. It is still an exhausting experience, but it has been one that motivated me to live and use my energy in far more conscious ways.

Roberta finished a graduate writing program in the mid-seventies but wrote irregularly in the next several years. It was while reading Stephen Mitchell's paraphrases of the Psalms while undergoing a whole year of chemotherapy for her first re-occurrence with cancer that she made a commitment to write regularly as a pathway for healing.

Roberta felt that David's Psalms gave her permission to wail. She started to write her own psalms that dealt with emotional and spiritual issues of her illness.

A tear is a doorway through which I can enter.

—Mother Meera

PSALM 13

Oh Lord, I am sinking in despair
  fearing you have forgotten me.

How long will my mind be confused
  and my heart in grief?

Turn towards me, mothering Healer, bring
  light to move from despair before my
  heart closes.

Gently comes your healing hand
  across my mind bringing what was needed
  before I knew myself.

Trust in your mercy opens my heart
  and I realize again your grace.

I am richly renewed.
Your mercy is deeper than my despair.

After writing these psalms, Roberta began to write about subjects and experiences other than cancer. Poem-making is an important way for her to remember that she is much more than illness and even more important, that her love of beauty and in-tense perceptions of life are a more accurate description of who she really is and what she offers to the world.

*

ALLAMAKEE MORNING

In this Allamakee morning,
a dog howls in the still dark hills,
a train whistle
rips the red velvet air,
a cock crows.

My brother is gone
to catch the sly trout
who hides in Frenchman's Creek.
I love him.

Roberta's second remission was ended abruptly when the cancer metastasized in June 1994. It was then she began to gather her poetry and polish it for a volume called *Star Eating Wolves*. She wanted to give these poems to her sons on Christmas. Roberta feels these poems are her important discoveries to share—they contain something of her essence. In the process of intentionally bringing them together, her daily experience of creativity grew in immediacy. She began to live her creativity rather than think about it.

If I am going to die, who is going to judge whether my poems are valuable? I finally climbed over the inner censor and gave myself permission to speak with freedom. I could enter a wonderfully quiet place and feel I was standing beside Rumi and could respond to his words. The words flowed from heart to paper.

THE FLOWER'S TONGUE

"A white flower grows in the quiet
Let your tongue become that flower."
                    —Rumi

*All through the night
I have breathed the moon,
sucking it down into my roots,
exhaling it into the center. At dawn,
through my leaves,
I beckon the rose-ash of clouds
to cradle my being—
see how the faintest shade of pink
gathers in the quiet.*

*On the fifth day of dancing
with the caresses of light,
I begin to reveal
the secret of whiteness.
Listen! Listen! It is in
your own breath!*

Roberta's inner quest intensified after the second remission and has continued. She and her husband, Eckford, a retired Episcopal priest, are both committed to live their lives more from *being* and to align themselves with what true healing means.

*When my cancer metastasized, I didn't know what to hope for any
longer. My spiritual advisor said maybe I had to hope for something
new—something I didn't know yet.
    That something new came very slowly after much grief, anger and
fear. I was so tired of cancer marker tests. I didn't want to live like that.
My life had to be something more than waiting for test reports and fear
of what they might tell me. There was a weariness that contributed to
my openness and that was connected to making choices that felt in harmony with my needs. It was through this process that I began to realize
that I was much more than just my body.
    Cancer slows me down and limits me. I can kick at the parameters
but this just wastes my energy. Having boundaries helps me to live my
life more by being rather than doing. I've done so much to help myself simply by gradually getting quiet within myself. I was always out
accomplishing things—I couldn't bear a tennis racket slap a ball with-*

out wanting to get out on the court and win. I was always striving for
the 4.0 in school. But I began to ask difficult questions and even with
all my intense feelings, I started to meditate on what might lie beyond.

MAYBE

Maybe we dance from this elegant place
   discarding our vulnerable bodies
      like old workclothes at the end of the day.

Maybe essence enters the air flying
   like monarchs in migration passed roses
   and rivers older than wood wizards.

Maybe meaning and magic stand up from
   the landscape like summer lightning,
   and for one holy moment

all questions have answers, all journeys a home,
   all living the roundness and warmth
   of a stone clutched tight in the hand.

Or maybe like four-year-olds we
   drop everything and simply run forward
   dazzled again!

Roberta reflects on this poem:

A thunderstorm in the Midwest, it is so dark and a burst of lightning
lights up that whole dark world. You've been sitting in darkness not
able to make out the landscape—even a familiar one. And then suddenly, wham-o! I imagine now that in dying, whenever that comes in
my life, there will be yet more meaning to discover. Maybe it won't be
logical meaning; maybe it will hold magic.

POEM-MAKING FOR CAREGIVERS

Poem-making when you are in a caregiving role can be a way for you to take care of yourself. Whether a journey of illness and healing occurs in a hospital or through care at home, creativity nurtures connection with self and others. Creative expression can be useful to all kinds of caregivers—doctors, nurses, therapists, family members and friends. Making a place on paper for your feelings of powerlessness, grief, love, and strength is a way to give a voice to your feelings and weave healing connections.

Sonia Usatch has been a caregiver and advocate for her son for the past eighteen years since he was struck with mental illness. He was studying acting at the prestigious John Drew Theater in East Hampton when, at age seventeen, he suffered a sudden onset of mental illness and returned home an entirely different person from the one she knew. Sonia experienced disbelief, guilt, shame and blame as the doctors pronounced their diagnoses. Fear and frustration followed as the illness escalated. At one point, he spent over five years in a state hospital. Three years into his hospitalization she wrote this poem:

ONIONS

five o'clock,
I am standing at my
kitchen counter
preparing the family's
evening meal

circles of onion
lie on a cutting board
like picture frames

suddenly and stubbornly
an image of my son

dragging
at the end of a long line
of saddened men
making their way
toward the state hospital's
dining room
to receive their evening meal

can I blame the onions for my tears?

Sonia talks about the need to write this poem to herself:

While I had no control over preparing my son's food, still I had to eat
and also feed the rest of my family, even as I imagined him in his lonely
environment. Why did this poem happen at this particular meal? I
think because I was addressing the profound question about blame out
loud once again. I heard myself going over the catastrophic situation:
What did I miss? Why did it happen to my child, to me?

The language of poetry gave a voice to the impossible questions and
to the search for nonexistent answers I couldn't find. Writing the poem
helped me not only through that dinner but to realize that creativity it-
self is a driving energy toward healing.

I was at the cutting board chopping onions and you know how a
wave comes up and there is no stopping it? I guess that is how the words
came out. The onions were a catalyst for the emotions that were layered
in my heart. The word "dragging" in the poem is appropriate on many
levels. Food is fuel for the body and it should yield energy. There is no
energy in institutional food. There is no zest or gusto. The atmosphere
can drag you down. Writing poems are my defense against dragging!

Sonia's son is in recovery, marking several years out of the
hospital. She has restored her energy and awarded herself the
gift of finishing her degree in community and human service.
She remains an advocate for her son but recognizes that she has
to have a turn at her life. She feels that she can be her own person within the framework of being his advocate and mother.

I've realized that I was not to blame nor is blame anywhere really use-
ful. The part of me that is dedicated to this person I love is always there
but one of the people I must love is myself. As each issue came up, the
agony lived inside of me until I was able to release it onto paper. Poems
are the pillow I cry into.

Here is a poem Sonia wrote recently that illustrates beautifully the connective strength of poetry as healer:

YELLOW YARN

you and I sit opposite
I slap a skein of
sun-yellow yarn
over your outstretched arms
and begin the winding

a rhythm, like lake water
sloshing, builds

my eyes close
sink back in time
and the yarn spirals
to a perfect sphere
like an unfurling infant

and the infant—you

moving in sync
with the unraveling yarn

suddenly, knots
interrupt flow
the yarn wears thin
wasting
threadbare, it breaks

*

I open my eyes
caress you
weaving you whole again

W*hat are circumstances but the*
touchstones of his heart? and what
are touchstones but provings of
his heart? but what are provings of
his heart but fortifiers or alterers
of his nature? and what is his
altered nature but his Soul?

—*John Keats*

Where communication had virtually ceased, Sonia used the yarn as a metaphor to show her son that healing is possible even when situations are worn thin and threadbare:

*   *I was able to explain to him that the yarn, like the illness which wore so*
*   *thin until it broke, could be knitted together again and that love, hope*
*   *and support would weave him whole again.*

LOSSES IN LIVING: BROKEN DREAMS OF CHILDHOOD, CAREER TRANSITIONS AND CHRONIC ILLNESS

The grief we need to heal may not be related to death but to other significant losses in our lives. Situations where our dreams have been deferred or dashed. It may be a sense of the loss of parts of our childhood. It might be the letting go of a career we enjoyed which defined us to a large extent. Or the difficulties and heartaches of coping with chronic illness.

Writing about these losses in words that condense and distill our experience, may release disappointment, protect us from cynicism, encourage our tenderness and sometimes offer us direction and hope.

Zawdie Ekundayo is thirty-two and has been living with HIV for six years. He manages an African-American bookstore in Denver, Colorado. Zawdie (pronounced "zah-DEE-a") offers personal commentaries on a local radio station and has taught political science and African-American studies at a community college. Although he has kept a journal for about sixteen years, Zawdie only recently began to explore poetry. He wrote the

following poem in a workshop where I had encouraged participants to write about the "poetic medicines" that would most
help their healing.

TO SLEEP WITH

All I want is someone to sleep with,
Someone to warm my toes and know I'm alive

All I want is someone to sleep with,
Someone to listen to me read poetry or short stories,
Someone to smell my breath and talk to me.

All I want is someone to sleep with,
Someone to cuddle with and to tug against for sheets,
Someone to rub my back and kiss my cheek, .
Someone to whom I can wish good night and bid good morning.

All I want is someone to sleep with,
Someone to ask about my dreams,
Someone to tell me how they slept,
Someone to feel my head and entangle my legs,
Someone to wake up to after a restful sleep.

All I want is someone, too

Zawdie says about this poem:

I am very literal and this is really the first poem I've ever written. It rep-
resented a leap for me to speak in this form. I was in touch with an emo-
tion. A yearning, a desire. But it's really a paring down or a clarifying
of my desire. My life has become a whittling away of all that is super-
fluous. It is not sex I am writing about; it is intimacy. When you are
dealing with HIV, that distinction becomes everything. There was a
time when my equation was sex equals death. For years I didn't touch
anyone. I couldn't. Anyone I wanted to be close to, I would think: I
love them too much to kill them. We all need love, we all need intimacy.

> *Sex is something that is terribly, terribly complicated. This poem is*
> *yearning for intimacy. Intimacy is something I need to heal—to be*
> *whole. My poem puts that yearning for intimacy plainly on paper.*
> *The poem tells what I need. I don't need flesh, particular organs, or a lot*
> *of other things but I do need to be touched, and held.*

Children feel a loss when a stable home environment is taken from them. The issue of not having a home is the basic theme in the following word collage poem about a time of family breakup and virtual homelessness for Pam, her mother and younger brother. Pam composes this fast-write poem as if she were a camera, scanning the spontaneous images of these essentially lost childhood years from ages five to nine.

FROM *SEEN THROUGH A DUSTY CAMERA LENS IN A VALLEY TOWN*

> *Dusty hot flat town—boring houses in a row—*
> *Lots of beer cans and cigarettes and shiny black hair molded from*
>   *Palmade*
> *Mighty Mouse to save the day*
> *Another house, where I am I now, still flat, weeds and dirt*
> *Another school*
> *Plastic cup thrown down in the dirt, abandoned as a shovel,*
> *Bonanza*
> *Another house big, dark always a T.V. always grass needing to*
>   *be planted,*
> *Always dried dog turds to step over, another school*
> *Another house, new people, very fat people, food frying, babies*
>   *crying, beer everywhere*
> *Another school*
> *The Twilight Zone*
> *Boxes packed, stacked and three twin beds all in one room includ-*
>   *ing mother and two children*
> *Cream of Wheat, toast in warm milk sugar cinnamon, hamburger*
>   *in warm milk over biscuits,*
> *Mickey Mouse Club, I Love Lucy, Leave It to Beaver*

A new home, green green grass, boxes unpacked, one person and
    one bed per room,
One family per house, mothers and fathers in every home down
    the block.
Another school . . .

                        —Pam Tolbert

Pam comments on how applying this kind of bare attention through writing to her childhood experience was helpful to her emotionally:

Overnight my father left our family and the house where we lived, which was owned by his parents. My father's parents threw my mother, myself and my brother out. My mother did not work or drive. For the next three and a half years, we lived in a whole string of houses where we rented rooms. My mother struggled to make enough money to support us. My younger brother and I added to her stress and in every home where we lived there were alcohol problems.

Writing this "camera scan" of those years helped me to see a lot of grit and tenacity in me to make it through such difficult times in a town that was so contrary to my sensibilities even as a child. There is much I can't feel about those years and this gives me a place to start. I could never get comfortable because I was never going to be in a place long.

I always have told my mother it wasn't her fault. She stuck by us and never gave up. She had a lot of integrity as a mother and I feel like I ended up with a lot of sensitivity, compassion, empathy, ability to do whatever is necessary in the grimmest circumstances rather than fold. My past did not equal my future. It felt never-ending as a child but it has changed.

The next poem speaks of the need to grieve, reflect upon and let go a profession that no longer is possible to maintain. How does one leave something that has become so familiar? Drawing a complete picture with your words of what is being given up may lead you toward claiming something essential in your life, something that you will always have with you.

★

ONCE A PERFORMER

Once I was a sly comedian's voice into a microphone.
Once I was the laughter of a piano's chords.
Once I was the beating hands of an audience applauding.
    Now I am muffled quiet between back drops, backstage.
Once I was a comic elfin face painted with make-up.
Once I was a spotlight glittering on white piano keys.
Once I was the heat and blinding glare of many spotlights.
    Now I am the curtained, dusty darkness backstage.
Once I was the wan face in a dressing-room mirror.
Once I was a white tuxedo and its sweat-stained lining.
Once I was a pink smear: make-up on a satin collar.
    Now I am the gray-green exit door opening, backstage.
Once I was a glossy photo promising a talent.
Once I was a joke routine, rehearsed, planned in advance.
Once I was an agent's phone number, dialed every day.
    Now I am the light of dawn outside an emptied theatre,
    And the deep breath of clean air filling my lungs
    While my mind still holds memory of applause.
                                    —*Bill Stephenson*

In the magic net of metaphor, Bill catches the pros and cons of
the performer's life. He shows us his enjoyment and the "back-
stage" dust. Noticing all the particulars of his previous life intensifies the poem. The use of metaphor literally shows Bill to
the door of change. How exciting and interesting is the performer's life as Bill describes it, how poignant and ultimately
beautiful is his exit from that life to a new dawn.

E X E R C I S E
Writing Through the Stages of Our Lives

1. Write your own poem that expresses something you long
for—something that is difficult and poignant. Zawdie, living
with HIV, wrote about longing for the unworried pleasure of

sleeping with someone. As an amputee I have imagined the simple thrill of walking with both bare feet in the sand and surf. You can begin your poem with the phrase, *"All I want . . ."*

2. Write your own "camera scan" poem that gathers material from a more difficult time in your life, a time when you gave up much because of circumstances beyond your control.

3. Focus on some valued activity in your life that you had to give up or leave—it could be a particular career, a sport, a hobby, something that you loved or enjoyed. Consider the pros and cons of that experience. Name all the particulars of that activity so that you reexperience it as you write. What pathway showed you to a new chapter in your life? What signs suggested your new direction? You can begin with the phrase: *"Once I was . . ."* and then fold into your poem, *"Now I am . . ."*

> It is healing to get brought back to knowing what you know.
>
> —Lisa Friedlander

CHAPTER SEVEN

THE PEACE OF WILD THINGS

Embracing the Earth to Tell Your Story

Stand still. The trees ahead and the bushes beside you
Are not lost. Wherever you are is called Here,
And you must treat it as a powerful stranger,
Must ask permission to know it and be known.
The forest breathes. Listen. It answers,
I have made this place around you.
If you leave it, you may come back again, saying Here.
No two trees are the same to Raven.
No two branches are the same to Wren.
If what a tree or bush does is lost to you,
You are surely lost. Stand still. The forest knows
Where you are. You must let it find you.

—David Wagoner

GIVING YOURSELF
PERMISSION TO BE WILD
AND MAGNIFICENT

Earth offers us powerful images and metaphors with which to tell our stories. Rather than thinking of the earth's resources as commodities like oil and wood, poetry suggests we consider the more intangible qualities which nature offers us, such as beauty and spectacle, turmoil and order, mystery and predictability.

A sense of beauty—wild and terrible or lovely and breathtaking—can be more healing than psychology currently acknowledges.

Close contact with nature through poem-making will strengthen your awareness of a healing connection to the earth. This healing relationship will help you create beauty in your life.

Infusing your poetry with earth imagery will help you reveal your unique voice and imagination. The stories of earth—and our stories—are interwoven, constantly changing in the cyclic process of birth, growth and death. A language for expressing these deep changes in your life can be found by tuning to the language of the earth.

Mirrorlike reflections exist between earth processes and your life. The natural world provides you with an excellent counseling center to help you discover greater meaning in your life.

Man knows that he springs from nature and not nature from him. This is an old and very primitive knowledge.
—*Loren Eiseley*

✱

Walt Whitman wrote about the deep relationship we have with the earth:

> Each of us inevitable,
> Each of us limitless—
>   each of us with his or her
>   right upon the earth,
> Each of us allow'd
>   the eternal purports
>   of the earth,
> Each of us here
>   as divinely as any is here.

In this stanza from her beautifully outrageous poem *ego tripping (there may be a reason why)*, Nikki Giovanni offers a spirited vision of her "limitlessness" that is glorious with imagery of earth.

> I sowed diamonds in my back yard
> My bowels deliver uranium
>   the filings from my fingernails are
>   semi-precious jewels
>   On a trip north
> I caught a cold and blew
> My nose giving oil to the arab world
> I am so hip even my errors are correct
> I sailed west to reach east and had to round off
>   the earth as I went
>   The hair from my head thinned gold and was laid
>   across three continents . . .

Poem-making and the natural world give you permission to be wild and magnificent. Your poetic musings of connection with the earth can take you beyond conventional ways of looking at yourself.

We are often so busy conforming to traditional notions of success that we miss this joyful opportunity to cut loose and feel our lives—to express our highest potential and explore our true legacy.

EXERCISE
An Outrageous Poem Using Images and Metaphors
of the Earth

Reread the stanza from Nikki Giovanni's poem or find the whole poem in her book *The Women and the Men*. Create your own poem using wild metaphors drawn from the natural world to present an outrageous, yet honest, picture of yourself.

INFUSING OUR POEMS WITH WHAT NATURE TEACHES US

A forest fire is awesome and frightening but clears the forest floor for new growth. What could this teach us about our own lives? How do we deal with the changes and challenges we face? What are disappointments and even disasters all about? Definitive answers to these questions are often not possible. Still, the insights we gain by observing nature, and the poems we make which include these insights, help us cope with our rage, grief and pain.

Metaphors and poetic images of earth can often *express* such feelings better than plain descriptive words, which seem to crack under the pressure of deep feeling. Feelings of grief might bring to mind images of winter's coldness. Pablo Neruda crystallizes a wintry grief image:

> Yes: seed germs, and grief, and everything that throbs
> frightened in the crackling January light
> will ripen, will burn, as the fruit burned ripe.

The earth is not a mere fragment of dead history, a stratum upon stratum like the leaves of a book, to be studied by geologists and antiquarians chiefly, but living poetry like the leaves of a tree, which precede flowers and fruit—not a fossil earth but a living earth.

—Henry David Thoreau

*

The poetry of earth offers us a chance to experience *something more* about life than our self-definition and ordinary language usually permit. Like the forest after the fire, this *something more* is full of new growth and unknown potential. We must invite this mysterious perspective into our lives if we are to grow. How to explore the mystery of the natural world?

I wrote a poem about weather—one of the most common preludes to conversation. Writing this poem led me to a new understanding about my fear of change and about how to be in tune with life from a very deep level.

MENTIONING THE WEATHER

Mentioning the weather
when we are bored,
uncertain, or just being polite
is not because we've been taught
to be boring, uncertain,
or polite.

We are trying to wake up!

Our words bubble up from
deep in the brain pan
of our animal nature
as we try to remember
a power that kept us
alert to what is,
looking up and around,
moving ourselves towards
the edge of our lives & life,
the intelligence to yield to
yet not be swallowed
by the terror tumbling past,
laying low—a deep impression
in the long grass.

Poem-making about the earth and her natural cycles can help you take time to *heal, renew, find balance* and *gain perspective.* Ancient poets knew this wisdom.

> *To everything there is a season,*
>   *A time for every purpose under*
>   *heaven:*
> *A time to be born,*
>   *And a time to die;*
> *A time to plant,*
>   *And a time to pluck*
>   *what is planted*
>
> *
>
> *A time to break down,*
>   *And a time build up;*
> *A time to weep*
>   *And a time to laugh . . .*
>   *—Ecclesiastes 3*

Writing about the earth will help you to center yourself between the extremes of self-doubt and selfishness. The earth shows how to release your potential and authentically express yourself, rather than giving too much of yourself away or holding too much inside. What do the salmon and oak tree teach? Salmon teach persistence—not to give up reaching your goal even when the world pushes against you. From the oak tree you can learn to draw from your deepest roots and express your purpose even as harsh winds strain your trunk and branches. What do you learn from a forest fern? Lightness, clarity and delicacy, perhaps. What about a stone? Here is a portion of a poem called *To a Stone,* written during a workshop:

> *Half encrusted in a mossy mound of green,*
> *I found a rock that speaks to me and sings.*
> *An imperfect stone nested just off the path,*
> *Unique in its plainness, it sings in my hand.*

*

Cupped in my hand, you share your calm,
Taking my heat while continuing cool.
Your molecules dancing a stillness and strength,
Your peacefulness calls me to join you there.

—*Diane Richard-Allerdyce*

EXERCISE
What Nature Teaches Us

Choose one aspect of the natural world which you feel has something to teach you. It could be an animal, plant or mineral. What specific quality does it express that speaks to you about your own life? Free write your impressions. Shape your favorites into a poem. Here are some possibilities to consider:

snow	breeze	diamond	rosebush	horse
turtle	mouse	badger	peachtree	grasshopper
granite	redwood	plankton	corn	thunderstorm

RECEPTIVITY AND PRESENCE: THE PRACTICE OF OPEN ATTENTION

Every part of the earth is sacred to my people.

—*Chief Seattle*

We are all made—plants and fish and cats and elephants and men—of organisms built of tissue that is built of cells. The life force is in the cells—protoplasm, made up of almost everything in the universe in infinitely minute particles. Now, because that protoplasm which, Huxley says, is the basis of life, is made up of almost everything in Nature, it responds to almost everything in Nature.

—Luther Burbank

Nature receives your feelings similarly to how the blank page is able to receive your words. Your pain or contentment can

∗

breathe when you camp in the woods, sit by a river, walk in a city park or write a poem.

But how to tune to the earth? How to use its energy to make healing poems? The answer is simple but difficult to achieve in our busy world: make time for yourself to be in a natural place, to breathe deeply and pay attention to where you are. You don't have to rush off to Yellowstone National Park or climb a high peak. Gather inspiration for your poems while you walk in your local park, garden in your own backyard, take a Saturday outing to the beach or sit and gaze out your kitchen window in the early morning hours.

Contact with the earth and poem-making is a way to learn about a practice of *open attention*. Open attention will make it more possible for:

* your creativity to flourish
* your connection with spiritual realities to integrate into your daily life
* your sense of beauty, joy and an entire range of feelings to awaken
* your sensitivity, intuition and insight to deepen
* your skill for making poems to grow

What is open attention? It is awareness. Learn to practice open attention by listening and seeing with your whole being. How can you deepen your skills of listening and seeing with your whole being? Key words that describe this practice of awareness are:

RECEPTIVITY AND PRESENCE

Receptivity and presence are like a tree. Imagine yourself as a tree. Become that tree. Roots, sap and trunk are your voice, body and life force that coalesce into your *presence* in the world. Branches and leaves represent your *receptivity*. Branches extend their leaves out to receive sunlight in the best possible way. The thin moon-shaped leaves of a eucalyptus turn broadly to the

The mountains, rivers, earth, grasses, trees, and forests are always emanating a subtle precious light, day and night, always emanating a subtle, precious sound, demonstrating and expounding to all people the unsurpassed ultimate truth.

—Yuan-Sou

sun in moderate weather but when it is hot and dry show only their thin edge to the sun.

Receptivity catches what is given to you. Presence gives shape and substance to what you receive.

> I drank a fertile alphabet
> and spoke a whole green pasture.
> —Cori Olinghouse, seventeen years old

Four things will strengthen and fine-tune your receptivity and presence. The first two are oriented toward the heart. They are part of your preverbal experience, and are universal feminine capacities:

* sensing and feeling

The second two are linked with mindful witnessing and are universal masculine capacities:

* noticing and naming

The first group are flowing and open and the second establish shape and expression for what you receive. These work together.

LYING IN A HAMMOCK AT WILLIAM DUFFY'S FARM
AT PINE ISLAND, MINNESOTA

> Over my head, I see the bronze butterfly,
> Asleep on the black trunk,
> Blowing like a leaf in green shadow.
> Down the ravine behind the empty house,
> The cowbells follow one another
> Into the distances of the afternoon.
> To my right,
> In a field of sunlight between two pines,
> The droppings of last year's horses

*

Blaze up into golden stones.
I lean back, as the evening darkens and comes on.
A chicken hawk floats over, looking for home.
I have wasted my life.

                                        —James Wright

Wright senses, feels, notices and names what is around him.
The poet allows and trusts what comes. This experience is not
a cognitive process: the poet does not self-consciously think,
"Now I will be receptive, now I will sense, now I will notice,
now I will name." All of these are an integral part of an *attitude* of
receptivity and presence—allowing your awareness to intuitively link with the living systems around you.

   Later, you may go back to change and improve your poem—
to make it truer to your intent. This creative process is compa-
rable to creation itself—just as there is endless variety in nature,
there are countless ways to shape what you make.

   David Wagoner says in his poem *Lost* (at the beginning of
this chapter) that you must let the forest find you. You must let
your poem come to you. Small and even obvious details are excellent places to begin. Wright receives what he sees and hears:

        Over my head, I see the bronze butterfly,
        Asleep on the black trunk
        *

        The cowbells follow one another
        Into the distances of the afternoon.

The invariable mark of wisdom is seeing the miraculous in the common.
                                        —Ralph Waldo Emerson

Cowbells merge with something larger—"the distances of
the afternoon." Receptivity is not a static state. It flows like a
river, allowing particulars to surprise you, to touch you, to per-
plex you, to change you, to thrill you, to expand your perspective—and sometimes, to give you the gift of healing poems.

   Wright hears the cowbell sounds expand into the afternoon
distances, he allows his feeling and awareness to go with this
experience, but he also remains *rooted* in a place. He is in the
hammock. Wright emphasizes this sense of being *present* in his

✳

body by the simple line that appears in the very middle of the poem:

To my right

We have to get quiet. We have to be still, and that's harder and harder in this century.

—Jane Kenyon

Presence asks that you know what is to your right. Poem-making is capable of grounding you because it helps you to know what is around you—and within you—and it makes a container to hold your experience. You must slow down and be present if you are going to make such a container, if you are going to feel and sense, notice and name. Open attention is not anything you need to "do"; open attention is something to let be.

Donna Kennedy is a features writer for the Living Section of the *Press-Enterprise* in Riverside, California. A journalist for twenty-five years, Donna is new to poem-making. She found poetic language while dancing on a visit to Trinidad on a hot summer night.

MIDNIGHT ON LAVENTILLE

*I sit at the center of the music
and it seeps into my bones like a damp night.
Bodies bouncing in pan rhythm,
one earnest Irish man at last where he belongs
pounding steel with his black brothers.
And me, my cup of corn chowder, my ginger shandy,
my green T-shirt bragging 'Despers, Despers, Despers Forever'
to the dirty cliff edges of Laventille
to the vine-sheltered shacks below
to the star pinholes above.
The music seeps into my bones like a damp night
on Laventille.*

This is what Donna says about the genesis of her poem:

✳
✳   *I went to the postcard table during John's workshop and chose a joyous*
✳   *card picturing a drummer and two dancers. Soon I was sobbing be-*

cause it reminded me of Krista and Ray—my dancer daughter and her husband, who is a percussionist. Krista has cancer and I have a deep fear of losing her and of losing dancing and magic in my life.

I spoke to the group about how the postcard reminded me of Krista and Ray and mentioned the experience I had at Carnival in Trinidad with them. John suggested I go there with my emotions and place myself right in the middle of that experience. I remembered the first night on the island, where I felt oneness with the earth beneath my feet and the stars and moon, and the people and the city below. The whole island was pulsing.

Ray has played steel drums since he was a teenager in Illinois, but it was remarkable he had been invited to play with the Laventille neighborhood band, Desperados. He was the only white man drumming among 120 black men and women.

At midnight we went up to the drum camp on this curving scary road to the top of Laventille Hill. We were way up high overlooking the city and the ocean. It is rumored to be dangerous up there but it didn't seem so to me. It was very bacchanal—everything open and sensual. All that mattered was the music.

When I was invited to go into the middle of the music with those three hundred steel drums pounding, it was the most incredible thing I ever felt, like being inside a heart. Everybody was smiling and sweating and the ground was shaking and there wasn't any difference between the ground and your feet and the stars. EVERYTHING was one.

The poem that I wrote was from the belly, not from the head. It is so hard for me to let go. Although I grew up in the desert with a mother who was close to the earth, I felt I connected with people, not the ground people stood on.

When I started to make this poem, I typed and sobbed, typed and sobbed. The drumming was a part of me again, and I was a part of the earth. I could feel in writing this poem—in the emotional way I got to it—that when I cap off the emotion, I shut off creativity. The creative things are very close to the emotional stuff. Letting that flow allowed this poem to come.

Sometimes I hear music haunting me, and then I have to fill that music with words.

—Claribel Alegría

Donna came to write this poem by taking risks. The risks she takes are always in moving from the periphery to the center of

*

her experience. First, she went up to an exotic and unfamiliar place to possibly dance under the stars. She didn't skirt the edges, she soon came to the center of the circle and danced. When she saw the postcard of the fabulous dancers and drummer, it evoked her tears at the workshop, and she went into that place of feeling. She went to her center, and from there the poem emerged.

EXERCISE
Making Contact with the Earth

I embrace emerging experience. I participate in discovery. I am a butterfly. I am not a butterfly collector.

—William Stafford

1. Sit with your back against a tree, with your senses alert and feelings open, and notice the details of what is around you. Experience yourself as a living organism with permeable edges, a part of everything that lives! Feel that in the universe all of life is flowing around and through you. Allow your impressions to arise directly from your contact with the tree and the ground and write a poem, or meditate on impressions to write about later.

2. Like Donna dancing in Trinidad, recall a dynamic, even ecstatic experience you've had in nature. Take your time to re-create that experience and shape a poem.

3. Visit a state park or a neighborhood nature trail or any natural place where you feel an affinity. Let that place find you as David Wagoner suggests; focus on that connection. Ask that place for a voice to use in poem-making to help you express the process of being found.

EXERCISE
The Language of the Land

The Okanagan word for "our place on the land" and "our language" is the same. The Okanagan language is thought of as the "language of the land." This means that the land has taught us our language. The way we survived is to speak the language that the land offered us as its teaching. To know all the plants, animals, seasons, and geography is to construct language for them.

—Jeannette Armstrong

1. Take one of the words below and imagine what it describes. If you choose the word "surf," for example, imagine yourself stepping into or walking along the surf. Say the word "surf" out loud. Free write everything about your physical impressions, feelings, thoughts or experiences that the word evokes within you. Write until that word comes alive for you.

2. Create a poem using earth words to explore and express your feelings and experience. Choose a feeling word (such as sadness or delight), experience word (such as sleep or play) or concept word (such as renewal or friendship) that you want to explore. Without using that word in the poem, communicate it by using the earth words on the list below.

marsh	tide	mountain	rivulet	shale	surf
billow	glacier	slope	swamp	moraine	ledge
fallow	grove	crust	plain	pond	knoll
slough	cave	thorn	flood	crescent	ravine
soil	ridge	grass	heather	cave	rock
sea	shoal	meadow	slough	current	dune
marsh	molten	pebble	mud	orchid	tundra
granite	lichen	hollow	hive	quarry	vine

The dynamic and evocative language of the natural world offers you the opportunity to discover a sane and ecstatic self. Nature and its language enfold us in meaning but do not insist on logic; they beckon us to sanity and joy by being noticed simply for the beauty they are: bronze butterfly and chicken hawk, cowbells drifting into the distance and the golden stones of horse shit.

✱

THE PRIMAL KNOWLEDGE
OF CONNECTIONS

> When the natural world reawakens in every fiber of our be-
> ing the primal knowledge of connection and graces us with
> a few moments of sheer awe, it can shatter hubris and isola-
> tion so necessary to narcissistic defenses. Once this has
> happened, ongoing contact with nature can keep these in-
> sights alive and provide the motivation necessary for con-
> tinued change.
>
> —Allen D. Kanner and Mary E. Gomes

Nature invites us to discover *connection*. This is the same invitation of poem-making: through playing with the lines of a
poem we begin to see the connections between different aspects of life, and these connections become catalysts for insight.

The process of writing weaves together our experience and
our imagination. As we write, these interwoven elements help
us to discover more about life, about nature, about our experience of loss and love—about how our life is ultimately connected to everything around us. Devices of poetry—sound,
imagery, rhythm, metaphor, personification—are all ways to
express natural connections. And conversely, attention to nature shows us a way to perceive poetic connections.

PEONIES AT DUSK

White peonies blooming along the porch
send out light
while the rest of the yard grows dim.

Outrageous flowers as big as human
heads! They're staggered
by their own luxuriance: I had
to prop them up with stakes and twine.

The moist air intensifies their scent,
and the moon moves around the barn
to find out what it's coming from.

In the darkening June evening
I draw a blossom near, and bending close
search it as a woman searches
a loved one's face.

—Jane Kenyon

Writing poetry surprises us with unexpected comparisons such as peonies and a loved one. Unexpectedness catches our attention. We say: "Yes . . . I can feel it's possible or I've felt that in flowers . . . but didn't have words to say it."

Read Jane Kenyon's poem a few times or have a friend read the poem to you. Savor the rich connections: peonies big as human heads, the moist air and the peonies' scent, the moon's interest in their scent, and the connection between the peony and a loved one's face. What connections do you see in the poem?

Your ability to sense nuances and connections is increased by developing your sensitivity. Direct contact with nature combined with poem-making is a way to strengthen your sensitivity and your ability to know and take care of your needs.

Trina Baker earned a master's degree in library science and works as an archivist at Lawrence Berkeley Labs. She is a tutor in an afterschool program and sings in her church choir. Tina wrote the following poem during a workshop I gave called *Living with Change, Rekindling Intimacy.* Her poem came out of a part of the workshop called *Transitions and Journeys of Solitude.*

The moment one gives close attention to anything, even a blade of grass, it becomes a mysterious, awesome, indescribably magnificent world in itself.

—Henry Miller

ALLUVIAL CHANGES

The delta stills in this shallow curve.
silt brown water under a blue sky,
no reflection of the sky like the ocean
no reflection of the pines like a lake,
the underwater slope so gentle

*

that the wakes of boats only softly
make the river's mouth rock and shimmer,
with its black and gold lights,
reflecting only color, no images.

Here the river, old, slow moving,
shifts—not yet ready for the sea change.
Not yet ready to leave the delta behind
for the depths of salt water.

The murky water must be walked into
to be known, toes exploring silken mud,
rocks few and far between, and smooth.
I stand ankle deep in the water
and cannot see my toes,
then sit in the warmth up to my neck,
giving only as much of myself
to the water or the sun as I choose.
And then, the sudden drop.

Trina had this to say about her poem:

Alluvial Changes *came out of a trip I made to the delta with a man I am no longer with. That visit was a healthy time and place in our relationship. I wanted to revisit that place in this time of transition.*

The delta is a place where river silt and minerals slow down and settle before they drop off into the open sea. In the poem, I walk into the alluvium—which is a combination of poisonous runoff of fertilizers and steer manure, but also contains gold and minerals that enrich the soil. Writing about this place was a way to sift through the good and bad in that relationship and to begin healing.

The delta is a place of transition in many ways: the bottom is unclear. You can't see what is going on. I had to feel my way out into it with my feet. I realize it is all right during this time to not know exactly where I am going. There was richness of experience I wanted to gather before moving on. Recalling that delta place helped to create a place of transition within myself.

*
*
*
*   *Writing about the delta made it possible to relax and see I wanted a*
time-out before I got back into taking risks.

Diane Richard-Allerdyce is an associate professor of English
at a university in Florida. She wrote this poem during a magical
five-day workshop at Omega Institute in Rhinebeck, New York.
Diane develops the extended metaphor of a lioness to call upon
a wilder part of herself:

LIONESS

I am still lioness
emerging to the daylight,
fierce with a living hunger
that carves its way
along my chest's lining—

> *I am the grassy plain*
> *below the lioness,*
> *the rippling of sunlight*
> *moving before her—*
> *I am the voice of the shadows*
> *between the lit places,*
> *damp and wide darkness*
> *rising to meet the grass tips—*
> *lifting all around each stalk*
> *and liking this lifting—*
> *darkness rising like earth itself rising—*

I am the lioness
moving
first slowly,
beginning to focus,
awakening to some half-remembered
sense that here is something
out there—
something I know how to do from

✦

the depths behind that lightning
at my core—

the memory returning
like a dream of darkness,
a shadow rising in the field before me
to meet the light—

I am beginning to move—
I am lioness beginning to move,
tearing pain in my side
returning—
yes I am wounded (I had forgotten)
my bones are on fire—

I am the light dancing on the grass plain—
light as weightless as the flame tips of fire.

Diane shifts back and forth from the direct voice of the lioness to a voice of the lioness' natural domain. These two voices create a contrast that allows the lioness to emerge and know herself, especially through a relationship to her environment. The structure of a poem—as you create and shape it—will help you embody the changes you want to make in your life or the changes being called forth in you. Diane describes her experience of making this poem:

The deeply buried feminine in those whose concern is the unbroken connection of all growing things is in passionate revolt against the stultifying, life-destroying anonymous machine of the civilization that we have built.

—Irene Claremont de Castillejo

Writing this poem I sought to access my primitive self, the self that doesn't hide behind academic titles and learning. As I entered into the metaphor of the lioness, I wanted the poem to express my process of becoming that animal. I sank into the metaphor and yet found myself resisting it. That's when it became helpful to switch in some stanzas to the gentler and subtle but still very important metaphors and images of the natural world.

The grass plain and shadows put the lioness in context. I realized later that those images could be the lioness's direct awareness of grass and shadows; the poem eventually became a growing unified awareness joining the lioness and her environment.

I felt the lioness's hunger as well as her guardedness because of her wound. I also felt her great urge to connect with the "here" of the earth, to wrestle with her domain. There was a desire to allow "the depths behind that lightning / at my core" entry into the world. That urge shows me that the experience of being wounded can even intensify or illuminate one's inner strength and power.

As I worked with these metaphors, I identified with that hungry and wounded image but could also step back and see the larger picture of the "rippling sunlight" and the "shadows between the lit places." Similarly, in any kind of conflict I experience, I step back in order to see more. I realized that the hunger was just the surface of a bigger plan of which the lioness is a part. As I identified with the fire in her—her wound, her hunger, her great urge to live—I saw that fire reflected in the weightless light on the grassy plain.

EXERCISE
Animals as Metaphor

Choose an animal—or anything in nature you feel an affinity with—as a metaphor. This animal may have qualities that are particularly important to you right now. As in Diane's poem, use your animal metaphor to express a way you would like to grow right now. Or use it to tell the story of a particular circumstance in your life that may need healing. Imagine everything you can about this animal: its habitat, how it moves, what it does, how it expresses. Go with your gut feeling—what animal embodies your current conflicts or yearnings?

| butterfly | eagle | bear | elephant | swan |
| spider | dolphin | wolf | deer | monkey |

✳

ECOPSYCHOLOGY AND POEM-MAKING: THE RECLAMATION OF DEEP LANGUAGE

The emerging field of ecopsychology is well expressed through the medium of poem-making. Ecopsychology and the poetry of earth are particularly concerned with:

> ✳ how physical, psychological and spiritual health are linked with creating a harmonious relationship with the earth.
> ✳ how understanding bioregions provides an opportunity for humans to see our healthy place living on the earth.
> ✳ how awareness of natural processes can teach us ways to live with painful aspects of our personal lives with more equanimity.

Natural places provide a place for us to retreat to and heal during personal crises. Wendell Berry's *The Peace of Wild Things* shows how the earth comforts us with grace and beauty.

THE PEACE OF WILD THINGS

When despair for the world grows in me
and I wake in the night at the least sound
in fear of what my life and my children's lives may be,
I go and lie down where the wood drake
rests in his beauty on the water, and the great heron feeds.
I come into the peace of wild things
who do not tax their lives with forethought
of grief. I come into the presence of still water.
And I feel above me the day-blind stars
waiting with their light. For a time
I rest in the grace of the world, and am free.
> —*Wendell Berry*

Suddenly, from behind the rim of the moon in long slow-motion movements of immense majesty there emerges a sparkling blue and white jewel, a light, delicate sky blue sphere laced with slowly swirling veils of white rising gradually like a small pearl in a thick sea of black mystery. It takes more than a moment to fully realize this is the Earth—home.

> —*Edgar Mitchell, Apollo astronaut, on seeing the earth while walking on the moon*

Poem-making is a way to gather and use ecological and psychological insights together in a dynamic way. Poems can tell the story of the rites of passage individuals and groups face on their earth journey; they can celebrate particular nonhuman life forms and our relationship with them; and they can speak about our profound relationship to mysteries of the earth and universe. Poems have served this purpose for a long, long time.

> *In the very earliest times,*
> *when both people and animals lived on earth,*
> *a person could become an animal if he wanted to*
> *and an animal could become a human being.*
> *Sometimes they were people*
> *and sometimes animals*
> *and there was no difference.*
> *All spoke the same language.*
> *That was the time when words were like magic . . .*
> *—Eskimo poem*

Indigenous people's wisdom about human and animal language. Homer recounting the dangerous sailing adventures of Odysseus to give a mythic foundation to community and individual quests, Vedic seers chanting sacred syllables drawn from vibration of the elements to raise consciousness—all of these gave voice to the energies of earth; voices that told of human beings connected with a larger field of life.

Ecopsychology calls upon us to rediscover voices of common sense, of magic, of story-telling, of sacred realities—all of these are found in the domain of poem-making and nature. The rediscovery of our place in the earth community is a way for us to understand a healthy relationship with ourselves. Wisdom is not found on a computer chip. It pulses within our heart, in the flow of being, through the precision of stars keeping their courses. Ecopsychology shows that wisdom is not the possession of any one person or group but is found when we realize our *relationship* to everything that is.

*

*As naturally as the oak bears an
acorn and the vine a gourd, man
bears a poem, either spoken or done.*

　　　　　—Henry David Thoreau

*The real work is becoming native in
your heart, coming to understand we
really live here, that this is really the
continent we're on and that our
loyalties are here, to these mountains
and rivers, to these plant zones, to
these creatures. The real work involves
a loyalty that goes back before the
formation of any nation state, back
billions of years and thousands of
years into the future. The real work is
accepting citizenship in the continent
itself.*

　　　　　—Gary Snyder

*As I look at the clouds,
whose presence just whispered something
against the long inscrutability of the sky,
they now recede, pull back behind
the slate blue cover of the world.*

*I see the ease with which nature
surfaces and dives,
bringing insides out and outsides in;
no day a kin to any other,
no light revealing without blinding
at some angle or distance from the heart.*

*In back or before me the common ground:
my ancestor, my future, my home;
the blood in my heart its ocean mate
and moon-tossed tidal chant.*

Do I play its music or am I the tune?
　　　　　—Lisa Friedlander

EXERCISE
Your Relationship with Nature—Writing Your Sense of Mystery

Was somebody asking to see the soul?
See your own shape and countenance, persons, substances,
beasts, the trees, the running rivers, the rocks and sands.
　　　　　—Walt Whitman

Reread Lisa Friedlander's poem and listen to the relationship she feels with nature. Her sense of belonging. The vitality of life flowing through her and around her. The ease and the awe. Meditate on something in nature that is simple. It could be clouds in motion. Wind through tree branches. Rain on a meadow. Flowers in your garden. Listen for the implicit music of these natural things. Watch the interaction of these different things together. Notice the very particular place in this interaction that draws your attention. Wendell Berry said, "I go and lie down where the wood drake/rests in his beauty on the water, and the great heron feeds." What does your chosen natural place tell you about yourself, about your relationship with nature? Invoke an open-eyed willingness to receive into your life a mysterious connection with the earth. Write about this.

BEING A VOICE FOR THE EARTH

Violent events of nature may cause pain and great upheaval, but these powerful acts do not foul the environment. The activity of ecological destruction seems to be reserved for humans. Your fears, rage and grief about environmental conditions, your desire to protect the earth and its inhabitants, your love for beauty, your stewardship for what happens to lakes and skies, can also be expressed through poem-making.

> *Even though many environmentalists act out of a passionate joy in the magnificence of wild things, few except the artists—the photographers, the filmmakers, the landscape painters, and the poets—address the public with any conviction that human beings can be trusted to behave as if they were the living planet's children.*
>
> *—Theodore Roszak*

William Wordsworth wrote almost two hundred years ago about humans being out of tune with the natural world:

> *The world is too much with us; late and soon,*
> *Getting and spending, we lay waste our powers:*
> *Little we see in Nature that is ours;*
> *We have given our hearts away, a sordid boon!*

*

This Sea that bares her bosom to the moon;
The winds that will be howling at all hours,
And are up-gathered now like sleeping flowers;
For this, for everything, we are out of tune;
It moves us not.—Great God! I'd rather be
A Pagan suckled in a creed outworn;
So might I, standing on this pleasant lea,
Have glimpses that would make me less forlorn;
Have sight of Proteus rising from the sea;
Or hear old Triton blow his wreathèd horn.

Y*o, earth, did I hear you say*
monsters are killing you?

—Kai, a child, reading a poem
over the radio

What do you feel about the lines, "Little we see in Nature that is ours;/We have given our hearts away, a sordid boon!" Do you feel sadness? Anger? A desire to connect with and celebrate earth's beauty? Do you want to protect the earth? What do you feel about your relationship to the earth and what we do to her?

Anita Brajdic, at my invitation to find a natural place she felt connected with, could only write about a place she once loved, now covered by a freeway:

FROM W*HERE* T*HERE* O*NCE* W*AS* W*HAT* I*S*
N*OT* E*ASILY* R*EMEMBERED*

Cranes and scrapers grind steady,
midstream of traffic like rocks
obstructing a migration
as urgent as salmon.
Battered swimmers seek the sea of office parks
then climb to foothill home
in an eternal loop to reach a final rest.
Who of them remembers the fertile ground before this river
cuts its way?
Who sees what is left at the core?
Our urban wounds,
blistering buildings
and dark tower with no eyes.

Does this lack of sight mean that we no longer desire
the center from where the river springs,
forgetting ourselves while flying in the diamond lane,
not keeping alert to hazards in the road ahead?

EXERCISE
Becoming the Earth's Voice

Joanna Macy, a Buddhist teacher and passionate environmental activist, developed a group process she calls "Council of All Beings." She invites a group of people to consider the fate of the earth and the profound level of environmental destruction occurring at this time not from the standpoint of our human species, but from the viewpoint of any nonhuman species. The idea for this exercise is drawn from that weekend-long process.

1. As a Coho salmon, or any other living thing, what would you have to say about protecting your waterways? About the way you are treated by humans?

2. Imagine what this creature would speak in a poem and write.

3. Try this exercise in a writing circle.

M*ore than any other of the human types concerned with the sacred, the shamanic personality journeys into the far regions of the cosmic mystery and brings back the vision and the power needed by the human community at the most elementary level. The shamanic personality speaks and best understands the languages of the creatures of the earth.*

—Thomas Berry

HOW THE EARTH MIRRORS OUR HEALING AND GROWTH

Earth mirrors for us what we go through in our own healing. Lisa McMongale grew up in central Pennsylvania on a farm with her mother, her grandmother and a lot of aunts and uncles. Lisa is now thirty-eight. Her sense of "place" is strong—she still lives in the home and on the rural land of her birth. She works in the lending service of a university library. Lisa studies languages, especially because she enjoys the sounds of the words.

*

The Black Walnut Tree is a poem that uses nature to evoke the process of emotional healing.

THE BLACK WALNUT TREE

Like a mother gathering scattered
toys at the end of the day,
I bend to pick up green
walnuts, the size and color of tennis balls
and pile them under the black walnut tree
for the squirrels that tear
the pulpy rind off to expose the woody shell
inside. In early August the yellowed walnut
leaves drop, the first to color, fall,
and skip with the wind across
the porch, scuffing dryly on the concrete floor.
The lowest limbs tower out of reach
unlike the maple's low
branches, perfect for climbing and siphoning
sweet sap for syrup and maple sugar candy.
A chain my grandfather tied
around a branch like a tourniquet
to hang a butchered pig until
the blood drained from its limp body
still snakes around the limb,
the chain so corroded after fifty
years of rain and snow, that if
I could reach it,
the rust would flake off
like dead skin onto my fingers.
I would climb a ladder to untie the chain,
but the tree grew around it,
and like all living things
made the wound a part of itself.

I asked Lisa to talk about her poem:

I was diagnosed with rheumatoid arthritis. I feel that this illness is at least partially connected to my own rigidity. Things had to be perfect or I didn't want them. I wouldn't bend. But I also didn't stand up for myself inside my family. I was reticent to speak. The chain around the tree was put there by my grandfather, and I think it expresses my rigidity and the limitations I've felt in my family structure.

When I started the poem it was the details that led me. Leaves scuffing across the porch. Details gave me direct contact with what the poem needed. The first part of the poem is a reference to motherhood and nurturing—gathering the walnuts for the squirrels. It's nurturing myself. Nurturing means that I am worth taking care of—even though I am not perfect. The walnut tree is a difficult tree—losing its leaves first in winter and getting them last in spring. It's not a tree you want to climb. Some people consider it a junk tree. It is harder to love such a tree, just as it was hard to take care of myself.

What the poem shows me is that the things that wound me and make me imperfect are a part of my experience. Rather than push them away and harden my attitude, I need to accept them, make them a part of my life, and move on.

This poem was the beginning of my healing. A few months after writing it I began therapy. It took me a long time to see what this poem meant, and I am still discovering things. I feel the answers were inside of me. Not so much answers as a process. The process of healing has deepened for me through my writing.

Unexpectedly you find it, welling upwards in the empty tree.

—Rainer Maria Rilke

LIVING IN A SENSUOUS WORLD AND WRITING ABOUT IT

Many poems in this chapter draw on rich sensual experience. Giving our fullest energy to the experience of perceiving nature with all of our senses, and then putting that experience into our poems, enhances this sensual quality. This life-affirming sensuous energy will shimmer and resonate in your writing.

Walt Whitman joined together the languages of sensuality and earth with ecstatic abandon:

I am he that walks with the tender and growing night,
I call to the earth and sea half-held by the night.

Press close bare-bosom'd night—press close magnetic nourishing night!
Night of south winds—night of the large few stars!
Still nodding night—mad naked summer night.

A workshop student, playing with words drawn from a bowl, made these poems:

Ancient souls collide,
embrace,
Bark and flesh meet,
dissolve,
home at last

Sun and Moon,
cling,
nude
boiling and dark
—Barbara Reese

Barbara's "poemlettes" show how the sexuality of life reverberates through everything in creation. The first one reminds us that sexuality is a celebration between our spirit and nature. The second poem shows an image of the intense nature of life—the erotically explosive and wild attraction of opposites.

Lisa McMonagle wrote this next poem about love-making. As she did in *The Black Walnut Tree*, Lisa allowed nature to help her respond to her physical and emotional wounds. Lisa makes the poem a place to reclaim herself, to break free of rigidity and give herself permission to respond with her whole body, with the powerful and soulful energies of her sexuality.

✴

CONTINENTAL DRIFT

I want to make love
on the bed of stones
beside that circle of rocks
ringing the black charcoal
remains of the fire we lit
that cold winter day we skated
on uneven, pitted ice
between brown, sphagnum moss-
covered banks over still water
running deep and translucent
as a dream below.

I want to feel
rocks shift
under my winged shoulder blades,
feel our hips grind together—
lapidary of our passion—
feel our skin, topsoil cushioning
our pelvises
the continental drift of our bodies.
                    —Lisa McMonagle

Erotic and sensual poems offer the opportunity to write directly
from our "earthiness." Lisa comments:

✴ I got the inspiration for this poem when I saw the rivers in Pittsburgh.
✴ As a kid I used to play at a creek that met with a smaller creek that
✴ went into a larger creek, and somehow in that moment of looking at the
✴ rivers, there was a connection in my mind with playing at those creeks.
✴   I kept thinking about rocks grinding together like a mini–continental
✴ drift or bodies making love. Life against life. Sound making sound. I
✴ think my relationship with my first boyfriend is a big part of this poem.
✴ He was very comfortable in the woods and so was I. We got away
✴ from my family and other people who tell us that there isn't magic in the
✴ world. I didn't feel the constraints of my religion in the forest.

*

We both ended up hurting each other a lot. Just as rocks or continental plates leave enormous marks as they slide upon each other, we left marks on each other as we moved out of each other's lives. So this poem is symbolic of that experience too.

I hadn't written an erotic poem before. When I did, something was liberated within me. This poem comes at a point in my life of learning to speak my truth. It's been a difficult thing—to speak for the real me. To say I am a sexual person—acknowledging I have a body. I ignored my body when it told me things. The rheumatoid arthritis was a direct message to take care of my body. That diagnosis, the creeks and forest, my remembrance of the joy and wounds of that first relationship, celebrating eroticism and the earth—expressing this frees me to speak for that part of me that has been hiding.

This poem was one of the easiest poems I ever wrote. I didn't labor over it. This one came to me whole. I think it came from the Muse.

E X E R C I S E
Celebrating Eroticism and the Earth

Explore the faint line between the sensuous and the sensual. The sensual is the sensuous imbued with sexuality. First begin with a sensuous description of a natural object like a stone, a river, a tide pool—and then, working with that piece, write your description as if to a lover, enhancing your sensuous description with erotic appeal.

CHAPTER EIGHT

POEMS OF WITNESS IN A CONFLICTED WORLD

Speaking the Truth, Going to the Heart

Writing poems offers me the possibility of attending, in great detail, to the very particular experience of another, while allowing me to own and nourish my own parallel processes. In reflecting back a person's rough edges, idiosyncratic thoughts, and courageous acts, perhaps I can facilitate both self-examination and self-love.

—Lisa Friedlander

SEEING THE WORLD WITH
THE EYES OF A POET

The profoundest of all sensualities
is the sense of truth
and the next deepest sensual experience
is the sense of justice.

—D. H. Lawrence

Actor Christopher Reeve, an eloquent champion for the handicapped, the environment and for compassion in American life, offers a courageously simple definition of "family values." Reeve says: "We are all family. And we all have value." His poetic conciseness is instantly clear and goes straight to the heart.

For a caring person it is difficult to find a language in our culture that offers a humane and noble way of responding to seemingly intractable problems like racism and homelessness.

Mean-spirited political and social views polarize us; harsh words deaden our sensitivity and the willingness to solve the problems we face. Individuals with fine solutions to offer feel unheard while people in positions of responsibility blame "others" for problems we all share.

Political groups and religions often squabble over trivialities and ideology, losing touch with their purpose and the original intent of their moral and spiritual traditions.

Advocates for social change remind us of our responsibility to one another and the need for justice—but the individuals who catalyze conscience *and* creativity are more likely to win our hearts and quicken our ability to feel.

How can we learn a language that helps us to feel more fully? Enter poets, poem-making and using your own creative voice to

I definitely feel there are many listening ears in our society and many people eager to use their voices in ways that lead to questioning and wonder. I feel that hunger every place I go, and I feel a receptivity in our culture to that hunger.

—Naomi Shihab Nye

*

speak the truth. What we discover in this creative language is something more powerful and lasting than instituting another program to solve a problem. Poetry offers a perspective that moves us beyond blame and indifference. What we can find is a common ground to stand on together and create better ways to live and understand one another.

> *People are beginning to understand that, especially in poetry, feeling transcends boundaries of race, culture, class, economics. They are also beginning to understand that intellect does not do that. On the other hand, the way we feel, the way we fear, the way we love, the way we hope—these are the same kinds of things for all of us. So poetry that is both intellectual and intuitive seems to me to be poetry that will get past any of the artificial boundaries which separate us.*
> —Lucille Clifton

Just as the poet is a menace to conformity, he is also a constant threat to political dictators. He is always on the verge of blowing up the assembly line of political power.
—Rollo May

Jack Hirschman is a poet of America's "third world." He lives close to, writes about and interacts with people who are forgotten by the mainstream, homeless people whom many of us avoid. We may feel powerless to do anything about homelessness. We may keep ourselves at a distance out of fear, lack of caring or a sense of problem overload. Homelessness *is* difficult. But our isolation and silence about it may be largely because we do not have an adequately human language to talk about homelessness; faces and hearts are forgotten.

Hirschman's poem captures the rhythms of human caring that allow us to draw closer to the life around us rather than shutting it out:

> HUMAN INTERLUDE
> for Terry Garvin
>
> She was standing against
>   the wall near
> the Tevere Hotel holding
>   a plastic cup
> as it began to rain.

I dug for a coin, walked
  up to her
and dropped it in.
    It fell to the bottom
of an orange drink.

I blushed, looked into her
  ravaged eyes and skin
    and hair prematurely
greying, and said
I was sorry, I'd thought

she needed some bread.
  "I do," she said
and smiled, "I was
    just having a little
    drink."

And we stood there
  laughing together
as we watched the raindrops fall
  on the orange lake
above the drowning money.
                    —*Jack Hirschman*

Notice how the poem personalizes Hirschman's encounter with the woman. He gives us details about Terry: where she is standing, what she drinks, how her face looks, what she says. Through simple detail, Terry becomes real. Hirschman includes himself in her life: he is vulnerable, blushing over his impulsive "helpfulness." He sweetens his "mistake" by recognizing it as a moment for two human beings to laugh together, noticing the poignancy of their experience.

To one degree or another, we have all known rejection. We have felt neglected. We probably have felt the distancing of those who do not want to acknowledge our pain or who walk away from us without a thought. We know the sadness that comes from not being understood by those closest to us. Yet we walk past others in need. Can you name the details of what you pass by in others?

EXERCISE
Looking at Your World with the Eyes of a Poet

There is a road from the eye to the heart that does not go through the intellect.

—*G. K. Chesterton*

Answer these sentence stems. Be a voice for others. Take time to consider who and what matters to you. Read it aloud. Rekindle your poetic voice and creative imagination through comforting those in your world whose conflicts you can feel. Use material you gather here to make poems. Be specific and detailed.

The artist, however faithful to his personal vision of reality, becomes the last champion of the individual mind and sensibility against an intrusive society and officious state.

—*John F. Kennedy*

What I long to see healed in my world is _____.

The beauty of _____ is a source of joy in my life.

The neglect of _____ makes me sad at heart.

I am determined to change the treatment of _____ in this world.

My heart is broken open by the loss of _____ in this world.

My creative spirit is kept alive by people who express the following: _____

_____ in this world.

Free write about a few of your responses. Just as Jack Hirschman is very specific in the poem *Human Interlude*, referring to a real person, shape your poem by being very specific about a particular person and circumstance.

HONORING MAJOR
TURNING POINTS
IN YOUR LIFE

I have something incomprehensible to say,
like bird song in the time of war

—Odysseus Elytis

In May of 1970, four people were shot dead and many others wounded at Kent State University. They were fired on by the National Guard during a protest of Nixon's invasion of Cambodia during the Vietnam War. I was fifteen. One of the students killed, Allison Krause, was a counselor at a summer camp for developmentally disabled children and young adults that my parents, Jim and Eleanor Fox, founded with Allison's aunt and uncle and other parents. My older sister Holly, who has Down Syndrome, attended "YES Camp" (Youth Enrichment Services) where Allison worked one summer.

Holly, a delightful person whose interesting mind and loving heart are as distant from war as I can imagine anyone being, is to me the perfect answer to injustice and hatred; she encourages hope for good and peace *by the way she is.* Her connection with Allison Krause brought something home to me about what mattered in life.

Elegies written for Allison, Jeffrey, Saundra and William could not return them to their parents or friends, could not return Allison to the children she taught and loved. But words of loss give a fierce voice to the tragedy of their deaths, as do poems written by Vietnam vets for their brothers and sisters who died by their sides in the war. Writing poems about how our history has affected us acknowledges our heartache and protects us from forgetting.

*

*If poetry gets too far towards the
realm of the aesthetic, the formal, and
the beautiful and doesn't acknowledge
the other sides of existence—the
history that we live in, the changes
and the darkness of history—then life
goes out of poetry, and it becomes an
escape.*

—David Mura

ALLISON

lured from corngreen commons
to gather lilacs & poppies
to stuff into gun barrels

but May had a darker meaning
& Allison of the flowers
fell on parking lot asphalt
her heart ripped apart

& what of spring?

rash volley of unreason
massacred spring

the commons where her kitten sprang
after butterflies
lies barren now

it's the winter of the generals
who would march us
over flowerless fields
to seek out foe   brother

it's the killing cold
of a world gone mad

still   the boot   the bayonet
—Alex Gildzen, 1970

The tragedy of Kent State, another harrowing legacy of the Vietnam War, was a turning point for me—at some deep level I made a choice that I would pursue the meaning I found in poetry as a way to heal. Kent State made me see poetry as *the only human expression using words that holds real promise.* Why? Because it speaks the truth and goes to the heart. The thread running through my love for poetry is a sense of conscience, *a capacity to witness*. Witnessing is a form of healing compassion which reminds me we are each unique and that we are all in this together.

EXERCISE
Telling the Story of Your Turning Points

What awakens your conscience and evokes your passion for making a better and more just world? Consider your beliefs and feelings about peace and human rights, women's progress, hunger, environment and health care, economic and political justice, self-determination for oppressed people, the freedom to express oneself artistically and spiritually.

   Is there an event that was a turning point in your life, that shaped how you wanted to live in the world? How did that event affect you personally? How does concern for others affect you personally? What place does your spiritual belief have in how you respond to suffering? What words, images or symbols come to mind to represent these things? Write a poem about whatever compels your heart.

Something has to die in order for us to begin to know our truths. Perhaps we have to lose our national fantasies.
— *Adrienne Rich*

POEM-MAKING AS A WAY
TO WITNESS TO SORROW
AND LOVE

> We are one, after all, you and I;
> together we suffer,
> together we exist,
> and forever will re-create each other.
> —Pierre Teilhard de Chardin

In the early 1980s American soldiers were sent to Lebanon. A car bomb delivered by an extremist group exploded inside

＊

All great questions must be raised by great voices, and the greatest voice is the voice of the people—speaking out—in prose, or painting, or poetry, or music; speaking out in homes and halls, streets and farms, courts and cafés. Let that voice speak and the stillness you hear will be the gratitude of mankind.

—Robert F. Kennedy

One of the things that I believe happens when poets bear witness to historical events is that everyone they tell becomes a witness too, everyone that they tell also becomes responsible for what they have heard and what they now know.

—Carolyn Forché

their compound, killing hundreds of men and injuring many others.

I thought about the mothers and fathers of those soldiers. Men who came to secure peace were asleep, dreaming in their beds when they were killed. Those soldiers' deaths and injuries in Lebanon brought no less grief to their parents than the grief of the Kent State students' parents, or that of the parents of all those who fought in the Vietnam War, whether American or Vietnamese, or the grief of any parent at any time in history whose child has died in war. Grief was the common legacy of all these families.

Sorrows of war do not bleed away gloriously into the ground of muddy battlefields. Sorrows of war return to *a particular place;* they go to the homes of mothers and fathers. The same errors of war are made again and again leaving us with feeling of anger and hopelessness. Writing poetry to express such feeling serves as a witness to the horrible events that take place in our lifetimes. Poem-making assures that the human suffering associated with such events will not be forgotten.

Soon after this awful event in Lebanon, I spoke with a friend and commented how sad and horrific it was, how senseless it felt. Stephen said, *"It hurts to the marrow."* His words triggered this poem:

THE MARROW OF WHO I AM

*"Forgiveness is holiness, by forgiveness
the universe is held together"*
                    —Mahabharata

i

*I hear the sorrow of mothers
abruptly leave this world,
escaping into whatever sky is above the door
they open to solemn military men,
who bring bad news like an ancient Greek chorus.
Tears of anguish spill onto sofas*

that do not matter anymore.
Grief rips the heart from every home's
special dream, as each mother suddenly wakens
into that unknown moment when masks are removed.

ii

The marrow of who I am
is a tree struck by the lightning
of anger and sadness, shattering
heartwood upon the earth.

The marrow of who I am
is made by the only Mother
who stands simply at each and every door,
listening to love's undying cry
melt into her very heart.

The marrow of who I am
is always creating new blood,
a life innocent to this world,
safe in the mystery of forgivenesses home.

Sofa and empty sky are wet with grief and soaked with sounds of sorrow. The second section of the poem has a different voice. Lines of incantation. Lines of painful truth. Lines of love. The death of a shattered tree, the Mother at the door, the resurrecting Christ-like nature of our blood creating marrow bone. I am not sure I understand this voice, but through writing, I am reaching to feel empathy for the sorrow and love of shattered strangers. That marrow is the voice of witness to sorrow and lasting love.

Your poems will continue to speak to you and others over time; the best healing work of a poem may happen years after you write it, unexpectedly. So it was with *The Marrow of Who I Am* when I sensed it might be just the right poem to read to Linda Wray, a workshop participant.

*

Linda is a woman in her early fifties of deep presence and poise. For twenty years Linda was the legislative aide to a prominent state senator. Now she is a grandmother, advocate for victim's rights, and gifted massage therapist. *The Marrow of Who I Am* spoke healing words to Linda because her daughter Teresa had been murdered.

Losing a child is the greatest grief. The murder of a child takes a mother beyond grief. My twenty-four-year-old daughter, Teresa, was beaten, mutilated and then raped by the violent husband she had left three months before. The poem came when I began to enter the deepest level of pain about the death of my child. I would wake up every day over the next year with tears in my eyes.

COMES THE DAWN

Will there ever come a dawn
without her screams in my ears?

While night tears
Seep from the heart, escape the eyes
while the soul dies
even in my sleep

Teresa's death left me fighting for custody of her three young children in the same court system that had sentenced her murderer to eleven years, then plea-bargained to a mere five years. There was no emotional respite for my other three daughters, my grandchildren and myself as the murderer was released from prison, the state paying his court expenses and air fare enabling an unsuccessful attempt to reclaim his children.

An electrical surge struck my soul when I heard The Marrow of Who I Am. *Particularly the lines "The marrow of who I am/is a tree struck by the lightning/of anger and sadness, shattering/heartwood upon the earth." This poem expressed emotion I had thought inexpressible and connected me to the emotions of another. No other medium in my life provides such a soul-touching link as poetry. Writing and read-*

ing poetry heals me in a way that multitudes of grief recovery groups and self-help books could not.

When I wrote "High Sierras" and "The Rose" I was on the banks of Mammoth Lake with a fishing pole. As I watched icy silver slivers of water caress my trout line, I sat trancelike, cradled in the crisp cold of snow-capped mountains. Intense sun rays set my cheeks on fire and penetrated my parka, sweatshirt and thermal underwear. I was enveloped in the cycles of nature. I felt in those moments the cycles of human life, Teresa's life. An ocean of grief hovered over my heart—the Pacific where my Teresa's ashes were scattered. Birth, life, death, Sorrow. Joy in nature—Tranquility. Such intense conflicting emotions. I picked up my notebook and began to write. Only poetry could express what I was feeling.

HIGH SIERRAS AT MAMMOTH LAKE

Fed a blue jay yesterday
   fluorescent
   vibrant hue
settled on my cabin gate
   I thought of you

a wolf crept upon the porch last night
   his yellow eyes beckoned me peer
deep within the soul of him
   beyond
   his scary veneer

caught a rainbow trout this morning
vivid green, pink and gray
   your presence
   engulfed me
when I released you today

the squirrel is busy gathering crumbs
I've thrown beneath the tree
   here

✳

*As the mind sinks into the heart there
are moments when we feel how
inseparable we are and always have
been. Perhaps even a sense of
connection that existed even before we
were born, a sense of the deathlessness
of our essential oneness.*

—Stephen Levine

*in nature's company
    you seem
    less dead
    to me*

THE ROSE

*Two dates are painful
    above all the rest
There are rituals I do
so they will be blessed.*

*Plant a rosebush
and kiss its thorns*

*This I do
in the month you were born.*

*And cherish your spirit
    as each bud
    comes alive*

*all through June
the month
    you
    died*

✳
✳   When I look at those poems written during that time at Mammoth
✳   Lake, I realize again that I can live soul-fully, joy-fully, meaning-
✳   fully, with a broken heart.
✳

A NON-EXERCISE
Writing About Sorrow and Love

Linda needed no "exercise" to allow these poems to well up
from her depths. What she needed and found was a safe place

where she could be with herself, with her sorrow and her love for Teresa. She allowed herself to feel the beauty of that place and was open to words that came. This is not an exercise you can think about "doing." If you have sorrow that needs expressing, find a place where you can go to just be. A place where you feel safe. Listen for your inner voice with patience. Like Linda, feel the cycles and presence of nature. Using poem-making as a way to witness to what happens in your life will gradually allow your grief to find a voice, and strengthen your connections with everything that lives and dies.

POEM-MAKING TO HEAL SOCIETAL WOUNDS

> It is with words we begin
> to know where we are,
> the details of existence
> reveal our code of connection.
>
> —Kimberley Nelson

What "details of existence" move you to speak the truth from your heart? How can you develop your compassion through writing? Explore these three things and the relationship they have to one another:

* language/words
* your creative imagination
* the particulars of the world you live in.

Poem-making will allow you to experiment with blending these elements. They are as closely woven together as the skin, muscle, bones, nervous, circulatory and endocrine systems that form the fabric of your body.

Once again children, with their emotional transparency, are our best teachers. We learn not only from their playfulness but

*

Truthfulness, honor, is not something which springs ablaze of itself; it has to be created between people.

—Adrienne Rich

I think every language has a musical core. I call our language the American language rather than English because the sounds of American language come from all our different ethnic communities, and these sounds are beautiful to me.

—Quincy Troupe

from paying attention to their intense struggle to make sense of the chaotic world they live in.

The following poem is written by my friend Poet in the Schools teacher Kimberley Nelson. Kimberley writes about "at risk" high school students, who include children in gangs. The poem illustrates how the use of words, creative imagination and the particulars of one's world, help these children discover the power language has to give their lives meaning.

Kimberley challenges them in her poem to share stories with one another, to not forget their history or ignore their world. She insists they name the details of their lives. She wants them to be more aware of a world beyond their own. She helps them to find a personal voice that breaks the enforced silence of gangs and reveals a new way to understand their circumstances.

The children are amazed that anyone would write about them. That someone would feel they are important enough to write about! They appreciate that Kimberley notices what happens in their lives and understands the tremendous difficulties they face. This is a portion from Kimberley's poem about her students:

NO PLACE FOR SOLITUDE
(from a speech made by Chief Seattle)

My class does not know the name Chief Seattle
or where on earth Cambodia is.
Like blind spots in our memory
this poverty of knowledge is dangerous.

Who decided this is not important
for them to know?
We talk about pride,
we read the words that trace his tribe
though we perish we become the earth.

It is abstract.
This is high school.

So we study the story a girl tells
about herself
and Cambodia
in twenty-nine lines.
Land War. Spirit War.
"I am Cambodia," she writes.

It is with words we begin
to know where we are,
the details of existence
reveal our code of connection.

And there's a light in their eyes
when the silence is burned.
They can see all around themselves
the past, the present, and future.
We all begin to know;

Africa, Pajaro, the liquor store,
a basketball court, Grandmother's house, the park,
Watsonville, Antarctica, the rodeo, home

Where we live, and the lives of our minds,
our relationships to trees, animals, and buildings,
to clouds, rivers, and shootings,
to neighbors, and strangers, and war,
to loneliness and oranges, to ancestors and the morning.

We learn from our stories
erasing the blind spots
that make myths of our lives

For we depend on each other, like words
saw horse, rocking horse, sea horse
I take meaning from you
near you, around me, at my side—
There's no place dedicated to solitude.

Here is what Kimberley has to say about the subject of her poem:

The reason I talk to my students about Chief Seattle is because many of them are in gangs. The only way to get them to share their stories with me is to share other people's stories. There is a vow of silence in gangs. Silence hides gang activities, so clearly telling stories unravels that. The witnessing expressed in my poem is a righteous resistance to silence that harms us.

Chief Seattle's speech is about the pride and love he had for his tribe. My students relate to his feeling of pride. I want to show them that his pride went beyond his own life and beyond his own people. As he put it, his love, the love of his people, actually became the surroundings, the trees, the grass, the sky. No matter what was done to his people, there was no way to get rid of them because they were embodied in nature. Chief Seattle took pride way beyond what these gang children envision for themselves; he turned pride into love.

My poem explores how we, as individuals, are like words shaped into language; our meaning derives from our relationships to others. Telling our stories helps us to define those relations in our lives. We are as necessary to each other for meaning as words are to one another for making sense.

What is my students' reaction hearing each other's stories? To breaking their silence? They express excitement. I took stuff from their poems and put it into mine: shootings, the basketball court, and Grandmother's house. It turns out they want the truth to be told.

We can learn from these troubled kids and support their desire to speak the truth and change their lives. A poem written by Dwight reflects on his chaotic past and determination to create a positive future:

I look forward to an America which will reward achievement in the arts as we reward achievement in business and statecraft.

—John F. Kennedy

WAS—WILL—NOT

*I was a thief, a gaffler, a
Hustler, a savage,
A money making machine
that loved counting cabbage.*

I was a Juvenile delinquent
who loved getting into trouble,
I Loved standing on corners
selling rocks like Barney Rubble.
I'd run down the block yelling
"yabba dabba doo" I got thirty little
friends and they can all run faster
than you. But that was then
and this is Now.
And I will not
will not
will not
go down
By the hands of another
.Man.

       —Dwight Young

Usually these kids get in trouble for what they say, but through poem-making they learn how to tell their truths and still be heard. They are finding a way to say what they think and feel—which often contains a lot of anger—and still be respected.

EXERCISE
Writing a Poem of Witness

1. Notice people who are marginalized in our society. What is their world made of? Kimberley noticed this about her students: *Africa, Pajaro, the liquor store, / a basketball court, Grandmother's house, the park, / Watsonville, Antarctica, the rodeo, home / Where we live, and the lives of our minds.* Like Jack Hirschman's attention to the homeless woman, Terry Garvin, pay attention to the details in the life of individuals you ignore or avoid.

2. Imagine what asks for healing or attention in this individual. What do you offer? What do you learn from this interaction with them? Shape these questions and details about their life into a poem.

Living Your Language: John and Lisa

Toni Morrison received the Nobel Prize for literature in 1994 and at the award ceremony spoke about the profound part language plays in sustaining the quality of our lives:

> *Language alone protects us from the scariness of things with no names.*
> *Oppressive language does more than represent violence. It is violence. It*
> *does more than represent the limits of knowledge. It limits knowledge.*
> *We die. That may be the meaning of life. But we do language. That*
> *may be the measure of our lives.*

What does this making of language have to do with justice and the well-being of a community? Christopher Reeve liberates those words "family values" from the potentially divisive and oppressive use of that phrase, by simply stating: "We are all family and we all have value." Poetic voices in this chapter who "do language" make something clear: each of our voices makes a difference in the world, we each have imaginative power.

The following stories and poems are from people who make poem-making a part of their commitment to help heal society's ills. For each of them, a creative use of language is a measure of their lives. I think their stories will inspire you to use poetry as a way to witness to the troubling realities around you.

John Dooley: Bringing Poetry to Prison

I think the American people want the truth, and they know that very often they aren't getting it, not only in politics but in the kind of entertainment they're being fed. There's this incredible longing to find something that really matters and that really helps us in our lives.

—Rita Dove

John Dooley grew up in San Diego. His childhood memories are of the wide open sky, the sea and dreaming. John remembers teachers who taught him to live by his heart. His father took a job as a management consultant overseas while John was growing up and his family lived for years in countries like Bangladesh and Thailand. Languages of water and of sky and the culture of Bangladesh poured into his being and have affected his life ever since his return from Asia.

John, forty-one years old, works as a education counselor in the school at a jail in Virginia. He has worked there with the school's founder, Ed Rollins, since 1978. Rough-hewn and noble-looking at 6'7", John is someone you would not want to mess around with, unless you were burdened with poor judgment. It is, however, John's humility, dedication to service and passionate voice that are most compelling as he speaks about his work:

We call our school at the jail "The Education Community." The word community is important to us. Old-fashioned words like sharing, caring and giving are important. These are magic words we forget, especially in prison. One thing a person must do in prison: make an absolute choice to live or flow off into some destructive world. You see the results of your decisions immediately.

People say to me, "How can you take it?" but working in prison has taught me about my own life. Each breath of air or sip of beer or laughter or loving touch is . . . whew! Awesome! I bring that sense of gratitude for life into work. I tell inmates I am not free until they are. I use words like tenderness and caring. Poetic words shake some egos up. We ask the men to think and care. We stress verbal and physical non-violence. We ask them to listen. I see how difficult it is for them to listen to themselves. That is one of the bitterest blocks: listening. I say, try it. It's okay. Listen. Education is self-awareness: to look at yourself in a mirror and to see yourself; to see that other people will be in your mirror, too. That's where sharing and caring come in. That's where writing becomes so important.

I say to them: writing will help you if you are not sure how to act, or if you feel mistrustful and angry. I suggest to them that if they write about it first, it might not come out the wrong way later to their neighbor or they might not say something damaging to a judge or parole officer.

Poetry can be anything: excitement about a single vocabulary word can be your poem. I tell them anything you do or share or give is your poem to write.

Each day is horrible in prison. There is nothing good in there. But sometimes, the insights in our hearts and souls will teach us. We start off with their everyday thoughts. I tell inmates: "Write your heart down."

Being a human being without forgiveness is like being a guitarist without fingers or being the diva without a tongue.

—Jimmy Santiago Baca

*

Poetry has a great digestive system and can consume and recycle almost anything.

—Stanley Kunitz

Writing clears a lot of mud and scum and abuse and anger. They see it in the writing and have no choice but to deal with it.

Every day we have conversations about the power of words. I encourage them to play with words. They'll create their own word and I'll make up a meaning. They get a glimmer of what it is like to create rather than destroy. Words can be fun, simple old-fashioned fun. They are powerful, too.

The passion and clear-eyed wisdom which John brings to his work as a teacher in prison is also apparent in his poem *A Prison Sharing.* In the poem he witnesses both the prisoners' lives and his own.

> within soul-less fog
> i,
> a tree   sipping
> walk, and ask
> "How might i talk with my Soul?"
>
> within a pit
> i,
> a dreamer upon the lips of the sky,
> breathe
> "Is what matters a good Heart and a
> compassionate service?"
>
> within human attack
> i,
> a stranger who always asks, "Show me Love!"
> remember my POW grandfather
> (who, upon returning after 5 long years, only
> shook my mom's twelve-year-old hand, in
> silence),
> and pray
> "Am I listening?"

within mind—assault
i,
a fragile wing seeking home,
balance and choose
"Is there love in my Heart?"

within skylessness
i,
a river refusing to burn,
offer
"How, with a shared joy, can i Be who i am?"

within the "In here there is no why!"–ness
i,
choosing thanksgiving
    balance
        a spiritual way,
give windows
    heart
        attention
            place
               audacity
               love
and ask
"Am i kind and tolerant and do i share goodwill?"

within a world of no-children, no-flowers
i
stand on the edge of my soul,
knowing your Soul.

[*the door closes behind me.*
     i'm going home now
     i have left them Behind, where I can't
     Be.
     Why do YOU want to Be in   here
     there?   ]

Lisa: Wearing Someone Else's Skin

Nursery rhymes, lullabies, jumprope jingles—the first poems in Lisa's life—bonded her to her mother, to her mother tongue, to intergenerational cultural rhythms. Childhood poems moved her body with their musical properties long before she moved language from her head into her hand and onto paper.

Lisa's paternal grandmother, a concert pianist, accompanied her untutored and ferocious dancing during her early years. She recalls the thrill of "The Hall of the Mountain King," in a section of *Peer Gynt*, which she asked her grandmother to play over and over again. The music impassioned her, not only through its mysterious melody, bewitching phrases and compelling rhythms, but also by its story. The journey into an unknown realm had "every muscle in my body vibrating with fear and stretching with curiosity."

As her life story unfolded, she danced, choreographed, taught dance, utilized movement as a therapeutic medium, wrote dance criticism and poems about dance. A sudden move to the West Coast eclipsed her fifteen-year-dance career. She earned degrees in movement therapy and clinical social work. She says, "It took another five years to understand what happened, and to emerge from my grievous loss of identity, purpose, and creative expression." Lisa says:

Writing poems showed me that I could channel my creative and expressive energies into language. It took me some time, however, to express my inner voice as honestly in words as I had in movement. For me, this creative transformation offered the developmental progress I'd already navigated as an infant and toddler speaking first through gesture and sound and then discovering the power of naming things and building narrative contexts in which I could organize my perceptions of the world.

My empathic experience of clients' stories can sometimes feel quite painful. Writing poetry about these experiences offers me an opportunity to gain some helpful detachment while crystallizing some of my impressions.

We discover our inner visions by bodying them forth . . . we body forth our ideals in personal acts . . . we body forth felt experiences in a poem's image and sound. We body forth our inner residence in the architecture of our homes and common buildings. We body forth our struggles and our revelations in the space of theatre. That is what form is: the bodying forth.

—M. C. Richards

I wrote a poem about Sarah, a newly married young woman with a bone condition called fibrous dysplasia. One night she limped painfully up the stairs to my office. As the tears trekked down her cheeks, she clutched her fists, describing her anger at people who expected her to move as quickly as they moved, accomplish tasks with more alacrity than she could manage. In truth, Sarah denied herself permission to confide her pain and ask for the consideration that she needed. She put her perception of other's needs before her own. The next day I wrote this poem, the closest I could get to wearing Sarah's skin and walking in her specially constructed shoes:

SMALL STEPS

Her bones confuse themselves,
hold soft and spongy parts that break.
The architecture of her life goes up
around a structure she can't count on.
Each step carries the full weight
of her eyes and heart and hope.
She feels each ragged edge of sidewalk,
each crack and puncture of the asphalt
as a challenge to stay whole.
She holds her steps like rosary beads,
smooth as syllables in a prayer.
She gets through each day on vigilance and faith,
shutting pain in the top floor of her soul
to pace and puff against the door.
She finds a witness in me,
someone to retell her story to her—
        no better ending
        nor a solid foundation—
with breath between the lines,
a heartbeat in the metre,
and a voice that moves beside her own.

This poem allowed me to recognize that my understanding of Sarah, my documentation of her suffering and the way she construed it, had important healing components. No, I couldn't remove her physical pain or the insensitivity of others in her work environment, but I could help channel her anger into assertiveness, and voice out loud what I heard between the lines so that she could create a more responsive context for herself. Interestingly, the week I wrote this poem, Sarah had also written poems, applied to audition for a music group, and gone swimming three times. I took great joy in witnessing Sarah's self-nurturing and healing potential move into the kinetic realm.

Writing poems offers me the possibility of attending, in great detail, to the very particular experience of another, while allowing me to own and nourish my own parallel processes. In reflecting back a person's rough edges, idiosyncratic thoughts, and courageous acts, perhaps I can facilitate both self-examination and self-love.

EXERCISE
Expressing Another Person's Struggle

Poetry is a conversation with the world; poetry is a conversation with the words on the page in which you allow those words to speak back to you; and poetry is a conversation with yourself.

—*Naomi Shihab Nye*

John and Lisa write poems in response to the hardships of people they come into contact with through their work. Writing poems allows them to witness to the struggles of other people. This is an enriching and healing experience, and you can do this kind of poem-making as well.

Write a poem about someone you know in a way that helps you to become more keenly aware of their struggle or difficulty. Find sound, rhythms, details and images to describe what this person is going through. What does this person's experience tell you about yourself?

THERE IS A SECRET ONE INSIDE US

Using Your Spiritual Voice to Heal

There is a Secret One inside us;
the planets in all the galaxies
pass through his hands like beads.

That string of beads one should look at with luminous eyes.

—*Kabir*

FINDING SACRED POEMS:
SOMETHING CLOSE
TO HOME

> The lesson which life repeats and constantly enforces is
> "look under foot." You are always nearer the divine and the
> true sources of your power than you think. The lure of the
> distant and difficult is deceptive. The great opportunity is
> where you are. Do not despise your own place and hour.
> Every place is under the stars, every place is of the world.
> —John Burroughs

You may or may not think of yourself as being spiritual, yet you feel compassion for the world. You may see how things relate and work together with sharp clarity. You may have a relationship with a meditation practice and/or teacher that is integral to your daily life. You may want to live simply, with integrity, to act in a way that helps your family, yourself and others to grow. You may walk the earth with wonder and reverence. You may feel uncertain and unsatisfied much of the time, longing for something more. You may wake up each day to discover more about yourself, more about life. You may feel all or some of these things at different points in your life.

Something *is* sacred about each of these experiences, and poem-making can help you to express that. But even more significantly, poem-making will help you to deepen your connection with what is at the center of all of these experiences, with your own center, with whatever name you give to universal mystery.

Making this connection will directly support your healing process. Why? What we most need to heal is not necessarily found in a new therapy, drug or diet. Those things might help

★

us to be more healthy; they might even cure us. All kinds of things are valuable in sustaining the quality of our lives and improving our health. But to heal, to begin to open to some sense of our wholeness—whether we are "cured" or not—whether or not we resolve a particular physical or emotional problem, seems to require that we give attention to this sacred mystery.

The particular situation you want to heal, whatever it is, can be related through poem-making to what Kabir called that "Secret One inside." Through his Psalms, David shares with God his full range of suffering and joy. The Psalms are a powerful example of sacred poem-making:

You cannot avoid paradise. You can only avoid seeing it.

—Charlotte Joko Beck

PSALM 86

> *Bow down Your ear, O Lord*
>   *hear me;*
> *For I am poor and needy.*
> *Preserve my life, for I am holy;*
> *You are my God;*
> *Save Your servant who trusts in You!*
> *Be merciful to me, O Lord,*
> *For I cry to You all day long.*
> *Rejoice the soul of Your servant,*
> *For You, O Lord, are good, and ready to forgive,*
> *And abundant in mercy to all those who call upon You.*

Poetry is the voice of the soul, whispering, celebrating, singing even.

—Carolyn Forché

David sings: "For I am poor and needy/Preserve my life, for I am holy." Although he is in extreme need, David does not forget that he is also holy—whole—and with this attitude he calls for God's intercession. As we discussed in Chapter One, paradoxes are beautifully contained within the vessel of a poem. That vessel is helpful to us when addressing our particular need for healing within a spiritual context. It can increase our awareness of our spiritual wholeness, even as we struggle with our pain and distress.

Poets from other sacred traditions also express this mysterious connection, this paradox of brokenness and wholeness. The following verses are by two Japanese women poets:

The way I must enter
leads through darkness to darkness—
O moon above the mountains' rim,
please shine a little further
on my path
                          —*Izumi Shikibu*

Although the wind
blows terribly here,
the moonlight also leaks
between the roof planks
of this ruined house
                          —*Izumi Shikibu*

Merely to know
The Flawless Moon dwells pure
   In the human heart
Is to find the Darkness of the night
Vanished under clearing skies.
                          —*Kojiju*

The moon is the image of enlightenment. That enlightenment is the center to which *all* experiences are related. These women recognized that their path of awakening was reflected in and sustained by the constant presence and cycles of the moon. Like David's awareness of his connection with God, these poets were aware of an essential wholeness, even though it is often made apparent by something as mundane as light shining through broken planks. They understood that the "Flawless Moon," or enlightenment, shines within the human heart.

The Japanese poems help us to understand the interplay of darkness and light in our lives, and to incorporate this under-

Y*et ruined as my house is, you live* *there!*

                          —*Thomas Merton*

✦

standing into our process of healing. Making poems which acknowledge your spiritual core is a transformative act that will
help you to heal.

You do not have to begin by writing either a Psalm or Zen
satori poem! A simple metaphor or image, drawn from your
own experience, may express your healing need and help you
to make your spiritual connection.

NAMING YOUR SPIRITUAL IMAGE: "I AM A SNOWFLAKE"

Mary TallMountain was born along the Yukon River in 1918.
Taken from her home by missionaries at the age of six because
of an outbreak of tuberculosis among her family and the
Koyukon people of her village of Nulato, Mary wrote poems
from midlife until her death in 1994. Her vibrant poems frequently referred to her roots and answered a deep ache she felt
in that early loss of home:

> *I am a snowflake. I drift*
> *into the dappled green depths*
> *of Mother Yukon*
> *with a thousand others.*
> *We melt and mingle,*
> *dancing the ancient circles.*
> *—Mary TallMountain*
> *from* Listen to the Night

The simple and universal image of the snowflake holds Mary's
individual longing to return "home." This is the spiritual genius
of poetic imagery. A poetic image makes it possible to express
spirituality in a way that is in tune with *your* inspiration and
needs. The universality of such images penetrates deeply and is
easily understood. Like Mary's snowflake in the Yukon, such images are found close to home. You can find them for yourself.

EXERCISE
Writing Sacred Poems Using Symbols, Image and Metaphor

Write a poem that includes a symbol, image or metaphor that
links or identifies you with something that is sacred to you.
Choose an image that feels attuned to your healing needs right
now. What will soothe or strengthen you? What will lighten
your heart or nourish you? You can use the metaphoric phrase
"I am . . ." or you can integrate this image or symbol into the
body of whatever poem you write. Free associate with the images you choose. Use all your senses to experience them. Examples might include:

star	rock	dove	river	lotus	flame
rose	bread	moon	roots	owl	breath

Come up with your own words that signify your connection to
the spiritual.

Phyllis Browne works for the Special Commission of the
United Nations. She wrote in a workshop:

I am a spark of fire.
My ancestors formed the molten center of the earth,
I dance among the tongues of bonfires,
leap at the hearthside,
gently warm the evening supper,

I slumber in the smouldering sunset campfire.
I am the flame of love igniting hearts,
the spark of inspiration that fires creative thought,
the fuel for dreams, desires, great causes.

Lighter and brighter, surer and purer,
a reflective facet of the Great Fire that is God,
I burn constantly, steadily, unquenchably, everlastingly,
a tiny beacon . . . shining everybody home.
                                        —*Phyllis Browne*

*The poet having to bring home
something, even in things common,
which is not obvious to surface
experience, avails himself of image,
symbol, whatever is just, beautiful,
meaningful, suggestive.*

—*Sri Aurobindo*

*

EXERCISE
Making a Poem of Spiritual Memory

Your connection with wholeness can be accessed through *re-membrance*. Hinduism, or what is known in India as "Sanatam Dharma" or the "Eternal Religion," says that *smriti*, or "divine memory," is within us all. This memory is ancient—but not like an artifact unearthed from antiquity. This is a "soul memory" of your original nature. Like an olive tree that continues to bear olives for thousands of years, this memory is alive in you now.

Write a poem that tells a remembrance of your divine origins. Use "I remember . . ." as a bridge to your soul memory. What will give you the guidance you need to access this memory? Consider your needs with regard to healing and enter those images that arise spontaneously within you. Trust that your soul memory will help guide you. Phyllis Baldwin, a therapist in Denver, Colorado, writes a poem of remembrance that is sensual and energetic:

> *I remember singing blood flowing into passionate seas.*
> *I remember silent flowers shouting of love—mouths and hearts open.*
> *I remember deep cathedral forests filled with mystery and moisture.*
> *I remember crystal autumns reflecting back the heat of summer—*
> *   red and yellow.*
> *I remember being an old woman, mother of my child, pregnant with*
> *   dark sorrows, love and laughter.*
> *I remember Light that endures, penetrates all limits and containers.*
> *   —Phyllis Baldwin*

I remember _____

I remember _____

I remember _____

Symbol, metaphor and remembrance—these are routes of return to that sacred place you've known before and where you may return "as if for the first time."

*W*e cannot discover ourselves
without first discovering the universe,
the earth, and the imperatives of our
own being.

*   —Thomas Berry*

RETURNING TO THE SACRED THROUGH LOVE, BEAUTY, WISDOM AND ECSTASY

There are states of being that evoke spiritual connection and can help rebalance us emotionally and physically. At times, beauty will help us most to heal, and at other times, we may need to call on wisdom to guide us toward healing. Is your heart constrained and creating problems in your relationships? Reading poets who express a deep love may help you to become aware of love's pathways, to grow sensitive to the language and poetic insight love evokes. You can then use your own poem-making to express, distill and integrate loving into your life so that your heart, rather than feel walled-in, may begin to open once again. We'll explore love, beauty, wisdom and ecstasy from this healing perspective, noticing how they are expressed in the poem-making of four people.

There are many things that call us out of ourselves and, in the moment we transcend our own boundaries, open us to the presence of the Beloved, to the background call of the cosmos.

—David Spangler

Love

> In the calm water of the love-nights,
> where you were begotten, where you have begotten,
> a strange feeling comes over you
> when you see the silent candle burning.
>
> Now you are no longer caught
> in the obsession with darkness,
> and a desire for higher love-making
> sweeps you upward.
>
> —Goethe

Love extends outward toward something or someone—and devotional love is giving of oneself *wholly* to what is beloved. This giving is not just in thought or word, but also in action.

✳

This upward sweep of loving reveals more of who we are and helps us to heal. Is there someone in your life you've wanted to love more? We can practice giving voice to love. Words of such devotional poems are often simple. Ellen Grace O'Brian wrote this poem about her son:

SOMETIMES AT NIGHT

Sometimes at night
a light shines, here,
in the middle of my chest
and I see you
Innocence is your face
Everything you have ever done
washes up
on this shore of love
you walk through it all
breathe in the salt air
step across the tangled kelp
enter another life.

Poems of devotion reveal that love is about gathering in *and* letting go. They often focus on a particular moment or experience of loving someone, using that moment to embody or signify something greater. Ellen reflects on the experience behind her poem:

When I wrote this poem I was thinking of my teenage son. My thoughts were concerned with recognizing his unique pattern of growth into adulthood and his separation from me. It's a huge letting go for me as a mother. The light shining in the middle of my chest is connected with my surrender to unconditional love for him and the bodily felt knowing of this love.

This letting go is about my faith in his connection with the Cosmic Mother and Father. The poem includes all the people I love. I brought to my heart all the other faces in my life. My son, like these other people, has his own path.

Poem-making makes it possible to touch my experience and the way I am in the world. There is a softening of my heart. The poem is a sacred memory that I carry into all my relationships. That is why writing a poem is so valuable. It is a vessel. The lines in my poem

> *breathe in the salt air*
> *step across the tangled kelp*
> *enter another life*

are about seeing my son's innocence; it is seeing my experience of letting go of an old relationship and opening to a new one with the light of the heart.

E X E R C I S E
Writing to Someone You Love or Whom You Feel Is Loving

Consider someone you love or feel devoted to; or someone you experience as possessing the quality of deep love and devotion. Bring a clear image of that person into your heart. Breathe deeply there with that person in mind and write to the person about your love—or about the devotional or loving person he or she is. What colors, tastes, sounds, symbols, feelings or images come to mind? Let the poem take on a life of its own and tell you about love.

Give a gift to your brother, but there's no gift to compare with the giving of assurance that he is the golden eternity. The true understanding of this would bring tears to your eyes. The other shore is right here, forgive and forget, protect and reassure.

—Jack Kerouac

Beauty

> Consider the lilies, for they neither toil nor reap. Yet
> Solomon in all his glory was not arrayed as one of these.
>
> —Jesus

Hollywood movie stars and racks of glossy magazine covers attempt to define beauty in our culture. But what is beauty *for you?* Psychology and medicine rarely acknowledge how beauty helps heal our psyches and souls. How has beauty helped to heal your life?

✴

Jesus often encouraged people to pay attention to something fairly subtle, as poets do. His poetic example of lilies is intended to emphasize faith in God's care for us; but his instruction to his followers may also be to make a place for beauty in their lives—and to consider what beauty conveys about what has value.

Noëlle Morris is a professional dancer and massage therapist. Her poem shows that for her beauty is not some ideal outside herself but something within her that is also found in the world. For Noëlle, beauty, and creating beauty, is what connects her to the Divine.

RUAH

> The Wind of the seaside slope blows my own Breath;
> The same Spirit which colors flowers
> and inspires the Life I feel between my Body
> which allows me to remember the Sadness
> of the lone girl walking through the Wind-
> swept slope beside the sea.

I continued to look at the flowers and in their living light I seemed to detect the qualitative equivalent of breathing—but of a breathing with no return to a starting point, with no recurrent ebbs, only a repeated flow from beauty to heightened beauty, from deeper to deeper meaning.

—Aldous Huxley

Noëlle says of her poem:

This experience came to me in the middle of the night. I was lingering between waking and sleeping. I saw my breath coloring flowers. I thought, "This isn't how things are in reality," but this is exactly how I perceived color happening and it seemed perfectly natural. The title of the poem is significant. "Ruah," in Hebrew, means breath-wind-spirit, it's all one word.

It was like those watercolor books I had as a kid—you put water on the page and color appears! I breathed and color appeared in flowers. If you move the breath in your body through yoga or massage, things start to happen. Breath moves and the body blooms information. I attend to that breath in both massage and dance.

I like the preposition "between" in speaking about the Life I feel because it's an impossible placement and it leaves my relationship to the divine elusive and in motion. As a dancer, a sense of placement is very important to me—where am I? Where is my breath? Is it in the flowers? Is it in me?

As the beauty of the wind and breath and spirit clears the density of my consciousness. I re-member (know again in my body) a very old sadness. It rises as a cry from deep within my body: uh—Uh—UH . . . I am ALIVE! While tasting this Life in full color, I can perceive with clarity the times and spaces where my deep longing for rich communion and joyful expression has remained in shadow, colorless and without motion.

The full movement of breath, echoed in the movement of my poem, is my journey towards wholeness. Movement is my active longing for the Divine. Without tasting some discomfort, such as this longing and loss, there can be little motivation for movement.

The function of poetry is not to teach truth of any particular kind, nor indeed to teach at all, nor to pursue knowledge, nor to serve any kind of religious or ethical aim, but to embody beauty in the word and give delight.

—Sri Aurobindo

The recognition of beauty in language is healing. The ancient Greeks said that "beautiful language" could induce *sophrosyne,* or a state of stability in psychic life. It is within that settled and steady presence felt in the body and mind that wisdom begins to emerge.

Wisdom

There are no holy places and no holy people, only holy moments, only moments of wisdom.

—Jack Kornfield

Wisdom means "to see" or "to know." It does not mean knowing facts or having an opinion. Wisdom is uncovered by being present enough to perceive the essence of your whole experience. This wisdom will help you attend to what matters in your life and understand the meaning of your life's changes. The practice of moment-to-moment *presence* is key. Seeing essence; knowing wholeness.

Poem-making helps to put your attention in the present moment. Line-by-line, breath-by-breath, moment-by-moment, you allow creative rhythms, sounds, feelings and insights to come. You learn to distinguish between a fresh insight and an

We invent nothing, truly. We borrow and re-create. We uncover and discover. All has been given, as the mystics say. We have only to open our eyes and hearts, to become one with that which is.

—Henry Miller

*

old conclusion when considering an answer to a problem you
face. Robert Frost said: "I have never started a poem yet whose
end I knew." This openness to the moment which poem-making encourages can help you discover answers you had no idea
were there.

Poem-making practiced as a method of discovery is nurtured
by patience. The practice of patience is what poet and journal-
writing teacher Nina Holzer calls "patient observation." We
don't know where our writing is headed, but we pay attention.
We make a quiet place within us to observe. A language of surprise comes to us not by acquired knowledge but through authentic growth. That can take time, but as successive rings mark
a tree's new year around the sun, wisdom will enter into your
writing.

Jim Fadiman is a transpersonal psychologist and teacher. He
has taught engineering and does business consulting. Poetry
doesn't affect his life often, but when it does he knows something important is happening. His poem *Illusions* began as the
result of heartache.

ILLUSIONS

There are no ex-lovers,
Only candles with wicks close-trimmed,
Glowing in vast spaces
Their light once filled.

There are no broken hearts,
Only places inside souls,
Where pain, stitched over,
leaves fine scars.

There are no lives lost,
Only times of separation,
As seeds fall from trees,
Asking no more than soft moist earth
To begin again.

Jim's poem distills an understanding that only real life cooks up:

*I wrote this while trying to pull myself up from a small pool of self-pity
I was sitting in. I was feeling bereft because a loving relationship seemed
to be ending. I was trying also to reopen real communications with an
old flame who was friendly, but so distant that I couldn't even get close
enough to be rebuffed.*

    *The first lines had crept into my mind the day before. I couldn't get
them to go away. I said them to my cordial but detached friend. She
said, "Yes, there's a poem in you. Find it."*

    *The rest of it burst forth that evening, truly catching me by surprise.
Then I could see what I was saying to myself was that "love never
dies." I never had any idea what that meant to me until I'd spelled it out
for myself.*

    *I recall vividly one other incident that this poem finally brought to
full awareness. Years earlier I'd had a serious car accident and was
badly banged up, graduating from a hospital to home care to an electric
wheelchair on my way toward recovery. Near Thanksgiving I received
a call from my high-school sweetheart. We'd parted with total misun-
derstandings and hadn't spoken for more than fifteen years. She heard of
my accident and called, because as she said (and I have to stop and
center myself, even to repeat it here), "We love so few people in our
whole lives, it is foolish to lose touch with any of them." Since then, she
and I have stepped over our apart years and are close again. She is
friends with my wife and children as well.*

    *I was blessed with her caring enough to track me down and give me
that lesson. The poem brought her wisdom into my present situation so
clearly that I felt awakened and freed. I was able to say aloud to myself
what I needed to remember—that the pain of feeling unloved is also, in
a wonderful redeeming way, always, at least in part, an illusion.*

    Wisdom does not fill us up with special knowledge others
lack; rather, it offers us the opportunity to understand what
lasts, to recognize life's illusions, and to place our personal experiences and difficulties in a larger context.

*A single atom of the sweetness of
wisdom in a man's heart is better than
a thousand pavilions in Paradise.*

        —Abu Yazid al-Bistami

✳

Ecstasy

My eyes are radiant with your spirit;
my nostrils fill with your fragrance.
My ears delight in your music,
and my face is covered with your dew.
Blessed are the men and women
who are planted in your garden.
who grow as your trees and flowers grow,
who transform their darkness to light.
Their roots plunge into darkness;
their faces turn toward the light.

—from *Odes of Solomon*

Solomon's experience of ecstasy is possible for us to experience as well. You may feel a sense of joyful rootedness when you're: Walking with someone you love. Receiving a child into your arms. Speaking with courage and honesty. Standing in a natural place. Working on something you care deeply about. Making love with someone. Singing to God. Feeling the delight of simple things. Sitting in meditation.

Even if we feel or glimpse this sense of joy, it is often difficult to find a way to sustain it in our lives. We live in a culture addicted to frenzy and transitory excitement. Ersatz "ecstasy"—howling at football games, winning the lottery, going wild on New Year's Eve, buying consumer products that promise to make us wildly powerful or alluring—these are not adequate replacements for authentic bliss and wildness—we know this.

The shadow side of such unfulfilled experiences contains depression, boredom and a feeling of emptiness. The message of poets is that we can find the miraculous *within* and experience the spontaneous connection to joy that is always available wherever we are. Sensuousness, spontaneity and curiosity, which are all part of poem-making, help us to slow down and notice the exquisite details of life; to break free and reclaim for ourselves a joy that wells up from within. Laura Golden Bellotti wrote a lovely poem about an afternoon walk that held ecstasy

I think we all have a core that's ecstatic, that knows and that looks up in wonder. We all know that there are marvelous moments of eternity that just happen. We know them.

—*Coleman Barks*

for her. In it she contrasts her spontaneous feeling of what is
holy with the reserve of formal religion.

THE RABBIS DO NOT LOOK AT ME

The rabbis do not look at me
but I am allowed to look at them
walking sober down the drizzling street
in broad-brimmed black hats and long black coats
careful eyes averting mine
pious eyes shunning mine
frightened eyes protesting mine
          that peer out recklessly beneath my black umbrella.

The rabbis cannot carry an umbrella
because it is Saturday
and it would be considered work
just as forbidden as looking at me
at my Jewish face
at my female face
at my unfaithful face
          exalted by the theft of three wet birds of paradise.

The rabbis turn their heads as I walk awestruck
past a small, homely house
gone wild with holy purple weeds
spilling purple dangerously
smearing purple over every wall of the tiny home
transforming the dwelling into a house of God's purple
a frenzy of forbidden radical glory
          the color of a cheap girl's lips.
                    —Laura Golden Bellotti

*The invariable mark of wisdom is
seeing the miraculous in the common.*
                    —Ralph Waldo Emerson

You can learn to evoke and express beauty, wisdom, love and
ecstasy by reading poets like Emily Dickinson, James Wright,
Rabindranath Tagore, Denise Levertov and Rumi. They represent only a handful of poets who write of the sacred. Their po-

*The continuous emergence of the God
beyond God is the mark of creative
courage in the religious sphere.*
                    —Rollo May

✳

ems speak to healing particular needs, and to a profound awareness of our holiness and oneness with the sacred. These poems
emit a state of consciousness that is meditative and have the potential to evoke meditative awareness in readers.

MEDITATION AND POEM-MAKING: PATHWAYS TO SILENCE, THE INNER VOICE AND THE UNKNOWN

> For each true poem born
> there is an origin;
> blessed ignorance of words that turn
> to splendid fire
> as stars in space will yearn
> to find on earth their upstretched twin.
> —John Fox

When meditation and poem-making are interwoven, it can be a
profoundly healing experience. Meditation enables you to listen more closely to your intuitive voice. Listening in this way
can inspire you to make healing poems—poems which reach
those places within you that need your attention.

Once a month for over ten years I've gathered with three to
seven people to sit and meditate for an hour and a half. We explore three mysteries of life:

* silence
* our inner voice
* the unknown

The thing we tell of can never be found seeking, yet only seekers find it.
—Abu Yazid al-Bistami

Specific similarities exist between meditative practice and
processes of healing, creativity and poem-making. As with
everything else in nature, silence, inner voice and the unknown
are not separate from one another; they are interdependent,

weaving together like threads in a single tapestry. These meditative elements can help in our healing and make our everyday
living more meaningful.

Silence

> Entrancement stills
> the active mind
> and realigns
> the inner self
> with the silent power
> of the tao.
> —Ellery Littleton

Observing silence is a way to quiet the mind and create a
place within yourself to *receive* language from deep levels of feeling. This receptive place where silence lives is found within the
heart—not your physical heart but what is known in yoga as
the fourth chakra, or spiritual heart. Yogis say this center is
found two finger-widths to the left of the breastbone in the center of your chest. Deepening silence within yourself nudges
your heart to open; which in turn makes receptivity to your inner voice more accessible and natural.

Meditative silence is like the lustre of green summer grass; to
appreciate this living silence, learn to listen actively. Enter into
silence and let it drink you.

*P*oetry comes out of silence and
yearns for silence. Like man himself, it
travels from one silence to another. It
is like flight, like a circling over
silence.

—Max Picard

> Elected Silence, sing to me
> And beat upon my whorlèd ear,
> Pipe me to pastures still and be
> The music that I care to hear.
> —Gerard Manley Hopkins

There is also nakedness to silence. Vulnerability can be troubling if one is accustomed to using layers of words to create an
identity in the world or to surround oneself with activity to

*

There is something nearer to us than Scriptures, to wit, the Word in the heart from which all Scripture comes.
                    —*William Penn*

avoid looking inside. To be with naked silence you must hold reverence for your anxiety, even your fear, because silence invites the unknown and that may not always seem like welcome company.

Loneliness might be felt when you enter meditative silence; loneliness that causes you to shy away from going deeper into silence. I've felt loneliness when meditating, but developing a relationship with silence allows me to see loneliness in a new way: it is sometimes a message for me to listen to silence *even more deeply.* This is difficult to do at first, because it is the opposite of what I feel comfortable doing. The more I relate with silence, however, the more it seems possible for loneliness to change and become a more complete feeling: *a sense of aloneness or solitude.* There is peace in solitude. Even when loneliness lingers, meditative silence encourages me, like seeing a companion waiting just ahead on the path, turning to call me.

Silence contains a whole landscape of inner space and inner time. You can spread out joyfully in your creative mind without any walls encroaching. Silence creates a kind of magical stage on which anything can happen.

A line of a poem might appear spontaneously as you waken or turn the corner on your way home. A foggy memory that compels you may suddenly come to clarity in an image imbued with feeling. Thoughts may take the entire floor of your magic stage as you see how they turn, jump and dance together.

If one does not rush to fill up the silence with small talk and busy activity, attention to inner silence often produces something simple and wondrous, something almost impossible: the rare insight, the acknowledgment of something frail and true, the solution to a problem you've hammered on too much and too long.

Inner Voice

> In writing poetry, all one's attention is focused on some inner voice.
>
> —Li-Young Lee

Your inner voice is not like the outer voice. The outer voice forms itself from genetic coding, early contact with the voices of others, intellect, emotion and geography. It is conditioned by belief and experience. Your outer voice takes shape as you hone talents and skills; it develops as you grow toward maturity. Your outer voice evolves from gurgling sounds of infancy to the words of your grown-up self. By contrast, the inner poetic voice has a timeless and unconditional quality; its archetype is the wise woman and sage. These old souls come into the world already complete; they are with us—and within us. This inner voice may come in different guises and has access to the secrets of humankind, the universe, and to your unique pathway through the world. The inner voice may tell us that awareness of our oneness with the sacred is our truest healing.

> *Remember the wind. Remember her voice. She knows the origins of this universe. Remember that you are all people and that all people are you.*
>
> *—Joy Harjo*

This intuitive wisdom already knows and bestows its guidance on you and in you. It is not necessarily verbal in expression: it speaks to you as knots in the belly, knocks on the heart's door, shivers up the spine, as a line of poetry that bursts into your ear coming from God knows where. Your inner voice finds creative ways to communicate with you, and this can be crucial to your healing experience.

The springs of the truest prayer and the deepest poetry, twin expressions of man's outward-going passion for that Eternity which is his home, rise very near together in the heart.

—Evelyn Underhill

When we are not sure, we are alive.

—Graham Greene

ENCOUNTER

Just down from the mountain, she has visions.
Just out of the forest, she has dreams.
Just off of the desert, she has omens.
Just into the harbor, she has songs.
Hungry, dirty, tired, unsteady on her feet,
*   she comes to tell.*
She spies my soul nestled in my listening ear
*   and fills it.*
"With this gift," she smiles, "you'll never
*   be the same."*

—Barbara Gellert

Your inner voice might speak to you as leaden heels and a fur-rowed brow—indications of a wise reluctance to enter a situation that is not good for you, or it may express as open-handed willingness to say "yes" to something new. Your inner voice may synthesize complexities of science and art into a few simple lines, get you somewhere on time, give you a prayer or answer one, show you something beautiful you've ignored for too long. All of these cues are "languages" spoken by the inner voice. Your inner voice is beyond the conscious mind's ability to capture, but you can listen for it as you become still, silent, and more trusting of the unknown in your life.

The Unknown

I love the dark hours of my being
in which my senses drop into the deep.
I have found in them, as in old letters,
my private life, that is already lived through,
and become wide and powerful now, like legends.
Then I know that there is room in me
for a second huge and timeless life.

—Rainer Maria Rilke

Most times in life we want to know what we are doing and where we are going. We have applied to enough job interviews, traveled in enough unfamiliar places and taken enough tests to believe that being prepared for the unknown is the best strategy. When it comes to creativity and tapping our deepest healing resource, however, the unknown is best approached with willingness to let go of our knowing.

We don't venture into the unknown in poverty. We can enter into it with our basic principles intact. We may bring with us the essence of what we love in life. But it's like meeting someone for the first time—most of all, we just need to show up with some interest and go from there. In bringing our problems to this spiritual dimension, we do not know what answers we will receive. The interesting question is: what will we discover?

One doesn't discover new lands without consenting to lose sight of the shore for a very long time.

—André Gide

The Stranger

You are a stranger to me
But I know you, know you
we traveled together once
were we two old men
or two young boys
I can't remember now

We rode the turtles of summer
deep into the lake

We warmed at fires at night
broken applewood in the snow

When I die
I want to be buried
with you
and my dog
and my toys of childhood.
—Lawrence Tirnauer

*

Trust shows the way.

     —Hildegard of Bingen

Larry doesn't *know* how he knows this "stranger," only that he does. What matters is the mysterious depth of memory and what it does to his imagination. Wholeness is felt in the presence of this "stranger," who has been part of Larry's consciousness from childhood and will continue with him into his elder years. The poignant energy of this poem emerges from not knowing yet trusting. Creativity and healing depend on openness to each new moment; on not knowing, not having all the answers.

Sell your cleverness and buy bewilderment;
Cleverness is mere opinion, bewilderment is intuition.

     —Rumi

EXERCISES
Writing About Silence, the Unknown and Your Inner Voice

1. Spend time in silence and being silent. Try being silent for a whole day if possible. Find a place that enhances your ability to listen to silence. A place you can meditate on your own or with a group. Go deep in the forest, along the beach, out in the desert or high on a mountain. Does silence feel different in each of these places? Go for a walk late in the evening in a place where it is safe and quiet. Take your time doing this. Don't hurry to write of your experience of silence. Get to know it. Let the silence guide you. Then free write what comes to you.

2. a. Write about things you know almost nothing about: deep sea diving, the simultaneous multi-tonal chanting of a Tibetan monk, the composition of stars—or whatever! *Imagine* yourself discovering something about those unknown things.

    b. Treat tomorrow as a completely new experience. What do you notice?

    c. What about the unknown most scares and interests you? Write this.

3. Read Barbara Gellert's poem *Encounter* again. Imagine yourself in a similar encounter with the unknown. What gift are

you given? Why will you never be the same? Gather these free writes from the above and compose a poem.

YOUR MUSE: THE POETIC MEDICINE OF CREATIVITY AND HEALING

Barbara Gellert and Larry Tirnauer both wrote about muselike figures. The muses in their poems open very different windows of truth to look through, but in both poems, healing and creative energies flow. The "poetic medicines" delivered to Barbara and Lawrence are just right for them, as if the muse knew what they needed. Giving attention to our muse will teach us how to *approach* our unique healing process. How can we best draw from these creative and healing energies? How do we recognize and welcome our muse?

Here are poems and stories from John Bowman and Ellen Grace O'Brian about where they each find the muse. Their different stories indicate that the muse can be found in both the mundane and the sacred.

John Bowman is Director of Communications at John F. Kennedy University, where I teach in the Graduate School of Psychology. Prior to working at JFK, John worked as a newspaper editor for thirty-five years. When the family-owned newspaper was bought by a large corporation, changes occurred and John's job was drastically redefined. It was difficult to adjust to his new situation, and John sought out therapy.

He realized in the course of therapy that he had staked his entire identity on his job. He *was* a newspaper editor, and that's all. Through therapy and with the help of his wife and friends, John found there was more to who he was than what he did. He asked himself: "What do I love to do?" The answer was *he loved to write.*

John had written poetry in high school and college. Writing lifted him during those years—being in contact with this creative process, he felt buoyant. His parents and friends, how-

*

ever, discouraged this interest, and with the responsibilities of life, writing poetry fell by the wayside as he entered into a successful newspaper career.

Now, in the throes of a career upheaval, his opportunity to write creatively returned when a friend gave him a journal for writing poetry. John says:

So I wrote. And I've been writing poems ever since. I initially thought I had wasted a lot of years, but as I started to write I realized I hadn't lost anything—it was just different. I had returned to something tremendously important to me. I wrote some poems out of anger about my job situation and what I saw happening to journalism. These arose from a depth of experience that I would not have been able to write from when I was nineteen. I've gone beyond my anger poems, and I am now discovering new territory in my poetry.

I didn't think making poems would be a spiritual experience, but it is. I go to a place where I am centered both emotionally and intellectually, and from there I can be silent so I hear that faint voice inside. From that centered place within comes poetry, and reading those words enhances my spiritual connection. Long after I've written a poem it has that kind of effect on me.

John took my course *Poetry Therapy: Reclamation of Deep Language* at JFK University and, while working on the healing muse exercise, came up with this interesting poem that expresses his hard-won freedom:

WITCH DOCTOR

*One morning a voice behind me
said, "You are a Holy Man."*

*I assumed serenity and, for a while,
felt elevated, chosen, separated from others
and dangerously better.*

I got over it. It was like the 24-hour flu.
When the fever broke, I was
on my feet again.

Today, I am asked about the healer in me.
I know that healing myself is going to take
so long that I'll never have time
to heal anyone else.

What does it all mean?
How does the Holy Man
connect with the Healer?
Are they the same? Are they one?

On the Namibian plain, termites will chew
up a fence post or a tree into a
7-foot-high mound of sawdust.

I feel like a 7-foot mound today
and I wonder how I can possibly
help the world. Then I catch
the eye of a tourist looking at me
and I feel healing humming in my dust.

John is breaking through into deeper levels of self-acceptance—
deep enough to feel that neither he nor his muse needs to be
anything extraordinary. That in fact his healing is the healing
gift he offers to the world. In being "nothing extraordinary," the
miraculous reveals itself.

The poem is almost incidental to the deep experience it evoked. Writing
this connected me to mystery. The poem surprised me when I realized I
am both the termite mound and the person looking at the mound. I am
the healer and the healed. That image seemed to really pull the poem to-
gether. I've been that tourist who felt fascinated and rekindled with
wonder by such a strange experience. I was really humming as I wrote
this poem!

The mound felt like a connection with earth, ashes and everything that is gritty in my life. This became my muse, my metaphor for healing.

Ellen Grace O'Brian welcomes the fertile dark, the place where her Muse appears, and she knows that a visitation of creative presence asks to be met and received through ritual:

MUSE

When she visits me
(it is not often now)
I make a simple offering,
rice from my kitchen, steaming
in a small white bowl.
She seasons it, pouring delicately
the dark salty sauce.
We do not talk but listen
(to some quieter things)
like the movement of clouds,
phantom freight trains
that connect, and ride low
across the evening sky.

There are clues here about greeting the Muse. Something about simplicity. Something about listening, *listening together.* Ellen says:

There is a preparation for this visit that happens in my own kitchen. Kitchen is an image for daily life. My own simple presence. Kitchen is the place where I bring forth nourishment—for something beyond myself. Something ordinary like rice (my daily life) is my simple offering. It is given flavor and savored.

There is longing in this poem: "When she visits me/(it is not often now)" is really about my yearning for her visit. I glimpse something in her visit that is very deep, like the quietness felt in listening to clouds, and my longing is to be in that depth.

EXERCISES
Meditation and Poem-Making

1. Choose a day when you do everything with less hurry. Consciously slow down when you: walk, talk on the phone, shop, play with a child, eat. Whatever it is, take your time. Feel how each activity holds a special kind of silence, an aspect that is unknown. Notice how everything you do, no matter how mundane, offers your inner voice the opportunity to express itself in a poem.

2. Participate in a meditation practice that attracts you or form your own meditation and writing circle.

3. Select a sacred poem by Rumi, Emily Dickinson, Walt Whitman, Li Po or one of David's Psalms (for instance) and memorize it. Make it a part of your daily life. For a week or month, use that poem as a guide into the experience of wisdom, beauty, love or ecstasy. Write your own poem to express your experience.

4. Create a ritual to invite your Muse. What will you offer? How will you prepare a sacred place? What happens when your muse arrives?

> Our Life is a faint tracing
> on the surface of mystery . . .
> —Annie Dillard

RESOURCES

For information about poetry therapy and for making contact with others interested in the healing potentials of poetry and poem-making, contact:

THE NATIONAL ASSOCIATION FOR POETRY THERAPY
P.O. Box 551
Port Washington, NY 11050, (516) 944-9791
The National Association for Poetry Therapy offers membership services such as publications, regional seminars, national conferences, national educational listings and certification training in poetry therapy through approved mentor supervisors. NAPT provides networking support among therapists, social workers, psychiatrists, healers, caregivers, physicians, nurses, teachers, librarians, storytellers, poets and anyone interested in the language arts for growth and healing.

The following centers offer workshop experience, educational programs and individualized training in poetry therapy:

THE CREATIVE RIGHTING CENTER
Sherry Reiter uses creative methods to conduct poetry therapy groups and train future poetry therapists. Poetry therapy training, one-on-one supervision, and an individualized training program are created in accordance with the guidelines of the National Association for Poetry Therapy. Long-distance mentoring is possible by fax, cassette and phone. Contact: Sherry Reiter, CSW, RPT, RDT, 1904 East First Street, Brooklyn, NY 11223.

THE CENTER FOR POETRY THERAPY TRAINING
The Center for Poetry Therapy offers comprehensive educational programs designed for therapists, teachers, clergy, poets and writers, librarians, and all others who use language arts in the service of growth and healing. The Center provides weekly classes in the DC Program, co-directed by Kenneth Gorelick, M.D., RPT, and Ruth Monser, MSN, RPT; monthly classes in the Poetry Therapy Training Institute (Potomac Program), directed by Peggy Osna Heller, Ph.D., MSW, RPT; and distance learning opportunities for national and international students in the Non-Residential Program, as well as workshops, and semi-annual intensive seminars. Center programs are consistent with the credential requirements of the National Association for Poetry Therapy. For information contact Peggy Osna Heller, 7715 White Rim Terrace, Potomac, MD 20854, (301) 983-3392, or Ken Gorelick, (202) 232-4338.

Pudding House Writers Resource Center

Pudding House is directed by poet Jennifer Bosveld and offers a wide range of poetry writing and application workshops, seminars, and one-on-one opportunities for those working on poetry therapy credentials or personal growth. Programs frequently open to all interested. Departments include: education, publications, and retreat. Poetry therapy peer groups are available. Extensive applied poetry library on site. Pudding House publishes *Pudding Magazine: The International Journal of Applied Poetry* and a variety of anthologies, chapbooks and educational materials. For information contact Jennifer Bosveld, 60 North Main Street, Johnstown, OH 43031, (614) 967-6060.

The Center for Journal Therapy

The Center for Journal Therapy teaches individuals, groups and communities to heal body, psyche and soul through writing. Founded in 1985 by Kathleen Adams, author of *Journal to the Self* and *The Way of the Journal*. The center offers a variety of training and workshops, including instructor certification training. Contact: CJT, Dept JF2, P.O. Box 963, Arvada, CO 80001, (888) 421-2298.

For more opportunities to explore writing and learn from the work of other poets, contact:

The National Writer's Voice Project of the YMCA of the USA
National Office
5 West 63rd St.
New York, NY 10023
(212) 875-4261
National Writer's Voice offers programs through YMCAs in local communities. Their mission is to "give voice to people through a democratic vision of literary arts and humanities. Our diverse array of programs and services aims to narrow the distinction between artist and audience, and between cultural institutions and the community, making the arts more accessible and life-enriching to the widest possible audience."

Associated Writing Programs
Tallwood House
Mail Stop 1E3
George Mason University
Fairfax, VA 22030
(703) 993-4396
AWP is a service organization that publishes the *AWP Chronicle* with interviews, profiles and articles directed toward the writer, the teacher of writing, and students of writing. AWP services writing programs across the United States and Canada, in particular providing job listings, a placement service and sponsoring an annual conference for those involved in the field of creative writing.

Poets & Writers
72 Spring St.
New York, NY 10012
(212) 226-3586
800-666-2268 (for California residents only)
Website: www.pw.org

California Office:
2140 Shattuck Ave., Suite 601
Berkeley, CA 94704
(510) 548-6618

Poets & Writers is a nonprofit literary organization that serves poets, fiction writers and performance writers through its various programs and publications. It publishes an excellent magazine called *Poets & Writers*. Poets & Writers can send information on how to publish, how to get copyrighted, find a literary agent and how to get money for writers. Poets & Writers has a Website with a wealth of information that includes addresses from *The Directory of American Poets and Fiction Writers*. They also feature popular Speakeasy forums.

POETS HOUSE
72 Spring Street
New York, NY 10012
(212) 431-7920
Poets House is a comfortable, accessible *place for poetry*—a 30,000-volume poetry library and a meeting place that invites poets and the public to step into the living tradition of poetry. Poets House resources and literary events document the wealth and diversity of modern poetry and stimulate dialog on issues of poetry and culture. Poets House publishes the annual *Directory of American Poetry Books*. The directory provides complete information about all of the poetry published within the diverse American poetry community, and includes a short description of each book and ordering information. Poets House is building a national archive of American poetry which is open to the public. Poets House was founded in 1985 by Stanley Kunitz and Elizabeth Kray.

WRITER'S CONFERENCE & FESTIVALS
P.O. Box 102396
Denver, CO 80250
Contact Kelleen Zubick: (303) 759-0519
A clearinghouse for information about writers and where to find them, where to improve and expand your writing skills, where to read what you write.

If you are interested in bringing poets and poetry to your local school or community, contact one of the organizations below for more information about possibilities.

TEACHERS AND WRITERS
5 Union Square West
New York, NY 10003
(212) 691-6590

CALIFORNIA POETS IN THE SCHOOLS
870 Market Street
San Francisco, CA 94102
(415) 399-1565
California Poets in the Schools is a superb statewide organization of professional poets who teach in K–12 settings and also serve the greater community. If you are a parent, teacher or administrator in California public schools, CPITS can bring poetry and poem-making to children in a dynamic and meaningful way.

SUGGESTED READING

Anthologies

Bernhardt, Mike, ed. *Voices of the Grieving Heart.* Cypress Point Press, 1994. This is a beautiful book. Write: Cypress Point Press, P.O. Box 56, Moraga, CA 94556.

Bly, Robert, James Hillman, and Michael Meade, eds. *The Rag and Bone Shop of the Heart.* NY: HarperCollins, 1993.

Bly Robert, ed. *The Soul Is Here for Its Own Joy: Sacred Poems from Many Cultures.* The Ecco Press, 1995.

Brown, Joe, ed. *A Promise to Remember: The Names Project Book of Letters.* Avon Books, 1992. Remembrances of love from the contributors to the AIDS Quilt.

Hirshfield, Jane, ed. *Women in Praise of the Sacred.* HarperPerennial, 1994.

Mitchell, Stephen. *The Enlightened Heart.* Harper and Row, 1989.

Moramarco, Fred, and Al Zolynas. *Men of Our Time: An Anthology of Male Poetry in Contemporary America.* University of Georgia Press, 1992.

Moyers, Bill, ed. *The Language of Life,* edited by James Haba. Doubleday Books, 1995.

Patterson, Lindsay, ed. *A Rock Against the Wind: African-American Poems of Love and Passion.* Perigee/Putnam, 1996.

Sewell, Marilyn, ed. *Cries of the Spirit* and *Claiming the Spirit Within.* Beacon Press, 1991, 1996.

Walker, Sue B., and Rosaly D. Roffman. *Life on the Line: Selections on Words and Healing.* Negative Capability Press, 1992.

Poets

Berry, Wendell. *Collected Poems 1957–1982.* North Point Press, 1985.

Dickinson, Emily. *Complete Poems.* Little, Brown and Co., 1960.

Elytis, Odysseus, trans. Edmund Keeley and Phillip Sherard. *Selected Poems.* Penguin Books, 1981.

Fox, John. *When Jewels Sing.* Open Heart Publications, 1989. Write: P.O. Box 60189, Palo Alto, CA 94306.

Hirshfield, Jane. *The Lives of the Heart.* HarperCollins, 1997.

Hughes, Langston. *The Collected Poems of Langston Hughes.* Alfred A. Knopf, 1994.

Kenyon, Jane. *Constance, Poems by Jane Kenyon.* Graywolf Press, 1993.

Lloyd, Roseann. *War Baby Express.* Holy Cow! Press, 1996.

Lorde, Audre. *The Cancer Journals.* Spinsters/Aunt Lute, 1980.

O'Brian, Ellen Grace. *One Heart Opening.* CSE, 1996. Write: CSE, P.O. Box 112185, Campbell, CA 95128.

Oliver, Mary. *House of Light.* Beacon Press, 1990.

Piercy, Marge. *Circles on the Water.* Alfred Knopf, Inc., 1982.

Rilke, Rainer Maria, trans. Robert Bly. *Selected Poems of Rainer Maria Rilke.* Harper & Row, 1981.

Rumi, Jelaluddin, trans. Coleman Barks and John Moynes. *Open Secret.* Threshold Books, 1984.

Whitman, Walt. *Leaves of Grass.* Modern Library.

Poetry Therapy

Hynes, Arleen McCarty, and Mary Hynes-Berry. *Biblio/Poetry Therapy: The Interactive Process.* North Star Press, 1986. A fine text for therapists and teachers.

Leedy, Jack, M.D. *Poetry as Healer: Mending the Troubled Mind.* Vanguard, 1985. A classic in the field of poetry therapy. Contact: Jack Leedy, 1049 E. 26th St., Brooklyn, NY 11210.

Guides for Writing (Adult)

Albert, Susan Wittig. *Writing from Life.* Jeremy P. Tarcher, 1997. A woman's guide for writing the unspoken story of her life.

Adams, Kathleen. *Journal to the Self.* Warner Books, 1990.

Adams, Kathleen. *The Way of the Journal.* Sidram Press, 1993.

Behn, Robin, and Chase Twitchell. *The Practice of Poetry.* HarperPerennial, 1992.

Bosveld, Jennifer. *Topics for Getting in Touch.* Pudding House Publications, 1994. Write: Pudding House, 60 N. Main Street, Johnstown, OH 43031.

Dion, Susan. *Write Now: Maintaining a Creative Spirit While Homebound and Ill.* Puffin Foundation, 1993. This is a gem. To request this book, write: Susan Dion, 432 Ives Avenue, Carneys Point, NJ 08069. Send only a 6 x 9 self-addressed envelope with $1.24 postage.

Goldberg, Bonni. *Room to Write.* Jeremy P. Tarcher, Inc., 1996. Superb ideas and guidance.

Lloyd, Roseann, and Richard Solly. *Journey Notes: Writing for Recovery and Spiritual Growth.* Harper/Hazelden, 1989.

Malone, Eileen. *The Complete Guide to Writers Groups, Conferences and Workshops.* John Wiley & Sons, 1996. An excellent comprehensive guide to help you find the writing connection that is right for you.

Rico, Gabriele Luser. *Pain and Possibility: Writing Your Way Through Personal Crisis.* Jeremy P. Tarcher, Inc., 1991.

Rico, Gabriele Luser. *Writing the Natural Way.* Jeremy P. Tarcher, Inc., 1983.

Smith, Michael C., and Suzanne Greenberg. *Everyday Creative Writing: Panning for Gold in the Kitchen Sink.* NTC Publishing Group, Lincolnwood, IL, 1996.

Stafford, William. *Writing the Australian Crawl: Views on the Writer's Vocation.* MI: University of Michigan, 1978.

Strand, Clark. *Seeds from a Birch Tree.* Hyperion, 1997. If you are drawn to write haiku, this lovely book will help you.

Ueland, Brenda. *If You Want to Write.* The Schubert Club, 1983.

Wooldridge, Susan G. *Poemcrazy.* Random House, 1995.

Guides for Writing (Children)

Heard, Georgia. *For the Good of the Earth and Sun.* Heinemann, 1989.

Krogness, Mary Mercer. *Just Teach Me, Mrs. K.: Talking, Reading and Writing with Resistant Adolescent Learners.* Heinemann, 1995.

Lewis, Richard. *When Thought Is Young.* New Rivers, 1992.

McKim, Elizabeth, and Judith W. Steinbergh. *Beyond Words: Writing Poems with Children.* MA: Wampeter Press, 1983.

Spirituality, Writing, Healing and Living

Aurobindo, Sri. *The Future of Poetry.* Sri Aurobindo Ashram, 1953.

Bachelard, Gaston. *The Poetics of Space.* Beacon Press, 1969.

Hirshfield, Jane. *Nine Gates: Entering the Mind of Poetry.* HarperCollins, 1997.

Hesse, Hermann. *My Belief.* Farrar, Straus and Giroux, 1974.

Holzer, Burghild Nina. *A Walk Between Heaven and Earth: A Personal Journal on Writing and the Creative Process.* Bell Tower, 1994.

Khan, Hazrat Inayat. *The Music of Life.* Omega Press, 1983.

Remen, Rachel Naomi, M.D. *Kitchen Table Wisdom*, Riverhead, 1996.

Remen, Rachel Naomi, M.D. *Community and Communion: The Voice of Community.* ISHI, 1992. Available from ISHI, P.O. Box 316, Salinas, CA 94924. An excellent commentary on poems from Commonweal cancer support center.

Richards, M. C. *Centering.* Wesleyan University Press, 1962.

BIBLIOGRAPHY

Anthologies

Anderson, Maggie, Raymond Craig, and Alex Gildzen, eds. *A Gathering of Poets*. OH: Kent State University Press, 1992.

Bass, Ellen, and Florence Howe, eds. *No More Masks! An Anthology of Poems by Women*. NY: Doubleday, 1973.

Dunning, Stephen, Edward Luedars, and Hugh Smith, comp. *Reflections on a Gift of Watermelon Pickle . . . and other Modern Verse*. NY: Scholastic Book Services, 1966.

Howard, Richard. *Preferences*. NY: Viking Press, 1974.

Longo, Perie, Don Campbell, Karin Faulkner and Toni Wynn, eds. *Waiting to Move the Mountain*. CA: California Poets in the Schools, 1994. Also see other anthologies from the poets in the schools program.

Martz, Sandra, ed. *When I Am an Old Woman I Shall Wear Purple*. CA: Papier Mache Press, 1987.

Williams, Oscar, ed. *A Pocket Book of Modern Verse*. NY: Washington Square Press, 1965.

Creativity, Poetics and the Writing Process

Cameron, Julia. *The Artist's Way: A Spiritual Path to Higher Creativity*. CA: Jeremy P. Tarcher, Inc., 1992.

Fadiman, James. *Unlimit Your Life*. CA: Celestial Arts, 1989.

May, Rollo. *The Courage to Create*. NY: Bantam, 1980.

Mayes, Frances. *The Discovery of Poetry*. NY: Harcourt Brace Jovanovich, 1987.

Rilke, Rainer Maria, trans. Stephen Mitchell. *Letters to a Young Poet*. NY: Random House, 1984.

Snyder, Gary. "The Real Work of Gary Snyder." *New Age Journal*, Vol. 5., No. 12 (June 1980), pp. 26–30.

Healing

Claremont de Castillejo, Irene. *Knowing Woman: A Feminine Psychology*. NY: Harper Colophon, 1974.

DeMaria, Michael B. "Poetry and the Abused Child: The Forest and the Tinted Plexiglas." *Journal of Poetry Therapy*, Vol. 5, No. 12 (1992).

✳

Heller, Peggy Osna. "The Three Pillars of Poetry Therapy." *The Arts in Psychotherapy*, Vol. 11, pp. 341–344 (1987).

Lerner, Arthur. *Poetry and the Therapeutic Experience.* MO: MMB Music, 1994.

McNiff, Shaun. "The Shaman Within." *The Arts in Psychotherapy*, Vol. 15, pp. 285–291 (1988).

Morrison, Morris R. "The Use of Poetry in the Treatment of Emotional Dysfunction." *The Arts in Psychotherapy.* Vol. 5, pp. 93–98 (1978).

Reed, M. Ann. "The Bardic Mystery and the Dew Drop in the Rose: The Poet in the Therapeutic Process." *The Journal of Poetry Therapy*, Vol. 6, No. 1 (1992).

Sullivan, Lawrence E., ed. *The Parabola Book of Healing.* NY: Continuum, 1994.

Poetry

Berry, Wendell. *Collected Poems 1957–1982.* CA: North Point Press, 1985.

Blake, William. *The Poetry and Prose of William Blake.* NY: Doubleday, 1970.

Bly, Robert, translator and adapter. *The Kabir Book.* MA: Beacon Press, 1977.

Cummings, E. E. *73 Poems.* NY: Liveright, 1963.

Cummings, E. E. *A Selection of Poems.* NY: Harcourt Liveright, 1926.

Cummings, E. E. *Complete Poems 1904–1962.* NY: Liveright, 1991.

Eliot, T. S. *Four Quartets.* NY: Harcourt Brace Jovanovich, 1943.

Elytis, Odysseus, trans. Edmund Keeley and George Savidis. *Axion Esti.* PA: University of Pittsburgh Press, 1974.

Elytis, Odysseus, trans. Olga Broumas. *The Little Mariner.* WA: Copper Canyon, 1988.

Fox, John. *My Hand Touches the Sea.* CA: Open Heart Publications, 1984.

Ginsberg, Allen. *Howl and Other Poems.* CA: City Lights Books, 1993.

Hirshfield, Jane. *Of Gravity & Angels.* CT: Wesleyan University Press, 1988.

Keats, John. *The Selected Poetry and Letters of John Keats.* NY: New American Library, 1966.

Kerouac, Jack. *The Scripture of the Golden Eternity.* NY: Corinth, 1970.

Lawrence, D. H. *Selected Poems.* NY: Viking Press, 1959.

Levertov, Denise. *Poems 1960–1967.* NY: New Directions, 1983.

Lloyd, Roseann. *Tap Dancing for Big Mom.* MN: New Rivers Press, 1985.

Lorca, Federico García, and Juan Ramón Jiménez, trans. Robert Bly. *Selected Poems.* MA: Beacon Press, 1973.

Neruda, Pablo, trans. Stephen Tapscott. *100 Love Sonnets.* TX: University of Texas, 1959.

Neruda, Pablo. *A New Decade: Poems 1958–1967.* NY: Grove Press, 1969.

Oliver, Mary. *Dream Work.* MA: Atlantic Monthly Press, 1986.

Rilke, Rainer Maria, trans. Gary Miranda. *Duino Elegies.* OR: Breitenbush Books, 1981.

Rilke, Rainer Maria, trans. Robert Bly. *Selected Poems of Rainer Maria Rilke.* NY: Harper & Row, 1981.

Rumi, Jelaluddin, trans. Camille and Kabir Helminski. *Daylight: A Daybook of Spiritual Guidance.* VT: Threshold Books, 1994.

Rumi, Jelaluddin, trans. Coleman Barks and John Moynes. *The Longing.* VT: Threshold Books, 1988.

Rumi, Jelaluddin, trans. John Moyne and Coleman Barks. *Unseen Rain.* VT: Threshold Books, 1986.

Rumi, Jelaluddin, trans. Kabir Helminski. *Love Is a Stranger.* VT: Threshold Books, 1993.

Rumi, Jelaluddin, trans. Coleman Barks and John Moynes. *We Are Three.* VT: Threshold Books, 1987.

Snyder, Gary. *Turtle Island.* NY: New Directions, 1974.

TallMountain, Mary. *Light on the Tent Wall.* CA: University of California, Los Angeles, 1990.

TallMountain, Mary. *Listen to the Night: Poems for the Animal Spirits of Mother Earth.* Freedom
    Voices Publications, 1995. Available from: TallMountain Circle, P.O. Box 423115,
    San Francisco, CA 94142.

Thomas, Dylan. *Collected Poems of Dylan Thomas 1934–1952.* NY: New Directions, 1957.

Whitman, Walt. *Complete Poetry and Prose of Walt Whitman.* NY: Pellegrini and Cudahy,
    1948.

Williams, William Carlos. *Selected Poems.* NY: New Directions, 1968.

Yeats, William Butler. *The Collected Poems.* NY: Macmillan, 1974.

Spirituality and Ecology

Berry, Thomas. *The Dream of the Earth.* CA: Sierra Club Books, 1988.

Ferrucci, Piero. *Inevitable Grace.* CA: Jeremy P. Tarcher, Inc., 1990.

Levine, Stephen. *A Gradual Awakening.* NY: Anchor, 1979.

Roszak, Theodore, Mary E. Gomes, and Allen D. Kanner, editors. *Ecopsychology: Restor-
    ing the Earth, Healing the Mind.* Sierra Club Books, 1995.

Swimme, Brian. *The Universe Is a Green Dragon.* NM: Bear and Company, 1984.

Tagore, Rabindranath. *Towards Universal Man: A Poet's School.* NY: Asia Publishing House,
    1961.

Yogananda, Paramhansa. *Autobiography of a Yogi.* CA: Self Realization, 1974.

PERMISSIONS

Chapter One

Chapter Two

✳

C h a p t e r   T h r e e

"*List*" by Dorian Brooks Kottler from *A PAUSE IN THE LIGHT* (Holy Cow! Press, 1980). Copyright © Holy Cow! Press 1980. Reprinted by permission of Holy Cow! Press, P.O. Box 3170, Mount Royal Station, Duluth, MN 55803.

"*Andalucian Wood*" by Catherine Firpo from VOICES OF THE GRIEVING HEART, edited by Michael Bernhardt (Cypress Point Press [P.O. Box 56, Moraga, CA 94556], 1994). © Catherine Firpo. Reprinted by permission of the author.

"*The Spirit of the Black Dog*" by Megan Schulz. © Megan Schulz. Printed by permission of Lisa Friedlander and Megan Schulz.

"*Cancer Ward—1990*" from STAR EATING WOLVES by Roberta de Kay (Acorn Press [P.O. Box 5062, San Jose, CA 95150], 1995). © 1995 by Roberta de Kay. Reprinted by permission of the author.

"*Psalm 13*" by Roberta de Kay from STAR EATING WOLVES © 1995 by Roberta de Kay. Reprinted by permission of the author.

"*Allamakee Morning*" by Roberta de Kay, previously published in BRAINCHILD #3, Springfield, IL, Spring 1976, and in STAR EATING WOLVES by Roberta de Kay. Reprinted by permission of the author.

"*The Flower's Tongue*" from STAR EATING WOLVES by Roberta de Kay; Acorn Press, P.O. Box 5062, San Jose, CA 95150. Reprinted by permission of the author.

"*Maybe*" from STAR EATING WOLVES by Roberta de Kay. Reprinted by permission of the author.

"*Onions*" by Sonia Usatch. © Sonia Usatch. Printed by permission of the author.

"*Yellow Yarn*" by Sonia Usatch. © Sonia Usatch. Printed by permission of the author.

"*To Sleep With*" by Zawdie Ekundayo. © Zawdie Ekundayo. Printed by permission of the author.

Excerpt from "*Seen Through a Camera Lens in a Dusty Valley Town*" by Pam Tolbert. © Pam Tolbert. Printed by permission of the author.

"*Once a Performer*" by William Stephenson, from SIMPLE GIFTS, compiled by Elaine Brooks 1996. © William Stephenson. Printed by permission of the author.

Chapter Seven

"*Lost*" by David Wagoner from *Riverbed* (Bloomington: Indiana University Press, 1972). © 1972 by Indiana University Press. Reprinted by permission of David Wagoner.

Excerpt from "*ego tripping (there may be a reason why)*" from THE WOMEN AND THE MEN by Nikki Giovanni (William Morrow & Co, 1979). Copyright © 1970. Reprinted by permission of William Morrow & Co.

"*Mentioning the Weather*" by John Fox. © 1993 John Fox. Printed by permission of the author.

Excerpt from "*To a Stone*" by Diane Richard-Allerdyce from SIMPLE GIFTS, compiled by Elaine Brooks 1996. © Diane Richard-Allerdyce. Reprinted by permission of the author.

"*I drank a fertile alphabet*" by Cori Olinghouse from A COLUMN OF AIR by Cori Olinghouse, © 1996. Reprinted by permission of the author.

"*Lying in a Hammock at William Duffy's Farm at Pine Island, Minnesota*" from THE BRANCH WILL NOT BREAK by James Wright (Wesleyan University Press, 1963). © 1963 by Wesleyan University Press of New England. Reprinted by permission of University Press of New England.

"*Midnight at Laventille*" by Donna Kennedy. © Donna Kennedy. Printed by permission of the author.

INDEX

Abandonment, image of, 79–80
Abusive relationships, 115–22
Acceptance, 144–46
    of loss, 23–24, 171–72
    in parent/child relationship, 104–7
Actherberg, Jeanne, 70
Action of writing poems, 116–17
Advertising, 12, 48
Affirmations, 90–91
Aging, feelings about, 141–43, 147–48
AIDS, 76, 185–86
AIDS quilt, 54
Alegría, Claribel, 203
Allamakee Morning, de Kay, 178
Allison, Gildzen, 230
All Marriages are Mixed, Dion, 130–34
Alluvial Changes, Baker, 207–9
Although the wind, Shikibu, 253
Amputation, as metaphor for loss, 21
Ancient souls collide, Reese, 220
Andalucian Wood, Firpo, 171–72
Anger, 99–105
Armstrong, Jeannette, 204–5
As I look at the clouds, Friedlander, 214
Associated Writing Programs, 280
Attention, 70, 73–74, 199
Attributes, naming of, 136–37
Aurobindo, Sri, 255, 261
Autumn, Rilke, 166, 168
Autry, James, 3

Baca, Jimmy Santiago, 243
Baker, Trina, *Alluvial Changes*, 207–9
Baldwin, Phyllis, *I remember singing blood
    flowing into passionate seas*, 256
Barely Breathing, Kreigler, 154–55
Barks, Coleman, 264
The bar of soap, Bolton, 62–63
Barrie, J. M., 96
Basho, *Winter Solitude*, 171

Beauty, 193, 257, 259–61
Beauty is everlasting, Moore, 137
Beck, Charlotte Joko, 252
Beitler, Noel, 39–41
    I miss you, 14
    Listen, 40
Bellotti, Laura Golden, *The Rabbis Do Not
    Look at Me*, 265
Beloved, Sing, and Deep Rivers Bend, Fox,
    139–40
Bernstein, Charles, 155
Berry, Thomas, 217, 256
Berry, Wendell, 215
    The Peace of Wild Things, 212
    To Know the Dark, 29
Bird Song, Marie, 156–57
Bistami, Abu Yazid al-, 263, 266
The Black Walnut Tree, McMonagle,
    218–19
Blake, William, *Joy & Woe are woven fine*,
    12
Bloch, Chana, *What shrinks inside us, these
    stones*, 102
Bly, Robert, 33, 127
    We did not come to remain whole, 94
Bolton, Elizabeth, *The bar of soap*, 62–63
Both Sides Now, Mitchell, 141
Bowman, John, 273–74
    Witch Doctor, 274–76
Brajdic, Anita, *Where There Once Was What
    Is Not Easily Remembered*, 216–17
Breakthroughs, 163, 168–69
Brodsky, Joseph, 25, 35
Browne, Phyllis, *I am a spark of fire*, 255
Bruchac, Joseph, *Half on the Earth, half in
    the heart*, 58
Budbill, David, *What I Heard in a Discount
    Department Store*, 101–2
Burbank, Luther, 198
Burroughs, John, 251

Burying the Gold, O'Brian, 117–22
busy place and bright, Weiner, 84

California Poets in the Schools, 26, 281
Cambodia, 239
Campbell, Joseph, 46
Cancer, xiii, 26–29, 44–47, 175–77
The Cancer Journals, Lorde, 13
Cancer Ward, de Kay, 175–76
Career transitions, 184, 187–88, 273–74
Caregivers, poem-making for, 181–84
Castillejo, Irene Claremont de, 9, 74,
    210
*The cat sleeping on the fence is famous to the
    birds*, Nye, 85
Caves, Sue, 54
The Center for Journal Therapy, 280
The Center for Poetry Therapy Training,
    279
Changes in relationships, 152–53
Chesterton, G. K., 228
Childhood abuse, healing poems,
    115–22
Childhood images, memory of, 73–74
childhood is a wobbly cardboard box, Fox, 74
Children, 63–64, 94, 114, 237–38
    creativity of, 95, 97, 108
    losses of, 184–87
    relationship with parents, 95–123
    "at risk," 238–41
Child-self, observation of, 123–24
The Circus Animal's Desertion, Yeats, 25–26
Clifton, Lucille, 4, 17, 226
    i am running into a new year, 36
Coleridge, Samuel Taylor, *The Rime of the
    Ancient Mariner*, 88
Collage, 162, 166–67
Comes the Dawn, Wray, 234
Communication, 9–11, 153
    child/parent, 97–99

★

Companion, poetry as, 5, 6–7
Comparisons, unexpected, 207
Compassion, 231, 237, 251
Concentration, 35
Connections:
　with earth, 194
　to joy, 264
　metaphors and, 65
　nature and, 206–11
　with sacred experiences, 251–52
　simile and, 61–64
　spiritual, 257
　universal, 55
　with wholeness, 256
Consonants, 89
The Continental Drift, McMonagle, 220–22
Conversation, cadence of, 85
Corso, Gregory, 90
Council of All Beings, 217
Courage, 30, 155
Crazy Jane Talks with the Bishop, Yeats,
　142–43
Crazy Jane Wants to Hear the Jazzmen of Po-
　etry Let Loose, Fox, 48
The Creative Righting Center, 279
Creativity, 40–42, 49, 53–55, 59–60,
　272, 273–77
　of children, 95, 97, 108
　and healing, 33–35, 182–83
Crises, existential, 24–26
Cry of pain, 13–18, 22–24, 30
cummings, e. e., 81
　who are you, little i, 97
Curiosity, 264
Cynicism, 165–66

David the Psalmist, 177, 252
Death, 173–75
　of loved one, 169–71
　of parent, 104
de Kay, Roberta:
　Allamakee Morning, 178
　Cancer Ward, 175–77
　The Flower's Tongue, 178–79
　Maybe, 180
　Psalm 13, 177
　Star Eating Wolves, 178
Destruction, ecological, 215
Details of life, 237, 264
Devotional love, 257–58
Dickinson, Emily, 81
　There is no Frigate like a Book, 60

Dillard, Annie, 37
　Our life is a faint tracing, 277
Diogenes, 97
Dion, Susan:
　All Marriages are Mixed, 130–34
　June Heat, 144–46
Divine memory (smriti), 256
Do Not Wipe Your Tears Away, Senkyrik,
　42–43
Dooley, John, 242–44
　i went to walk upon, 85
　A Prison Sharing, 244–45
Dove, Rita, 4, 242
Dreams, 78, 184
Duncan, Robert, A Song of the Old Order,
　149–50
Dust Bowl, Hughes, 38
Dylan, Bob, 136

Each of us inevitable, Whitman, 194
Earth, 193
　voice for, 215–17
Ecclesiastes, To everything there is a season, 197
Ecological destruction, 215
Ecopsychology, 212–15
Ecstasy, 264–66
ego tripping (there may be a reason why), Gio-
　vanni, 194
Einstein, Albert, 61, 81
Eiseley, Loren, 193
Ekundayo, Zawdie, To Sleep With,
　184–86
Elected Silence, sing to me, Hopkins, 267
Elytis, Odysseus, 229
Emerson, Ralph Waldo, 201, 265
Emotions, 75, 83–84
　release of, 49–53
　See also Feelings
Empathy, 247–48
Encounter, Gellert, 270
Ending of relationship, 139–40
Energy, 81
Enjambment, 85
Enlightenment, moon as image of, 253
Entering the Dark Places with Innocence, Peter-
　mann, 44–45
Entrancement stills, Littleton, 267
Environmentalism, 215
Eroticism, 222
Eskimo, In the very earliest times, 213
Evans, Robert, On Runners, 112–14
Even To This, Fox, 22

Exercises:
　Animals as Metaphor, 211
　Becoming the Earth's Voice, 217
　Capturing Images, 37–39, 73–75
　Celebrating Eroticism, 222
　Connecting the Personal with the Universal,
　　55
　Creating a Collage to Reveal Your Feelings,
　　166–67
　Expressing Another Person's Struggle, 248
　Expressing Your Suffering Courageously, 19
　Finding Poems in the Resting Places of Your
　　Healing Journey, 168
　Finding Your Sacred Place, Companion and
　　Natural Medicine, 5–9
　Healing the Past by Revisiting Images, 80
　Images of Painful Feelings, 77
　Integrating Disparate Elements in Your Rela-
　　tionship, 134–35
　The Language of the Land, 204–5
　Listening Well, 41
　Looking at Your World with the Eyes of a
　　Poet, 226
　Making a Poem from Images of Grief, Pain
　　and Hope, 167–68
　Making a Poem of Spiritual Memory, 256
　Making Contact with the Earth, 204
　Making Word Choices (Or Not Letting the
　　Good Ones Get Away), 89
　Meditation and Poem-Making, 277
　Opening to a Feeling of Solace and Spiritual
　　Support, 168
　Opening to the Way Your Child Is, 98–99
　An Outrageous Poem Using Images and
　　Metaphors of the Earth, 195
　Playing with Line Breaks and Line Lengths,
　　86
　Poem of Want and Poem of Acceptance, 107
　Poetry and Relationships, 10
　The Power of Healing Metaphors, 68
　Reclaiming Feelings, 43–44
　Recognizing the Essence of Your Partner, 140
　Releasing Emotions, 51–53
　Sacred Object, List of Particulars, Container
　　for Memory, 173
　Seasons of Love, 152–53
　Seeing Beyond Death - "Her Spirit Is Still
　　with Us Forever," 174–75
　Simile - Making Connections in Your Daily
　　Life, 64
　Special Objects and Places of Childhood, 123
　Telling the Story of Your Turning Points, 231

Time Well Spent—Writing Poems About Parenthood, 114

Turning On to What You See, 72

What Nature Teaches Us, 198

"When I Am Old I Shall Wear Purple," 147–48

Words That Cry Out, 17–18

Write a Poem of Longing, 157–58

Writing About Silence, the Unknown, and Your Inner Voice, 272

Writing About Sorrow and Love, 236–37

Writing a Love-Making Poem, 148

Writing and Ritual—A Salve for Your Wounds, 147

Writing a Poem of Witness, 241

Writing Sacred Poems Using Symbols, Image and Metaphor, 255

Writing the Vulnerable Thing You Didn't Say, 147

Writing Through the Stages of Our Lives, 188–89

Writing to Someone You Love or Who You Feel is Loving, 259

Writing with Passion, 49

Your Childhood Voice and Qualities, 123–24

Your Relationship with Nature—Writing Your Sense of Mystery, 214–15

Existential crises, 24–26

Experience, 4

externalization of, 34

Fadiman, Jim, *Illusions*, 262–63

Family values, 225, 242

Fear, silence and, 51

Fear snatched my voice away, Kriegler, 50–51

Feelings, 3, 33, 62, 198–201

expression of, 74–80, 100–107, 129

Fern Hill, Thomas, 88–89

Finding What You Didn't Lose, Fox, 16

Firpo, Catherine, *Andalucian Wood*, 171–72

The Flower's Tongue, de Kay, 178–79

Forché, Carolyn, 232, 252

For each true poem born, Fox, 266

For Isaac, Rigg, 164

Fox, Holly, 229

Fox, Jim and Eleanor, 229

Fox, John, 20–24

Beloved, Sing, and Deep Rivers Bend, 139–40

childhood is a wobbly cardboard box, 74

Crazy Jane Wants to Hear the Jazzmen of Poetry Let Loose, 48

Even To This, 22

Finding What You Didn't Lose, 16

For each true poem born, 266

Listen to the deep cello, 157–58

The Marrow of Who I Am, 232–34

Mentioning the Weather, 196

Your arrival occurs at night, 38

Fragility, 29–30

Franck, Frederick, 70

Frankl, Viktor, 165

Free verse, 82

Friedlander, Lisa, 189, 224

As I look at the clouds, 214

Friendship, Keane, 61–62

Fromm, Erich, 44

Frost, Robert, 262

Love at the lips was touch, 83–84

Frustration, 99–104

García Lorca, Federico, *My heart of silk*, 8–9

Gellert, Barbara, 273

Encounter, 270

Gestalt of poem, 80

Gide, André, 271

The Gift, Hirshfield, 87–88

Gildzen, Alex, *Allison*, 230

Ginsberg, Allen:

Howl, 81–82

Wales Visitation, 82–83

Giovanni, Nikki, 113

ego tripping (there may be a reason why), 194

The Women and the Men, 195

God, 23–24, 161

Goethe, Johann Wolfgang von, *In the calm water of the love-nights*, 257

Gomes, Mary E., 206

Grahn, Judy, *Paris and Helen*, 136–38

Greene, Graham, 269

Grief, 23–24, 42–43, 76–77, 161–89, 195

of parents, 232, 234

Guidance, from poetry, 3, 29

Haas, Kris, 166–67

Haas, Robert, 35

Half on the Earth, half in the heart, Bruchac, 58

Hall, Donald, 78, 160

Harjo, Joy, 7, 269

Harrington, Anne, *Jammed/Crammed/ Damned*, 75–77

Harrison, Jim, 57, 99

Hauptmann, Gerhart, 53

Healing, 12, 217, 251–52, 272, 273–77

of childhood abuse, 115–22

creativity and, 33–35, 40–41

poetry and, xiv, 4, 49, 70, 86–87, 161

Heart, spiritual, 267

Heart of Water, Misciagna, 65–66

Heller, Peggy Osna, 12

Henry, Mark, *Second Anniversary*, 105–7

Hesse, Hermann, 2

High Sierras at Mammoth Lake, Wray, 235–36

Hildegard of Bingen, 272

Hill, Hyacinthe, *Reaching Toward Beauty*, 142

Hinduism, 256

Hirschman, Jack, *Human Interlude*, 226–27

Hirshfield, Jane, *The Gift*, 87–88

HIV infection, 185–86

Holzer, Nina, 262

Home, loss of, children and, 185–87

Homelessness, 226–27

Hope, 163, 164

Hopkins, Gerard Manley, 81

Elected Silence, sing to me, 267

Howl, Ginsberg, 81–82

How the days went, Lorde, 73

Hughes, Langston, *Dust Bowl*, 38

Human Interlude, Hirschman, 226–27

Huxley, Aldous, 3, 260

Island, 21

Hymn, Kerouac, 70–72

I am a snowflake. I drift, TallMountain, 254

I am a spark of fire, Browne, 255

I am he that walks with the tender and growing night, Whitman, 219–20

i am running into a new year, Clifton, 36

I am the poet of the Body and I am the poet of the Soul, Whitman, 13

I am water rushing to the well-head, Kenyon, 64

I ask all blessings, Anon. Navaho, 5

I ask for a human language, Robertson, 9

I don't have much knowledge yet in grief, Rilke, 24

I drank a fertile alphabet, Olinghouse, 200

If you don't know the kind of person I am, Stafford, 34

★

I have lived on the lip, Rumi, 35
Illness, 44–47, 145–46, 163, 175–80
Illusions, Fadiman, 262–63
I love the dark hours of my being, Rilke,
    270
Image of Myself 3, Jones, 55
Images, 36–39, 59, 69–80
    from earth, 193, 195, 253
    of loved one, 137–38
    spiritual, naming of, 254–56
I miss you, Beitler, 14
Inner voice, 266, 269–70
Inside a bubble, Weiss, 96
Insight, 11, 24, 195, 213
In the calm water of the love-nights, Goethe,
    257
In the very earliest times, Eskimo, 213
Intimacy, 132–34, 140–48, 185–86
Intuition, 13, 66
*I remember singing blood flowing into passionate
    seas*, Baldwin, 256
Island, Huxley, 21
It's O.K. for the rich and the lucky to keep still,
    Rilke, 18–19
I wake to sleep, and take my waking slow,
    Roethke, 33
i went to walk upon, Dooley, 85

Jacobsen, Rolf, *Let the young rain of tears
    come*, 44
Jammed/Crammed/Damned, Harrington,
    75–77
Jefferson, Lara, 32
Jesus, 259–60
Jiminez, Juan Ramon, *Music*, 64, 65
John F. Kennedy University, 273–74
Jones, Ira B., *Image of Myself 3*, 55
Jong, Erica, 90
Joy, 264
Joy & Woe are woven fine, Blake, 12
June Heat, Dion, 144–46
Jung, Carl, 153

Kabir, *There is a Secret One inside us*, 250
Kai (child reading a poem on radio), *Yo,
    earth*, 216
Kanner, Allen D., 206
Keane, Carolyn, *Friendship*, 61–62
Keats, John, 21, 184
Kennedy, Donna:
    Midnight on Laventille, 202–4
    Ritual, 104–5

Kennedy, John F., 228, 240
Kennedy, Robert F., 232
Kent State University, 229–30
Kenyon, Jane, 202
    I am water rushing to the well-head, 64
    Peonies at Dusk, 206–7
Kerouac, Jack, 259
    Hymn, 70–72
Khan, Hazrat Inayat, 6
Kinnell, Galway, 60
Knowledge, intuitive, 66
Kojiju, *Merely to know*, 253
Kornfield, Jack, 261
Kottler, Dorian B., *List*, 170
Krause, Allison, 229
Kreigler, Onie:
    Barely Breathing, 154–55
    Fear snatched my voice away, 50–51
Kunitz, Stanley, 243

Lagoni, Laurel:
    Marriage, 150–51
    Waterfall, 151–52
Lamson, Glo, 4, 49
Language, poetic, 9–10, 47–53, 55, 242
    beauty in, 261
    metaphoric, 65
    of natural world, 193, 204–5
Lawrence, D. H., 225
Layout of poem, 80–83
Lebanon, massacre of soldiers, 231–32
Lee, Li-Young, 269
    See a peach bend, 72
Let the young rain of tears come, Jacobsen,
    44
Letting go, and acceptance of loss,
    171–72
Levertov, Denise, 81
Levine, Stephen, 236
Lewis, Richard, 94, 95, 108
Life, turning points in, 229–31
Line breaks, 17, 59, 63, 80–86
Lioness, Richard-Allerdyce, 209–11
Lisa (dancer), 246–48
Lisa (student), *Terribly Loud Screaming Kept
    the House Awake*, 115–16
List, Kottler, 170
Listen, Beitler, 40
Listening, 199
    to inner voice, 266
Listening creates holy silence, Remen, 41
Listen to the deep cello, Fox, 157–58

Littleton, Ellery, *Entrancement stills*, 267
Loneliness, xiv, 17, 153, 268
Longing, 153–54, 155, 157–58
Lorde, Audre:
    How the days went, 73
    The Cancer Journals, 13
Loss, 20, 39–41, 161, 184–89
    death of loved one, 169–71
Lost, Wagoner, 192, 201–2
Love, 126, 135, 143–44, 257–59
    witness to, 231–37
Love at the lips was touch, Frost, 83–84, 85
Loved one, 135–40
    death of, 169–71
Lovemaking, 147, 148, 220–21
The Lover, Olalla, 96
Lying in a Hammock at William Duffy's Farm,
    Wright, 200–201

McCarriston, Linda, 101
McMonagle, Lisa, 217
    The Black Walnut Tree, 218–19
    The Continental Drift, 220–22
Macy, Joanna, 217
Mahabharata, 232
Marie, *Bird Song*, 156–57
Marriage, 127, 132–34, 148–53
Marriage, Lagoni, 150–51
The Marrow of Who I Am, Fox, 232–34
The Mask, Rigg, 162–63
Mass media, 47–48
Maxwell, Florida Scott, 100, 163
May, Rollo, 42, 226, 265
Maybe, de Kay, 180
Meaning, xiv, 153
    line structure and, 83–84
Medicine, poetic, 3, 8–9, 273–77
Meditation, 35, 266–73, 277
Meera (Mother), 177
Memory, 173, 256
Men, 129–30
    relationship with parents, 105–7
Mentioning the Weather, Fox, 196
Merely to know, Kojiju, 253
Merton, Thomas, 253
Metaphors, 59, 61, 64–68, 184, 188
    animals as, 211
    from earth, 193, 195
    of loss, 20
    for loved one, 137
    and vulnerability, 141
Midnight on Laventille, Kennedy, 202–4

Miller, Alice, 123
Miller, Henry, 207, 258, 261
Milosch, Joe, *Why is a scar on a man a mark of distinction*, 26–29
Minty, Judith, 59
Misciagna, Orion, *Heart of Water*, 65–66
Mitchell, Edgar, 212
Mitchell, Joni, *Both Sides Now*, 141
Mixed feelings, images and, 78–80
Moon, as image of enlightenment, 253
Moonbeams, Roberts, 144
Moore, Marianne, 87
    Beauty is everlasting, 137
Moore, Thomas, 27, 40, 160
Morris, Noëlle, *Ruah*, 260–61
Morrison, Toni, 242
Mother and Child, Oles, 78–80
Mother - Eyes Cast Down, Weiner, 102–4
Mura, David, 230
Muse, O'Brian, 276
Muse, poetic, 6–7, 162–63, 273–77
Music, Jiminez, 64, 65
My eyes are radiant with your spirit, Solomon, 264
My Familiar, TallMountain, 7
My heart of silk, García Lorca, 8–9
Mystery, 166, 213, 214–15, 251–52

Naming, receptivity and, 200–201
The National Association for Poetry Therapy, 279
National Writer's Voice, 280
Natural medicine, poetry as, 3, 8–9
Natural speech, flow of, 84–85
Nature, and poetry, 193–222
Navaho (anon.), *I ask all blessings*, 5
Nelson, Kimberley, 81, 237, 241
    No Place For Solitude, 238–40
Neruda, Pablo, *Yes: seed germs, and grief, and everything*, 195
New Blues from a Brown Baby, Sharp, 84
Nonacceptance, intimacy and, 144
Nonverbal images, 162–63
No Place For Solitude, Nelson, 238–40
Noticing, 200–201
Novalis, 63, 258
Nye, Naomi Shihab, 225, 248
    The cat sleeping on the fence is famous to the birds, 85

Objects, 168–69
    special, of childhood, 123

O body—, Remen, xiv
O'Brian, Ellen Grace, 273
    Burying the Gold, 117–22
    Muse, 276
    Sometimes at Night, 258–59
Ode: Intimations of Immortality, Wordsworth, 82–83
Okanagan language, 204
Olalla, Veronica Paz, *The Lover*, 96
Oles, Carole, *Mother and Child*, 78–80
Olinghouse, Cori, *I drank a fertile alphabet*, 200
Oliver, Mary, 24
Olson, Charles, 25
    These Days, 16–17
Once a Performer, Stephenson, 188
Onions, Usatch, 181–83
On Runners, Evans, 112–14
Others, experiences of, 247–48

Pain, 20–24, 170–71
    cry of, 13–18, 30
Pain's terrorwide eye, Willkie, 15–16
Paradox, 12–13, 23, 252–53
Paredes, Adriana, *Unbroken Promise*, 109–13
Parenthood, 95–123
Paris and Helen, Grahn, 136–38
Passion, writing with, 48–49
Patience, 262
Paz, Octavio, 48
The Peace of Wild Things, Berry, 212
Penn, William, 268
Penna, Nick, *Waiting in Line*, 96
Pennebaker, James, 14
Peonies at Dusk, Kenyon, 206–7
Personal stories, 53–55
Petermann, Susanne, 44–47, 89
    Entering the Dark Places with Innocence, 44
"Phantom pain," 20–21
Picard, Max, 267
Picasso, Pablo, 97
Piercy, Marge, 64
    To Have Without Holding, 128
    Unlearning Not to Speak, 49–50
Playfulness, 62
Poem-making, 15–16, 29–30, 33–34, 35, 48, 129, 143, 163, 166, 261–62
    for caregivers, 181–84
    and emotions, 49–53, 74–80, 161–62
    and healing, 116–17
    and illness, 44–46, 175–80

and love, 257
    meditation and, 266–73
    nature and, 193–222
    and relationships, 116, 128, 135, 136
    and social change, 225–28, 237–48
    and spirituality, 251, 254
    as witness, 231–37
Poetic elements, 36–39
Poetic tools, 59–91
Poetry, xiii, 2, 3–5, 21–23, 53, 60, 134, 161, 230, 267
    sharing of, 50, 135
    See also Poem-making
Poet's House, 281
Politics, 225–26
Power, truth and, 13
Praise, expression of, 137–40
Presence, 199, 202–4, 261
Pride, 240
Priorities, shift in, 25
Prison, poetry in, 243
A Prison Sharing, Dooley, 244–45
Psalm 13, de Kay, 177
Psalm 86 (Bible), 252
Pudding House Writers Resource Center, 280

The Rabbis Do Not Look At Me, Bellotti, 265
Radiology Report, Petermann, 45–46
Reaching Toward Beauty, Hill, 142
Reality, 13, 65
Receptivity, 199–202
Reese, Barbara, *Ancient souls collide*, 220
Reeve, Christopher, 225, 242
Rejection, 227
Relationships, 9–10, 127, 240, 257
    with earth, 193–222
    intimate, 128–53
    metaphoric, 65
    parent/child, 95–123
    of words, 88–89
Relativity theory, 81
Religion, 225
Remembrance, poem of, 256
Remen, Rachel Naomi, 134
    Listening creates holy silence, 41
    O body—, xiv
Repetition of words or sounds, 88
Resilience, 29–30
Rhythm, 83, 138
Rich, Adrienne, 55, 231, 238
Richard-Allerdyce, Diane:

★

Lioness, 209–11
To a Stone, 197–98
Richards, M. C., 30, 88, 126, 246
Rigg, Dedee:
    For Isaac, 164
    The Mask, 162–63
    The Winter Garden, 164–65
Rilke, Rainer Maria, 13, 36, 91, 219
    Autumn, 166, 168
    I don't have much knowledge yet in grief, 24
    I love the dark hours of my being, 270
    *It's O.K. for the rich and the lucky to keep
        still*, 18–19
The Rime of the Ancient Mariner, Coleridge,
    88
Ritual, 147
Ritual, Kennedy, 104–5
Roberts, Elizabeth I., *Moonbeams*, 144
Robertson, Georgia, *I ask for a human lan-
    guage*, 9
Roethke, Theodore, 65, 102
    I wake to sleep, and take my waking slow, 33
    This shaking keeps me steady, 41
Rollins, Ed, 243
The Rose, Wray, 236
Roszak, Theodore, 215
Ruah, Morris, 260–61
Rumi, Jelaluddin, 24
    A white flower grows in the quiet, 178
    I have lived on the lip, 35
    Sell your cleverness and buy bewilderment, 272

Sacred experiences, 251
Saint-Exupéry, Antoine de, 23
San Diego Writing Center, 26
Schulz, Megan, *The Spirit of the Black Dog*,
    173–74
Seattle (Chief), 198, 238, 240
Second Anniversary, Henry, 105–7
See a peach bend, Lee, 72
Seeing skills, 199
*Seen Through a Dusty Camera Lens in a Valley
    Town*, Tolbert, 186–87
Self, 66–68, 197
Self-care, in relationship, 155
Self-discovery, 128
Self-pity, 23
Self-respect, 155
Sell your cleverness and buy bewilderment,
    Rumi, 272
Senkyrik, Jodie, *Do Not Wipe Your Tears
    Away*, 42–43

Sensation, 36–39
Sensitivity, 30, 109, 207
    of children, 95
Sensuality, 219–22, 264
Sexual relationship, 136, 148
    HIV and, 185–86
Sexuality, 220–22
Shake off this Sadness, Unamuno, 11
Shakespeare, William, 61
Sharp, Saundra, *New Blues from a Brown
    Baby*, 84
Shikibu, Izumi:
    Although the wind, 253
    The way I must enter, 253
Silence, 240, 266, 267–68, 272
Simic, Vesela, 108–9
Simile, 59, 60–64, 138
Sinetar, Marsha, 141
Slater, Lauren, 29
Small Steps, Lisa, 247
Smriti (divine memory), 256
Snyder, Gary, 65, 69, 214
Social change, 225–28
Societal wounds, healing of, 237–48
Solitude, 268
Solomon, *My eyes are radiant with your
    spirit*, 264
Sometimes at Night, O'Brian, 258–59
A Song of the Old Order, Duncan, 149–50
Sorrow, witness to, 231–37
Sounds, repetition of, 88
Spangler, David, 257
Speech, poetic, 30
Spender, Stephen, *What is precious, is never
    to forget*, 11
Spirit, after death, 173–75
The Spirit of the Black Dog, Schulz, 173–74
Spirituality, 34–35, 251–77
Spontaneity, 264
Square Black Box, Stephenson, 168–69
Stafford, William, 204
    If you don't know the kind of person I am,
        34
    *This is the field where the battle did not
        happen*, 6
Star Eating Wolves, de Kay, 178
Stephenson, Bill:
    Once a Performer, 188
    Square Black Box, 168–69
Stevens, Wallace, 34
The Stranger, Tirnauer, 271–72
Strona, Anna Louise, 154

Surprise, 3–4, 62, 63, 128, 262
    children and, 97, 98

Tagore, Rabindranath, 62, 132
TallMountain, Mary:
    I am a snowflake. I drift, 254
    My Familiar, 7
Tan, Amy, 5
Teilhard de Chardin, Pierre, *We are one,
    after all, you and I*, 231
Tell me a tale, I'll tell you a tale, Winkle,
    129–30
Tenderness, 127
Tense, shifting of, 80
Terribly Loud Screaming Kept the House Awake,
    Lisa, 115–16
There is a Secret One inside us, Kabir, 250
There is no Frigate like a Book, Dickinson, 60
These Days, Olson, 16–17
"Third world," American, 226
This is the field where the battle did not happen,
    Stafford, 6
This shaking keeps me steady. I should know,
    Roethke, 41
Thomas, Dylan, *Fern Hill*, 88–89
Thoreau, Henry David, 153, 195, 214
Time, passage of, parents and, 107–14
Tirnauer, Lawrence, 273
    The Stranger, 271–72
To a Stone, Richard-Allerdyce, 197–98
To Have Without Holding, Piercy, 128
To Know the Dark, Berry, 29
Tolbert, Pam, *Seen Through a Dusty Camera
    Lens in a Valley Town*, 186–87
To Sleep With, Ekundayo, 184–86
Transitional times, 112–14
Troupe, Quincy, 238
Truth, xiii, 9–10, 13
    about abusive relationships, 116
    American people and, 242
    troubled children and, 240–41
Turner, Mary Kay, 66–67
    The Well, 67–68
Turning points in life, 229–31

Ullman, Dana, 8
Unamuno, Miguel de, *Shake off this
    Sadness*, 11
Unbroken Promise, Paredes, 109–11
    Spanish version, 111–12
Uncertainty, 166
Underhill, Evelyn, 269

Universal connections, 53–55
The unknown, 266, 270–72
Unlearning Not to Speak, Piercy, 49–50
Usatch, Sonia:
    Onions, 181–83
    Yellow Yarn, 183–84

Vietnam War, 229, 230
Viorst, Judith, 132
Voice, xiv, 3, 69–70
    of child-self, 123–24
    for earth, 213, 215–17
    inner, 269–70
    and relationships, 127–28
Voigt, Ellen Bryant, 108
Vowels, 89
Vulnerability, 30, 140–48, 175, 267–68

Wagoner, David, *Lost*, 192, 201–2
Waiting in Line, Penna, 96
Wales Visitation, Ginsberg, 82–83
War, sorrows of, 232
Was somebody asking to see the soul?, Whitman, 214
Was—Will—Not, Young, 240–41
The way I must enter, Shikibu, 253
We are one, after all, you and I, Teilhard de Chardin, 231
Weather, poetry of, 196–97
Weber, Caitlan, 89
We did not come to remain whole, Bly, 94

Weiner, Elsa:
    busy place and bright, 84
    Mother—Eyes Cast Down, 102–4
Weiss, Greta, *Inside a bubble*, 96
The Well, Turner, 67–68
Welwood, John, 135, 145
Western poetry, changes in, 81
What I Heard in a Discount Department Store, Budbill, 101–2
What is precious, is never to forget, Spender, 11
What shrinks inside us, these stones, Bloch, 102
A white flower grows in the quiet, Rumi, 178
Whitman, Walt, 69, 81
    Each of us inevitable, 194
    I am he that walks with the tender and growing night, 219–20
    I am the poet of the Body and I am the poet of the Soul, 13
    Was somebody asking to see the soul?, 214
who are you, little i, cummings, 97
Wholeness, 48, 252–53, 256
Why is a scar on a man a mark of distinction, Milosch, 26–29
Wilder, Thornton, *Our Town*, 95
Williams, William Carlos, 81
Willkie, Cathy, *Pain's terrorwide eye*, 15–16
Winkle, Jack, *Tell me a tale, I'll tell you a tale*, 129–30
The Winter Garden, Rigg, 164–65

Winter Solitude, Basho, 171
Wisdom, 213, 257, 261–63, 269
Witch Doctor, Bowman, 274–76
Witnessing, 231–37
The Women and the Men, Giovanni, 195
Woodman, Marion, 140
Word choice, 18, 50, 59, 86–89
Word spacing, 17
Wordsworth, William:
    Ode: Intimations of Immortality, 82–83
    The world is too much with us, 215–16
Wray, Linda, 234–36
Wright, James, 60
    Lying in a Hammock at William Duffy's Farm, 200–201
Write Now: Maintaining a Creative Spirit While Homebound, Dion, 130
Writing of poetry, xiii, xiv, 3–4, 30, 40, 41–42, 51, 134
    children and, 95, 114
    tools for, 59–91
See also Poem-making

Yeats, William Butler, 24, 135
    Crazy Jane Talks with the Bishop, 142–43
    The Circus Animal's Desertion, 25
Yellow Yarn, Usatch, 183–84
Yes: seed germs, and grief, and everything that throbs, Neruda, 195
YES (Youth Enrichment Services), 229
Yo, earth, Kai, 216

ABOUT THE AUTHOR

John Fox is a certified poetry therapist and a lecturer in the Graduate School of Psychology at John F. Kennedy University in Orinda, California. He is the author of two volumes of poetry, *My Hand Touches the Sea* and *When Jewels Sing* (audiotape). John teaches in the California Poets in the Schools Program. John has presented workshops at Omega Institute, Esalen Institute, Hollyhock, Common Boundary and throughout the United States. If you are interested in sponsoring a workshop by John for your conference, center or group, or would like to receive information about his schedule, please contact John Fox, CPT, P.O. Box 60189, Palo Alto, CA 94306.